Coming Out
of the Classroom Closet:
Gay and Lesbian Students,
Teachers, and Curricula

Coming Out of the Classroom Closet: Gay and Lesbian Students, Teachers, and Curricula

Karen M. Harbeck, PhD, JD
Editor

Coming Out of the Classroom Closet: Gay and Lesbian Students, Teachers, and Curricula, edited by Karen M. Harbeck, was simultaneously issued by The Haworth Press, Inc., under the same title, as special issues of the *Journal of Homosexuality*, Volume 22, Numbers 3/4, 1991, John P. DeCecco, Editor.

Harrington Park Press
An Imprint of The Haworth Press, Inc.
New York • London

ISBN 1-56023-013-4

Published by

Harrington Park Press, 10 Alice Street, Binghamton, NY 13904-1580

Harrington Park Press is an imprint of The Haworth Press, Inc., 10 Alice Street, Binghamton, NY 13904-1580.

Coming Out of the Classroom Closet: Gay and Lesbian Students, Teachers, and Curricula was originally published as *Journal of Homosexuality,* Volume 22, Numbers 3/4, 1991.

Library of Congress Cataloging-in-Publication Data

Coming out of the classroom closet : gay and lesbian students, teachers, and curricula / Karen M. Harbeck, editor.
    p. cm.
    Originally published: Journal of homosexuality : vol. 22, no. 3/4.
    Includes index.
    ISBN 1-56023-013-4
    1. Homosexuality and education — United States. I. Harbeck, Karen Marie.
LC192.6.C66   1991
370.19'345 — dc20
                                                       91-39814
                                                        CIP

Coming Out
of the Classroom Closet:
Gay and Lesbian Students,
Teachers, and Curricula

Dedicated
to
Lesbian and Gay Educators,
Past, Present, and Future

CONTENTS

Introduction   1
Karen M. Harbeck, PhD, JD

Addressing the Needs of Lesbian, Gay, and Bisexual Youth:
The Origins of PROJECT 10 and School-Based
Intervention   9
Virginia Uribe, PhD
Karen M. Harbeck, PhD, JD

Educators, Homosexuality, and Homosexual Students:
Are Personal Feelings Related to Professional Beliefs?   29
James T. Sears, PhD

Liberal Attitudes and Homophobic Acts: The Paradoxes
of Homosexual Experience in a Liberal Institution   81
William P. Norris, PhD

Gay and Lesbian Educators: Past History/Future Prospects   121
Karen M. Harbeck, PhD, JD

Living In Two Worlds: The Identity Management Strategies
Used by Lesbian Physical Educators   141
Sherry E. Woods, EdD
Karen M. Harbeck, PhD, JD

From Hiding Out to Coming Out: Empowering Lesbian
and Gay Educators   167
Pat Griffin, EdD

Images of Gays and Lesbians in Sexuality and Health
Textbooks   197
Mariamne H. Whatley, PhD

Teaching Lesbian/Gay Development: From Oppression
to Exceptionality   213
Anthony R. D'Augelli, PhD

Educating Mental Health Professionals About Gay
   and Lesbian Issues   229
         Bianca Cody Murphy, EdD

HIV Education for Gay, Lesbian, and Bisexual Youth:
   Personal Risk, Personal Power, and the Community
   of Conscience   247
         Kevin Cranston, MDiv

Index   261

Table of Cases   273

ABOUT THE EDITOR

Karen M. Harbeck, PhD, JD, is a lecturer at Clark University in Worcester, Massachusetts, and a fellow at the New England Resource Center for Higher Education, University of Massachusetts. She recently completed a major study of the employment of gay men as educators in preschool through university settings. Dr. Harbeck maintains a private law practice throughout Massachusetts, specializing in the legal needs of lesbian and gay clients. Her work has focused on the historical and contemporary treatment of women and minorities in American education from an interdisciplinary background of history, law, anthropology, and education.

Coming Out
of the Classroom Closet:
Gay and Lesbian Students,
Teachers, and Curricula

Introduction

Karen M. Harbeck, PhD, JD

Over the past few decades our society has experienced radical social and technological change. New values and beliefs have been asserted about individual freedom, minority rights, human relationships, and global involvement. Schools have become a major arena of social conflict, as one group asserts traditional values, and the other demands that children be prepared for changes in technology, society, and the environment. One major issue that exemplifies this conflict within the educational system is the topic of homosexuality.

Several social and historical factors have combined to make the controversy over homosexuality and education one of the most publicly volatile and personally threatening debates in our national history. Since colonial times, American education has emphasized religious and moral development as a primary goal. Thus, teachers, as role models for impressionable youth and as employees of local government, often faced a wide variety of forbidden behaviors, such as prohibitions on smoking, drinking, dancing, dating, marriage, and pregnancy, that was unequaled in any other profession. In fact, monitoring the activities of the teacher has been an affirmative community responsibility, rather than a mere prurient interest.

Clearly then, both sexuality and homosexuality have been major threats to the traditional cultural ideology set forth in the schools. Homosexuality has been viewed as a sin, a sickness, or a crime. Additional scientific theories advanced in the early 1900s also explained it as a genetic defect, a mental disorder, or a learning disability. Since the 1960s, however, lesbians and gay men have joined other disenfranchised minority groups in our society, such as Blacks, women, and teachers, to assert their civil rights, personal freedoms, and social entitlements. The struggle is far from over, however, as we see from the resurgence of conservative political influ-

---

In addition to thanking the contributing authors, the Editor would like to express her appreciation to Dr. Jodie L. Wigren, Carol C. Barnes, Claire A. Murray, Dr. Arlene A. McGrory, and her sisters, Linda and Anita, for their support and assistance.

1

ence. It is not surprising, given this historical context, that the men and women — and young students — who had same-sex desires chose to remain invisible rather than face the harsh consequences of the previously almost unrestricted power of educational administrators and the extremes of community intolerance. Sadly, even today, most gay and lesbian educators and students remain invisible — for some because of this very real experience of hostility, and for others because of internalized oppression that leads to self-doubts and fears.

This book is about empowerment and it is a collection of recent research. As such, we view it as a beginning contribution to an ongoing discussion rather than a completed endeavor. In fact, it may be the first collection of research on homosexuality and education in educational history. All too often, both the scholars who might have undertaken such studies and the potential participants in that research have been dissuaded by threats to their tenure, promotion, reputation, and personal safety. This fact was made very clear as I corresponded with the few authors who had written early articles on the topic, only to learn that most of them were heterosexual individuals who undertook the research out of compassion for a relative or friend harmed by the system, or for conservative administrators who wanted clarification of their rights. Even these scholars spoke of the hardships that they had endured once this research had been published, including one's threatened loss of custody of her children during a bitter divorce.

Every contributor to this volume is aware of the potential professional and personal harm that might result in being affiliated with a homosexuality and education project. I think that it is reasonable to say that we are all emboldened by our predecessors, supported by our friends and colleagues, and strongly motivated to address the prejudice, ignorance, and discrimination that cause pain to gay and lesbian teachers, administrators, and students. Because several of the articles included in this book discuss the detrimental effects of the invisibility of gay and lesbian issues and individuals and internalized homophobia, some readers may feel that we are critical of our colleagues who do not feel safe making their sexual orientation a public matter. On the contrary, we feel a tremendous compassion for this perspective. We do hope, however, that whenever an opportunity arises to educate people about homosexuality and bisexuality, those who can risk it in that moment will do so for the sake of gay, lesbian, and bisexual youth and for each other.

As the research on gay, lesbian, and bisexual issues in education comes out of the closet, the real cost of homophobia and invisibility in our society is becoming more apparent. Recent estimates by the Department of Health and Human Services, for example, suggest that of the over 5,000 suicides annually by young men and women between the ages of 15 and 24, over 30% of them may be directly related to emotional turmoil over sexual preference issues and societal prejudices surrounding same-sex relationships. Other current studies, including the lead-off article in this volume by Virginia Uribe and myself entitled, "Addressing the Needs of Lesbian, Gay, and Bisexual Youth: The Origins of PROJECT 10 and School-Based Intervention," reveal that gay, lesbian, and bisexual adolescents and young adults in our society are frequently struggling with the numerous and very serious consequences of social disapprobation and isolation. In addition to higher than average instances of suicidality, these young people also experience higher levels of substance abuse, sexual abuse, homelessness, parental rejection, emotional isolation, drop-out risk, low self-esteem, prostitution, physical and verbal abuse, and sexually transmitted diseases. As a response to this shocking reality, Uribe and other concerned individuals within the Los Angeles Unified School District developed the first school-based counseling, intervention, and education program for homosexual and bisexual youth. As the article discusses, PROJECT 10 seems to have had a tremendous impact on most students and educators within the school district. The general student population demonstrates greater sensitivity to and acceptance of diversity and sexual preference. The gay, lesbian, and bisexual participants report higher levels of self-esteem, academic success, social acceptance, interpersonal connections, and safer sexual practices. The success of PROJECT 10 demonstrates that low cost, school-based intervention programs are possible and that they are effective in addressing the previously ignored hardships of lesbian, gay, and bisexual adolescents.

In his article, "Educators, Homosexuality, and Homosexual Students: Are Personal Feelings Related to Professional Beliefs?" James Sears provides three perspectives on how homosexuality is frequently dealt with in the schools. First, Sears presents comments by gay and lesbian students about how their teachers and counselors respond — or fail to respond — to issues concerning homosexuality. Next, Sears provides questionnaire and interview data gathered from counselors, and then beginning teachers, about their feelings and professional responsibilities with regard to homosexual students and incidents of prejudice. Sears concludes that while these educators believe that they can and should adopt a supportive stance in dealing with homosexuality, in fact, personal prejudice, lack of knowledge, and fear prevent them from being very effective resources for students.

In another attitudinal survey, possibly the first of its kind, William Norris and his colleagues have undertaken the ambitious task of a campus-wide assessment of the beliefs and behaviors of all students and employees in relation to the lesbians, gay men, and bisexuals at a college. As reported in "Liberal Attitudes and Homophobic Acts: The Paradoxes of Homosexual Experience in a Liberal Institution," in the face of increasing hostility towards women, minorities, and homosexuals in society in general, and because of some specific incidents of discrimination and intolerance that occurred on the campus of this very liberal, liberal arts college, the administration took the enlightened view that an in-depth study of the situation would greatly facilitate efforts to intervene and to educate. Because the questionnaires for students and for employees were so detailed, Norris is able to provide insight into each group's specific concerns. Additionally, the data suggests that gender and race play an important role in the types of prejudice (beliefs) and discrimination (actions) that one might experience in light of one's real or perceived sexual preference orientation.

The research presented in this volume suggests that we have greater social support and legal protections than is normally assumed, and that our invisibility and internalized oppression may play major roles in limiting our freedoms. In my article entitled "Gay and Lesbian Educators: Past History/Future Prospects," for example, I review the history of case law on gay and lesbian teacher dismissal and credential revocation. Since the 1960s there has been a strong legal precedent for retention of homosexual educators unless they have been involved in some indiscretion or unprofessional conduct. Additionally, since the early 1970s, this legal precedent has been augmented by active support for gays and lesbians from teachers' unions and special interest litigation groups. This support has provided a balance against school districts' prior superiority in access to legal talent and money, thus making school administrators much more eager to negotiate a resolution to a conflict rather than face the high cost of litigation. Since legal policy issues concerning homosexuality are rarely mentioned in the textbooks and courses taken by school administrators, it is very important that we inform them—and ourselves—of our rights. If we do not assert them, we do not have them.

In the Woods and Harbeck phenomenological attitudinal study of lesbian physical education teachers, these educators also realize that there has been a liberalization of attitudes towards lesbians and gay men, but they remain convinced that as lesbian physical education instructors they would be immediately terminated from their employment if their sexual orientation were disclosed. In "Living In Two Worlds: The Identity Management Strategies Used by Lesbian Physical Educators," Sherry Woods and I present the extreme circumstances of these lesbian educators who struggle to hide their sexual orientation while working in close, physical contact with their same-sex students in a profession that has been traditionally labeled as lesbian because of a stereotype that athletic women are masculine. When faced with this threat to their livelihood, most of these women created sharp divisions between their personal and professional realms. This same phenomena was mentioned as a frequent coping mechanism for teachers who participated in Pat Griffin's empowerment project. As reported in her article, "From Hiding Out to Coming Out: Empowering Lesbian and Gay Educators," with reflection upon their circumstances and support from their group members during the 15-month process, all of the participants were able to be much more visible as gay and lesbian educators. Although these participants enjoyed several benefits from the empowerment process, probably the three most significant were a heightened sense of self-esteem, a greater ability to serve as a resource for gay and lesbian youth, and a surprising level of acceptance and positive outcomes when they did risk disclosure. While both Woods/Harbeck's and Griffin's research speak to the powerful influences and constraints of internalized homophobia, Griffin's research corroborates my findings that lesbian and gay educators have many more freedoms if we are able to assert them. Clearly, telling an oppressed group that they have rights is insufficient until it is coupled with the extensive self-exploration and affirmation that comes from working through these personal and societal issues in a supportive setting.

While the prior articles explore people's attitudes and actions with respect to homosexuality, Mariamne Whatley takes a completely different perspective by analyzing the influences that perpetuate these beliefs in "Images of Gays and Lesbians in Sexuality and Health Textbooks." Like the articles that follow hers from Anthony D'Augelli and Bianca Cody Murphy, the author is concerned about the lack of adequate and appropriate representations of gay men and lesbians in curricula and textbook materials. Whatley argues that some progress has been made, but like other minorities, exemplars of homosexuality remain isolated and ghettoized within the larger context of a textbook. Similarly, the images that are presented compound issues of homophobia with those of racism, sexism, ageism, and ableism by portraying most homosexuals as young, white, able-bodied, politically active males.

While also exploring themes of empowerment and homosexuality in curricula and textbooks, Anthony D'Augelli, in "Teaching Lesbian/Gay Development: From Oppression to Exceptionality," provides a positive alternative for gay and lesbian undergraduates during the time in their lives when they are actively exploring their sexuality. D'Augelli's course structure and process focus on exceptionality, empowerment, and oppression. It critiques the invisibility of homosexuality and the hidden negative curriculum in traditional undergraduate courses.

In her essay on "Educating Mental Health Professionals About Gay and Lesbian Issues," Bianca Cody Murphy also explores the failings of traditional curriculum, this time in schools of psychology, medicine, social work, and counseling. While ethically bound by the tenants of their professions to be informed and compassionate towards minority clients, most mental health professionals remain woefully uneducated and unprepared to help with issues concerning homosexuality. Murphy outlines the failings in the academic programs and inservice training, and then discusses methods to improve the situation with a variety of written materials and course/seminar designs. Murphy concludes with the three elements that she finds essential to effective intervention: increased information; an exploration of the interplay between the lesbian/gay client's self, sexuality, and our homophobic society; and the interaction between the attitudes, beliefs, and sexual orientation of the client and the therapist.

And finally, in his article, "HIV Education for Gay, Lesbian, and Bisexual Youth: Personal Risk, Personal Power, and the Community of Conscience," Kevin Cranston explores the failings of current HIV/AIDS prevention programs with respect to the unique needs of gay, lesbian, and bisexual youth. Cranston argues that in the process of attempting to diminish the perception that AIDS is primarily a gay disease and thereby heighten the awareness of heterosexuals to their potential susceptibility to HIV infection, significant opportunities are being lost to discuss gay, lesbian, and bisexual issues and to meet the developmental needs of sexual minority youth. Cranston proposes a model of HIV prevention education that includes broader self and group empowerment training, social skills development, peer support networks, and access to risk reduction health care materials. Through greater self-efficacy and support from a community of like-minded individuals, Cranston believes that gay, lesbian, and bisexual youth will feel empowered to make positive choices for their mental and physical well-being.

It is our hope that this volume of research on homosexuality and education will serve three major functions: address the lack of available research on the topic; encourage lesbians, gays, and bisexuals in education as they struggle within the system; and provide concerned individuals with some of the knowledge needed to empower themselves and to educate others. Although the research does verify the existence of negative attitudes and incidents of discrimination directed at lesbians, gay men, and bisexuals, it also speaks to the very powerful limitations that we as a minority have incorporated into ourselves in the form of internalized homophobia in the face of societal oppression. While acknowledging our victimization, we also choose to affirm our power. Similarly, by our choice of professions we affirm the power of education as a mechanism for personal and societal change. As we educate and empower ourselves through research and advocacy as described in this volume, we heighten our effectiveness in the struggle to educate others about our positive alternative lifestyle.

In conclusion, I would like to take this opportunity to express gratitude to the men and women who, over the past two decades, have lobbied their educational organizations to include support for lesbians and gay men. Although at times reluctant advocates, the legal assistance and political clout contributed by the National Education Association, the American Federation of Teachers, the Modern Language Association, their state and local affiliates, and several other groups, have greatly enhanced the quality of life for gay and lesbian educators and their students. As one example, several of the contributors to this volume were brought together at the first session on "Homosexuality and Education" presented in San Francisco at the American Educational Research Association national meetings in April of 1988 that was organized by James Sears. This opportunity provided all of us with a stronger network of colleagues and friends, whose collective effort made this volume possible.

Addressing the Needs of Lesbian, Gay, and Bisexual Youth: The Origins of PROJECT 10 and School-Based Intervention

Virginia Uribe, PhD

Fairfax High School, Los Angeles, CA

Karen M. Harbeck, PhD, JD

Clark University and University of Massachusetts, Boston

SUMMARY. This research chronicles the formation and expansion of a counseling and educational program for gay, lesbian, and bisexual youth called PROJECT 10 at Fairfax High School. A model program was tested during the academic year 1985-1986, and is now being implemented throughout the Los Angeles Unified School District and in other schools across the nation. Fifty self-identified homosexual students were interviewed in order to clarify the needs of lesbian, gay, and bisexual teenagers in relation to their school experiences. Additionally, a questionnaire study of 342 respondents from the general student population was undertaken in order to chart

---

Virginia Uribe is nationally known as the founder of PROJECT 10, the first school-based program in the nation to address the needs of lesbian, gay, and bisexual youth. She holds a PhD in Counseling Psychology from Sierra University and has been a science teacher at Fairfax High School for over thirty years. Correspondence and requests for the PROJECT 10 Handbook may be addressed to her at: 7850 Melrose Avenue, Los Angeles, CA 90046. Karen M. Harbeck is the editor of *Coming Out of the Classroom Closet: Gay and Lesbian Students, Teachers, and Curricula.* She holds a PhD from Stanford University, two master's degrees, and a JD from the University of Santa Clara Law School. She currently teaches a course on gay and lesbian issues in education at Clark University. Correspondence may be addressed to the author at: P. O. Box 1809, Brookline, MA 02146.

the beliefs and attitudinal changes of those teenagers who experienced school-based educational programs that portrayed homosexuality and bisexuality as variations on a continuum of human sexual expression and emotional attachment. Suggestions for further research are discussed.

In November of 1984, Fairfax High School experienced a very common phenomena, and they chose to respond to it in a very uncommon manner. The school, located on a street of "New Wave" and "punk" specialty shops, is nearly adjacent to the City of West Hollywood, California, which has a large population of gays and lesbians. Fairfax High has a student body of approximately 2500 students of mixed racial and ethnic background.

The incident involved an openly gay male student who had been transferred to Fairfax from another school. From the day he entered, "Chris" was physically abused by peers, and verbally abused by teachers and peers alike. Finally, "Chris" dropped out of school entirely and turned to the streets, becoming one more casualty of a system that neither understood, nor cared about him. His rejection was a systematic repeat of his experiences at four previous schools.

This incident was so offensive to some members of the faculty and administration that it prompted an investigation into the educational history and background of "Chris H.," age 17, Black, male homosexual. Two counselors, seven former teachers, and the head of a group home where he lived were located and questioned. "Chris" had been forcibly ejected from his home at age 14 for admitting that he was gay. He had been on the streets for about a year until he was placed in a juvenile detention home and eventually in a group residential home for lesbian and gay adolescents. All his former teachers and counselors described him as "sweet," "nice," and of average intelligence, with no particular learning disabilities. The only reason that anyone gave as to why he encountered so much trouble in school and at home was that he was gay. The story was always the same. He would enter a school and the students would begin harassing him immediately. If he defended himself, either verbally or physically, he was taken to the dean's office and reprimanded. The adults added to this by making innuendoes or other subtle remarks about his homosexuality. "Chris" had experienced so much abuse at one school that there was a letter in his file, written by an administrator at the Gay and Lesbian Community Services Center, registering a protest about "gay bashing" that had taken place at the campus. The response of the school was to transfer "Chris" out.

Mobilized by this evidence that homophobia was alive and active in the educational system and, in fact, that it was institutionalized in a manner that was predictable and systematic, the senior author was charged by the administration with developing a model program to work with self-identi-fied gay, lesbian, and bisexual youngsters in the school setting. PROJECT 10, named after Kinsey's (1948) estimate that 10% of the population is exclusively homosexual, was originally envisioned as an in-school coun-seling program providing emotional support, information, resources, and referrals to young people who identified themselves as lesbian, gay, or bisexual or who wanted accurate information on the subject of sexual orientation. A second goal of the program was to heighten the school community's acceptance of and sensitivity to gay, lesbian, and bisexual issues. Subsequently, PROJECT 10 has become a district-wide and nation-wide forum for the articulation of the needs of lesbian, gay, and bisexual teenagers.

There are countless numbers of "Christophers" and "Christines" in our nation's schools. For them, junior and senior high school is often a time of isolation, humiliation, and pain. Those who openly admit their sexual orientation or who depart from traditional sex-role stereotypes of masculinity and femininity are verbally harassed and physically abused. Those who conceal their homosexual feelings experience loneliness and alienation, a splitting of their gay, lesbian, or bisexual identity from the rest of their personality. Most conceal their sexual feelings because of internal confusion, pain, and the fear of rejection and hostility. By devel-oping elaborate concealment strategies these young people are often able to "pass as straight," but at some significant, unmeasurable cost to their developmental process, self-esteem, and sense of connection.

Cultural taboos, fear of controversy, and a deeply-rooted, pervasive homophobia have kept the educational system in the United States blind-folded and mute on the subject of childhood and adolescent homosexual-ity. The paucity of literature, intervention, and understanding in this area is a national disgrace. Young men and women struggling with their sexual orientation during a time of intense physical, social, and developmental change are failed by physicians, educators, mental health professionals, and clergy who breach their ethical and professional obligations by being uninformed and unresponsive to the special problems and needs of these youth. While many of these young men and women are able to excel or at least get by in this difficult exploration, many of those failed by the sys-tem face an inordinately high risk of suicide, parental rejection, peer abuse, homelessness, school drop-out, drug abuse, and prostitution. Research indicates that adolescent homosexuals are either treated as though they do not exist or as objects of hate and bigotry. The traditional support structures that serve all other children do not serve gay, lesbian, and bisexual youth.

This study is limited in its theoretical framework to the process of stigmatization and its effect upon the adolescent homosexual's personal and social development in school. It will demonstrate that institutionalized homophobia exists and is perpetuated in schools, and that it systematically damages adolescent gay, lesbian, and bisexual youth both personally and academically. Cost-effective remedies are possible and can be reasonably implemented with the result that positive models of self-esteem replace the negative models that now exist for gay, lesbian, and bisexual teenagers.

BACKGROUND DISCUSSION

One of the major functions of the school as an institution is to assist in the child's growth of autonomy as a social individual. Implied in this is the development of the sense of self. This sense of self, which begins in infancy, includes not only internal intrapsychic components but also the management of social roles. Adolescence involves the expansion of this ego identity, particularly in the realm of social roles.

For the adolescent homosexual, such expansion includes the realization that one is a member of a stigmatized minority group. This process alone is daunting since gay, lesbian, and bisexual youth are denied access to information about human sexuality and alternative lifestyles, in part, because of the belief by some that merely having this information could cause young people to become homosexual or bisexual. Ironically, in the one court case that extensively explored the relationship between childhood influences and homosexuality, the testifying experts and the judge agreed that a child's sexual orientation was firmly established by age five or six at the latest (*Joseph Acanfora v. Board of Education of Montgomery County, et al.*, 359 F. Supp. 843 (1973); *aff'd* 491 F. 2nd 498 (4th Cir. 1974); *cert. denied*, 419 U.S. 836 (1974)). It also was agreed that a child's parents, who were probably heterosexual in orientation, were much more major role models than any teacher or textbook material so that the danger was minimal in terms of school-related influences. Given these scientific and legal conclusions, the court mentioned that young children who are gay, lesbian, or bisexual would probably benefit from access to information and role models in order to facilitate their optimal development (see also Harbeck, 1987).

This developmental process is further complicated by the isolation of the gay, lesbian, or bisexual youth. While most members of minority groups, whether ethnic, national, religious, racial, or gender-related, usually enjoy the support of and enculturation by other family and community members, the homosexual or bisexual young person is usually alone in this process of exploration and identification. In fact, they quickly come to realize that the mere expression of sexual confusion or same-sex attraction can be grounds for intense parental and peer hostility and/or rejection. Thus, while many minority groups are the target for prejudice (beliefs) and discrimination (actions) in our society, few persons face this hostility without the support and acceptance of their family as do many gay, lesbian, and bisexual youth.

It is the basic assumption of this study that homosexuality is a normal variation in both sexual orientation and sexual behavior. Negative attitudes toward homosexuals are primarily the result of homophobia, a prejudice similar in nature and dynamic to all other prejudices including anti-Semitism, racism, and sexism. The problem is that sometimes an attribute by which an individual is assigned group membership is a stigma so discrediting that it in effect reduces or denies the individual's other social identities. Homosexuality is such a stigma in our society. Thus, the primary developmental task for the adolescent gay, lesbian, or bisexual is adjustment to a socially stigmatized role in isolation without adequate, honest information about themselves or others who are like them during a time of tremendous physical, social, emotional, and intellectual change. Although individuals react with great diversity and resistance to societal pressures, most pass through a period of great turmoil during their teen years that is greatly compounded by negative stereotypes and lack of information about same-sex attractions.

The mental health and social development of gay, lesbian, and bisexual youth is further compounded by the often invisible nature of one's sexual orientation. Most persons who belong to a particular racial group or who are physically challenged in some manner, for example, cannot hide their status as a member of that minority group. Their challenge lies in coping with the preconceived notions of all persons with whom they come into contact. Most gay, lesbian, and bisexual persons, however, face the constant and complex choice of potentially posing as "normal" among other normals in order to distance themselves from these negative preconceived stereotypes. This gives rise to a socialization process involving learning to hide. Martin (1982) describes the predicament of the adolescent homosexual who is in the process of acquiring an integrated identity and who may encounter serious obstacles such as social isolation, rejection of self, prejudice, and discrimination on the road to a hopefully stable sense of self identity. Certainly the developmental task is formidable, and this is further complicated by actual experiences of prejudice and discrimination in housing, educational benefits, medical assistance, employment, physical and emotional security, and other forms of societal oppression directed against lesbians, gays, and bisexuals. For those children who reveal their same-sex attraction, school often means a place for verbal and physical abuse from teachers and fellow students and other homophobic practices that undermine their ability to learn and frequently causes them to drop out of school altogether.

> Every child learns not only what is expected of the various social identities he or she is being raised to but also the groups that society abhors. In adolescence, young homosexually-oriented persons are faced with the growing awareness that they may be among the most despised. They are forced to deal with the possibility that their actual social identity contradicts most of the other social identities to which they believe they are entitled. As this realization becomes more pressing, they are faced with three possible choices: they can hide, they can attempt to change their stigma, or they can accept it. (Martin, 1982, p. 57)

Each of these possibilities is less than optimum. Adolescents who accept the negative images attached to a homosexual identity are at risk for incorporating them within their own repertoire of behaviors. For example, they may assume the affectations of the promiscuous lifestyles they believe are socially expected. Those who hide typically experience damaged self-esteem, distancing from family and peers, and self-conscious attempts to avoid disclosure. This strategy of deception distorts almost all relationships the adolescent may attempt to develop or maintain and creates an increasing sense of isolation. The adolescent realizes that his or her membership in the approved group, whether it be the team, the church, the classroom, or the family, is based on a lie. Withdrawal from group membership is often the consequence of this isolation, and the effects of this withdrawal persist into adulthood. Finally, those who attempt to change the stigma face the possibilities of conflict with parents and school authorities, social ostracism, and even threats to their physical safety.

Most adolescents have not finalized their sexual orientation identification, and they are not willing to risk the ridicule and harassment that accompanies being open about their sexuality. Thus, they opt for concealment and hiding. The rewards for being normal are so great that those who can pass will. Thus, educators should keep in mind that for every gay, lesbian, or bisexual youth that they identify in the school, there are countless others who remain invisible and in need of support, acceptance, and informed assistance. The following interview excerpts reflect these conflicts.

> *John, age 17, Caucasian.* I have been able to tell my parents that I'm gay, and they are accepting but certainly not enthusiastic. Some of my friends know, but most don't. I'd never tell the people in my church youth group because they wouldn't understand. I still go to church dances, but I hate it. I just do it for my parents. I'm involved in school activities, because some kids around here know I'm gay; I'm afraid they would make it a big issue if I ran for school offices though.

> *Hack, age 17, Chinese.* The only way I have been able to deal with being gay is to throw myself into school activities. I am "Mr. Popular," and I hate every minute of it. Only one person at school, a lesbian, knows about me. My parents found out but they refuse to believe it. I don't like the social pressures on me. I have to go to school functions that for me are a total sham.

Techniques developed by adolescent gay, lesbian, or bisexual youth for coping with their sexual preference identities are as varied as the individuals themselves. Some drop out, while others try to excel in academic and social circles.

> *Eleanor, age 18, Caucasian.* My parents don't know about me, and for now I don't see that it would do any good to tell them. I have never dated a guy. I've dealt with being a lesbian by throwing myself into my work. My parents think I'm going to be a doctor, so they leave me alone. I'm very wary of close friendships because they will find out about me, and I'm not ready for that. I guess I'm just not very sociable.

A major aspect of hiding is the ever-present need to self-monitor. Unconscious and automatic behaviors, especially those relating to gender, are brought to the forefront of conscious attention. Gay, lesbian, and bisexual teenagers date members of the opposite sex, make up elaborate and sometimes false stories about dating, and employ many other techniques in order to hide their sexual preference. Each successful act of deception, each moment of monitoring which is unconscious and automatic for most heterosexuals, serves to reinforce the belief in one's difference and inferiority.

The experience of acquiring a homosexual or bisexual identity places the teenager at risk for dysfunction, in part because of the stigma attached to homosexuality in contemporary American society. Gay, lesbian, and bisexual adolescents may be at a higher risk of dysfunction because of their unfulfilled developmental needs for identification with a peer group, lack of positive role modeling influences and experiences, negative societal pressures, and their dependence upon parents and educators who may be unwilling or unable to provide emotional support concerning the issue of homosexuality.

Like all stigmatized individuals, the adolescent homosexual needs someone to talk to. Centuries of discrimination preclude the presence of adult role models to whom the young person can turn. The schools, one of the most important traditional structures in a young person's life, have maintained a dark silence on the subject of homosexuality. As a result, adolescent homosexuals and bisexuals are denied access to accurate information about their own sexuality that in the context of the current AIDS epidemic is especially ominous.

One study has been conducted by the New York City Gay/Lesbian Community Clinic (Paroski, 1987) to ascertain the needs and health care requirements of gay, lesbian, and bisexual adolescents. One hundred twenty-one self-identified homosexual adolescents were questioned over a period of 18 months. They reported using self-initiated exploration and personal contacts to learn about the homosexual lifestyle. A significant finding with serious implications for health care concern is that most males in the sample used sexual activity as a method of exploring homosexuality, thus placing themselves at extremely high risk for sexually-transmitted diseases.

Another area of ominous concern is the issue of adolescent and young adult suicide (ages 15 to 24), which is finally receiving the attention it deserves by educators and the public. In the recent Department of Health and Human Services Report on the Secretary's Task Force on Youth Suicide (1989), it was estimated that gay and lesbian youth are five times more likely to attempt suicide than their heterosexual peers. Kourany's (1987) study of the randomly sampled impressions of psychiatrists further suggests that the suicide attempts of gay, lesbian, and bisexual youth may be more injurious and lethal than those of their heterosexual counterparts. Thus, it may be the case that over 30% of the more than 5,000 annual suicides by young adults are compounded by issues of sexual orientation and sexual identity (National Center for Health Statistics, 1986).

In their recently published study of homosexual and bisexual male youth, Remafedi, Farrow, and Deisher (1991) have not only documented this alarming suicidality, they have also discerned some characteristics or milestones that may reflect a greater risk of suicidal tendencies in young males. Young men with more feminine gender role characteristics and those who recognized their same-sex orientation at an early age and acted on those sexual feelings seem to face the highest risk of self-destructive behavior, although an immediately precipitating factor seems to have been extreme family problems.

The Remafedi, Farrow, and Deisher study further confirms Remafedi's earlier research (1987) and that of others that documents an unusually high relationship between homosexuality and sexual abuse, drug abuse, homelessness, prostitution, feelings of isolation, family problems, and school difficulties. For example, in his 1987 study, Remafedi found that nearly half of the subjects reported a history of sexually-transmitted diseases, running away from home, or conflict with the law. Those less than 18 years of age experienced higher rates of substance abuse, high school drop-out, and conflict with the law than did older participants. Unfortunately, none of the literature explores the powerful influence of the school experience, and thus, no attempt is made to assess the manner in which the school experience might be changed to aid these troubled youth during a time of extreme turmoil and developmental risk.

One important source of additional material on the experience of teenage gays and lesbians was testimony obtained from the National Gay and Lesbian Task Force in Washington, D.C., and from the Institute for the Protection of Lesbian and Gay Youth, Inc., in New York City. This study included testimony presented by Damien Martin, Joyce Hunter, and Steve Ashkinazy to the Governor's Task Force on Lesbian and Gay Issues, and the New York State Task Force on Gay Issues on January 17-18, 1985. The testimony was derived from youths entering the Institute for the Protection of Lesbian and Gay Youth, and suggested isolation, family violence, school homophobia, stress, shelter, and sexual abuse are the main concern of many adolescent homosexuals.

Testimony from Kevin Berrill of the National Gay and Lesbian Task Force reported on the anti-gay violence among 2,000 gay men and lesbians nationwide. Among those surveyed, more than 90% had experienced some type of verbal and physical abuse. Nearly half the males and nearly one fifth of the lesbians had been harassed or attacked in high school or junior high school. This testimony also substantiated research by other organizations that indicated anti-gay violence is widespread, particularly in the secondary schools.

Finally, there are a few sources of primary material that are personal narratives by students describing their high school experiences, and these may provide the most accurate description of what it is like to be a gay, lesbian, or bisexual teenager in the American school system. These books are *One Teenager in Ten* (Heron, 1983), *Reflections of a Rock Lobster* (Fricke, 1981), and *Growing Up Gay in the South* (Sears, 1990). The impact of peers' negative attitude and behavior upon a teenager's self-concept is dramatically demonstrated in these narratives.

In conclusion, the most salient aspect of a review of literature on adolescent homosexuality and bisexuality is the startling lack of material until recently. While there is a representative body of material on the development of a homosexual identity and the stigmatization process, there are few empirical studies on the effects of stigmatization upon the adolescent homosexual. It appears that the literature substantiates the fact that school-based homophobia is psychologically damaging, but the nature and extent of the damage has yet to be determined. That no correlation studies on suicide, substance abuse, and sexual identity conflicts have been undertaken suggests that homophobia extends to the field of scholarship as well.

Studies on lesbians or the inclusion of lesbians in the existing studies are noticeably absent. This is also true for the Black and Hispanic segment of the adolescent homosexual population. In fact, factors related to race, ethnicity, religion, and geographic location, as well as teenagers from different backgrounds or in different stages of sexual self-identification, need to be explored.

THE FORMATION OF PROJECT 10

It is apparent from the experiences of "Chris," mentioned earlier in this article, and other students that school-sanctioned homophobia is widespread and is a major contributor to the medical and psychosocial problems of adolescent gays, lesbians, and bisexuals. Our intent was to reduce the effects of anti-gay and lesbian discrimination by creating a model counseling program for both homosexual and heterosexual youth in the Los Angeles Unified School District, consisting of education, school safety measures, human rights advocacy, drop-out prevention strategies, and use of community resources. Finally, we hoped to increase the body of basic information on the subject of school-sanctioned prejudice and discrimination, and provide a rationale for future research. The implications of attitude formation and school-based homophobia are substantial. Experimental studies on intervention techniques and attitude development are important research problems for the future.

From the onset, the study involved a dual approach. One was an investigation into the extent and effect of the stigmatization process upon lesbian and gay teenagers in the schools, and the second was a practical approach which involved developing a model program and working with self-identified homosexual youngsters in a school setting.

First, it was necessary to break through the wall of silence that surrounded the subject of homosexuality so that the target group could be reached. Second, a safe and supportive atmosphere had to be provided so that youngsters could talk about their sexuality in a non-threatening way. Third, a non-judgmental posture had to be developed that could serve as a guideline in dealing with gay and lesbian youth.

Some gay and lesbian students who attended Fairfax High School were invited to meet weekly at lunch time on an informal basis. Before long the group had grown to twenty-five or more "regulars." These early meetings were spent in rather unstructured "rap" sessions, discussing problems that were encountered in the school setting. The plight of "Chris," whom many of them knew, was discussed along with the similarities his case bore to so many others. Although none of this was measured quantitatively, preliminary observations indicated that most of the students reflected the societal attitudes of discrimination against them. Low self-esteem, feelings of isolation, alienation, and inadequacy were common. Although most in this early group were very intelligent, few were performing at a level consistent with their native capacity. Many were involved in self-destructive behavior, including substance abuse and attempted suicides, and were on the verge of dropping out of school. One of the most significant facts was their feelings that they existed in a box, with no adults to talk to, no traditional support structures to lean on for help in sorting out their problems, and no young people like themselves with whom to socialize. In effect, these young homosexuals perceived themselves to be stranded in an environment that shunned their very existence.

Many who claimed they were not "overt" in their mannerisms remembered being called "faggot" or "dyke" as early as their elementary years. Those who departed from traditional sex-role stereotypes were especially punished. For those who concealed their homosexual feelings, their recollections were of loneliness and alienation, a splitting of their homosexual identity from the rest of their personality.

Most did what they could to conceal their sexuality because to affirm it was too painful. They devised elaborate concealment strategies, and the result of these strategies was to cripple them emotionally and socially. It was especially noteworthy that all of them felt that their social development had been seriously inhibited by their homosexuality.

At the beginning of the academic year 1985-86, PROJECT 10 began to be implemented in increasing degrees of visibility. A brochure was prepared and distributed throughout the community, and a core group of teachers, administrators, and counselors was trained. The advisory board felt that visibility was very important, a fact made easier by an article in the *Los Angeles Times* in November, 1985, that was followed by publicity in many local area school papers and extensive media coverage on television.

The publicity was significant for two reasons. First, it heightened awareness of a program that dealt with a subject that was totally invisible in the schools. Second, it became a gauge of public reaction to the program. The response has been overwhelmingly positive, with fewer than ten negative calls being recorded initially.

Although the district was very supportive, it did not allocate any funds for the program. Consequently, outside funding has been obtained annually from the City of West Hollywood and from incorporating as a 501 (c) nonprofit corporation, Friends of PROJECT 10. These monies have supported library materials, a hotline, incidental costs of publicity, awards, and scholarships sponsored by PROJECT 10. During the academic year 1986-1987, over 200 students availed themselves of counseling and information services.

In the academic year 1987-1988, PROJECT 10 was expanded throughout the junior and senior high schools of the Los Angeles Unified School District. Many factors contributed to this expansion, such as, board members sympathetic to the special needs of this target group, a general desire to attack the problem of school dropouts, and an increasing awareness of the menacing AIDS epidemic among the teenage population.

Accordingly, a bulletin was distributed to each principal informing him or her of the expansion of PROJECT 10. Following that bulletin a packet of information was distributed to each head counselor. This packet included student-oriented booklets that had been printed by the Office of Guidance and Counseling and signs to be posted in the office.

A total of 210 schools, including magnet and continuation schools, were invited to participate. Involvement is measured by a staff training session or by an indication that the material is being made available and the program is receiving some visibility. Each school where this has occurred has reported that between four and ten students have sought information in the first month. Student response is measured by student-counselor (or other staff member) contact, student contact with the PROJECT 10 coordinator, usually by phone, or a call to the PROJECT 10 information line. A total of 277 responses from outside Fairfax High School was tabulated from September 20, 1987, to December 30, 1987.

Generally speaking, the response has been poor in predominantly Black and Hispanic schools, indicating the need to develop particular strategies for working with the minority communities. These same areas seem to have a high level of denial and cultural resistance to AIDS education efforts as well (Bean, 1987).

INTERVIEW RESULTS

Two interview samples were collected between 1984 and 1987 (see Uribe, 1988, for a more complete discussion of the studies and their findings). The first sample was limited to 50 respondents, all of whom identified themselves as gay, lesbian, or bisexual. The purpose of this study was to ascertain some of the problems, attitudes, and experiences of these youth, particularly as they related to the school setting. The second sample consisted of 342 randomly selected students at Fairfax High School who were surveyed after PROJECT 10 had been in place for one school year. The purpose of this was to assess any positive or negative responses to the program from the general school population.

All the respondents involved in the gay, lesbian, and bisexual youth study (Sample #1) either attended Fairfax High School or attended another school and had made contact with the program. The study was limited to 50 respondents because it was felt that a larger sample would not have yielded significantly different results. Although an attempt was made to obtain an equal number of males and females, the final study consisted of 13 females and 37 males. They were all senior high school students, and their ages ranged from 16 to 18. Twenty were Caucasian, one Asian, one Armenian, one Afghanistani, seven Black, two Filipino, and eighteen Hispanic. Included in the Hispanic group was one male student who spoke no English and who had to communicate with the aid of an interpreter.

The interviews were conducted in an informal style over a period of several months and covered four major areas: their school experiences as self-identified homosexuals, with particular emphasis on perceived or real acts of discrimination; their relationship with their families; their involvement with alcohol and other abusive substances; and their concern with health matters, particularly AIDS and other sexually transmitted diseases. It is important to note that the latter concern emerged as one of the main reasons for making contact with PROJECT 10.

Of the 37 males, 35 were already sexually active with other males. The average age for the first sexual experience was 14 years, and in the majority of cases this was with an unknown male. Twelve of the respondents acknowledged having sex with women. It was interesting to note that reasons for this were ascribed to loneliness and isolation rather than to confusion over sexual orientation. None of the males in this sample had his first sexual experience in a "safe" manner, and none was still with his first sex partner. The impact of the AIDS epidemic had not made major changes in their sexual behavior by the time the interviews began, although some of the students who had friends in the "organized" gay community were more cognizant than others about "safe sex" practices. Although follow-up studies are necessary, the males who were in the sample for the longest period appeared to be responding to intensive educational efforts to modify their sexual behavior. This underscores the importance of the program.

Among the 37 males, only two had a positive relationship with their families over the issue of being gay. In all cases, the families knew about their sexual orientation, and the situations varied from extreme family disruption to forcible expulsion from home. Fifteen of the boys were living with friends, two admitted to living with "sugar daddies," and three were in residential or foster homes for gay adolescents.

Their involvement in alcohol and substance abuse was startling, with 36 of the 37 respondents admitting problems in the area. Equally startling was the fact that half of the study participants acknowledged engaging in suicide attempts in the years prior to the interview. Although a few (8) had sought help from school personnel, the majority sought help outside the schools. Without exception, those seeking help from private sources denied their sexual orientation to them. It appeared that the treatment for sexually transmitted diseases was obtained from free clinics and other services rather than family doctors.

The sample response indicated that there was widespread verbal and physical harassment in school. While some harassment began in elementary school, it increased significantly in frequency and intensity beginning in 7th grade and continuing throughout secondary school. Teachers as well as students participated in verbal harassment. Each respondent knew at least one or more students who had dropped out of school because of physical and verbal abuse that he or she had encountered. As a group, the respondents singled out their junior high school years as the most painful for them. Coming out to themselves, without psychological or social support, was described as "a time when I wanted to die," "a period where I just wanted to blot out all my feelings," or "a time when I felt like I was suffocating."

Their early sexual experiences were not recalled as happy events; rather they were often violent, guilt-ridden experiences that parallel the "date rape" experiences of many young women:

> *Greg, Caucasian, age 18.* I knew I was gay when I was eleven years old, but I didn't have sex until I was 14. I met some guy at a party, and he asked me if I wanted to go over to his apartment and watch T.V. It seemed like the end of the world. We went to his place, and he gave me some liquor. I didn't know what to do so I drank it. Then he started fooling around with me. I thought I was supposed to go along with it. I could have decked him, but somehow I was so scared that I just couldn't do anything. I thought I could run away from him, but I didn't know where I was, and I would have been too ashamed to tell anyone what happened.

Greg was particularly upset over the fact that his superior physical advantage was neutralized by the intimidating circumstances of the moment.

> When it was all over, he took me home. I gave him a wrong address, and then walked home. For weeks I was scared I'd catch something from him. I hated myself and started drinking more and more. Last year in my health class someone from the Rape Treatment Center said they get calls from guys who have been in situations like mine. I wish I had known about it, because the hardest thing for me was that I couldn't tell anybody. That was the lowest point in my life.

The responses of the 13 self-identified lesbians were considerably different from the responses of the men. Only 5 of the women had experienced sex with another woman. Although all of the young women self-identified as lesbian, there was a general reluctance to associate with the label. Further questioning revealed negative societal attitudes connected with the word "lesbian" that had not yet been shed by the respondents.

None of the women reported violent sexual encounters, but all reported considerable emotional pain over the issue of coming out to themselves. Seven reported having problems with alcohol, and three reported serious suicide attempts. Only two reported having verbal harassment directed toward them, but all reported knowing first-hand of instances of anti-gay discrimination from both teachers and fellow students. Each respondent knew at least one other person who had dropped out of school because of harassment.

Eight of the lesbian respondents reported having told their parents of their sexual orientation, and in each case their parents told them that it was a passing phase that would go away. It is interesting to note that this parental response was made to the young women, while it apparently was not a parental response directed towards the males in the study sample.

The most prevalent sentiment voiced by the young women in the sample was extreme isolation: "I feel like an oddball, not like anyone else"; "If I told any of my friends, they probably wouldn't have anything to do with me"; "There probably isn't anyone else like me."

The responses from Sample #1 participants substantiates claims by advocates for gay, lesbian, and bisexual youth that homophobia exists in the schools in a way that is predictable and systematically damaging. Overt discrimination, in the form of verbal and physical harassment, occurs with such regularity that it is an accepted part in the life of any openly gay male. Although such discrimination is apparently directed more toward gay males than toward lesbians, the majority of adolescent homosexuals of both sexes felt that the concealment of their sexual orientation was the safest course whenever possible.

In the study of the general student population at Fairfax High School, over 500 questionnaires were distributed in health and science classes in 1986. These classes were chosen because they were easily accessible and because they contained a cross-section of the students. Of the questionnaires distributed, 342 were returned. The results indicated that the PROJECT 10 program had been widely discussed (61%) with teachers in other classes, and that the majority of students felt that the subject of homosexuality was an appropriate topic for discussion.

The results also revealed that a majority of the respondents (56%) knew a gay, lesbian, or bisexual person, and they felt that there should be some outreach to gay and lesbian students on every campus. Seventy-nine percent felt that the greatest benefit of PROJECT 10 was that it provided all students with a place to get accurate information on gay, lesbian, and bisexual issues.

When asked whether the effect upon Fairfax High School had been positive or negative, 51% responded positive, 11% felt the effect had been negative (gives the school a bad name), and 38% were unsure as to the effect. Overall, the sample revealed a remarkable lack of resistance to the program.

The second part of the sample consisted of subjective evaluations maintained for the three years of the study. They came after discussions of homosexuality and bisexuality in health classes and after showing a sympathetic portrayal of a gay high school student in a made-for-TV movie *What If I'm Gay?* In these evaluations, that numbered over 300 during the time period, a shift was recorded indicating increased understanding and tolerance of homosexuality. Although the results suggest that attitudes about homosexuality and bisexuality can be changed through education efforts, more extensive research is required to assess the depth and longevity of this attitudinal change.

CONCLUSIONS

The gay and lesbian students who participated in the Sample #1 study confirmed that damage is done by school-based homophobia and that it negatively affects the self-esteem of adolescent homosexuals and increases the likelihood of self-destructive behavior. The most glaring fact emerging from the samples is the need for intensive education about safe-sex practices among teenage male homosexuals. The sample strongly suggests that information routinely received in health classes is insufficient and that a major educational effort should begin in junior high school. One-to-one counseling on the AIDS issue and close, careful monitoring appear to be the most effective, and perhaps the only, way to educate about the potential consequences of unsafe sex.

Furthermore, it should be of concern to school-based health practitioners and family physicians that students perceive them as actively hostile or, at best, unavailable resources for medical, psychological, and safe-sex information and assistance. The effect of these attitudes is to dissuade many young homosexuals from seeking adequate medical assistance. When they do seek assistance, these students admit that they rarely reveal their sexual orientation to the helping professional. Thus, while the authors are heartened by the recent article on adolescent sexuality by Bidwell and Deisher (1991) that urges family physicians and medical practitioners to be more alert and sensitive to the special needs of gay, lesbian, bisexual, and transsexual young people, the problems remain significant and largely unaddressed.

Also inadequately attended to are the counseling, drop-out, substance abuse, and suicide prevention needs of gay, lesbian, and bisexual students. The article by Sears (1992) in this volume speaks eloquently to these students' perceptions and the attitudinal limitations of the counseling and teaching professionals who are ethically bound to serve this population, but who fail them every day. Similarly, the articles by Harbeck (1992) and Woods and Harbeck (1992), also in this volume, demonstrate why gay and lesbian educators and administrators often feel too much at risk to reveal their sexual orientation and, thus, to serve as positive role models for adolescent homosexuals and bisexuals.

Another alarming feature of this study is the evidence that young gay males are frequently initiated into homosexual activity in a "date rape" situation involving substance abuse and a lack of safe sex practices. Not only must health care and education professionals address the self-esteem issues that heighten the likelihood of this sort of victimization, they must also more actively provide information and services to assist persons coerced into sexual activity and/or who have been raped.

While this study of homosexual males is dramatic because of the reports of their actively self-destructive behavior in light of the potentially lethal consequences of AIDS, it is important to realize that lesbian students face somewhat different, but equally difficult and lethal circumstances. Many of these young women have realized that their emotional and sexual feelings are strongest for members of their own sex, and yet they remain in a developmental limbo because of isolation and cultural taboos about female sexuality. Additionally, these women have attempted to articulate their feelings to their parents, and almost to a person they have been met with a dismissal of their feelings as merely "a passing phase." Without positive role models and information, these young women are defeated by the belief that their lesbian feelings are bad and "will pass" if not acted upon. Clearly, the high number of young women in this study who reported attempting suicide highlights the silent pain and confusion of their unique circumstances.

The study of the general student population at Fairfax High School suggests that negative attitudes and stereotypes toward homosexuals and bisexuals can be altered with educational intervention, a finding substantiated by Price (1982) in his study. The general student study also revealed that gay and lesbian teachers can have a very positive effect upon attitudes toward homosexuality — both for heterosexual and homosexual students — if these teachers affirm rather than conceal their sexuality. In this way, discussions seemed to move from a purely intellectual level to a heartfelt, humane, and tangible situation that elicited more personal and emotional exchanges that led to greater acceptance and insight.

PROJECT 10 was developed against a background of institutional homophobia and the effects of the stigmatization process upon gay, lesbian, and bisexual adolescents. The positive results obtained by PROJECT 10 substantiate the belief that low-cost remedies to anti-gay prejudice and discrimination are possible, that controversy surrounding this issue can be minimized, and that a commitment to human rights and the needs of these young people demands that remedies be pursued.

Furthermore, the authors believe that the impetus for such remedies should arise within the school district, in light of the professional and ethical obligations of teachers, administrators, and school-board members to provide school-based assistance and quality education for all students. If such programs are not initiated voluntarily within the schools, advocates for lesbian, gay, and bisexual youth's rights to equal educational opportunity have suggested that a litigation strategy should be pursued through the state courts (Dennis and Harlow, 1986). While the authors personally prefer education, not litigation, it is clear from the information available on suicide rates, drop-out risk, low self-esteem, health risks, substance abuse, and the plethora of other problems often experienced by gay, lesbian, and bisexual adolescents that intervention must occur immediately in every school in this nation. The pain and hardship suffered by adolescent gay, lesbian, and bisexual youth is no longer invisible, and our lack of action is no longer professionally or ethically acceptable.

REFERENCES

Bean, C. (1987). Minority AIDS Project. Telephone Interview, 20 November.

Bidwell, R., & Deisher, R. (1991). Adolescent sexuality: Current issues. *Pediatric Annals, 20*(6), 293-302.

Dennis, D., & Harlow, R. (1986). Gay youth and the right to education. *Yale Law and Policy Review.*

Fricke, A. (1981). *Reflections of a rock lobster.* Boston: Alyson Publications.

Harbeck, K. M. (1987). *Personal freedoms/public constraints: An analysis of the controversy over the employment of homosexuals as school teachers,* Vols. I and II (Doctoral dissertation, Stanford University). *Dissertation Abstracts International 48* (7), 1862A. (University Microfilms No. DA 8723009.)

Harbeck, K. M. (1992). Gay and lesbian educators: Past history/future prospects. In K. Harbeck (Ed.), *Coming out of the classroom closet: Gay and lesbian students, teachers, and curricula.* New York: The Haworth Press, Inc.

Heron, A. (1983). *One teenager in ten.* Boston: Alyson Publications.

Kinsey, A. C., Pomeroy, M., & Martin, C. E. (1948). *Sexual behavior in the human male.* Philadelphia: Saunders.

Kourany, R. F. (1987). Suicide among homosexual adolescents. *Journal of Homosexuality, 13*(4), 111-117.

Martin, D. (1982). Learning to hide: The socialization of the gay adolescent. In S. Feinstein, J. Looney, A. Schwartzberg, & A. Sorosky (Eds.), *Adolescent psychiatry* (pp. 52-65). Chicago: University of Chicago Press.

National Center for Health Statistics (1986). *Vital statistics of the United States.* Vol. 2: Mortality, Part A. Hyattsville, MD.

Paroski, R. (1987). Health care delivery and the concerns of gay and lesbian adolescents. *Journal of Adolescent Health Care, 8,* 188-192.

Price, J. (1982). High school students' attitudes toward homosexuality. *Journal of School Health, 52,* 469-474.

Remafedi, G. (1987). Adolescent homosexuality: Psychosocial and medical implications. *Pediatrics, 79,* 331-337.

Remafedi, G., Farrow, J., & Deisher, R. (1991). Risk factors for attempted suicide in gay and bisexual youth. *Pediatrics, 87*(6), 869-876.

Sears, J. (1990). *Growing up gay in the South: Race, gender, and journeys of the spirit.* New York: The Haworth Press, Inc.

Sears, J. (1992). Educators, homosexuality, and homosexual students: Are personal feelings related to professional beliefs? In K. Harbeck (Ed.), *Coming out of the classroom closet: Gay and lesbian students, teachers, and curricula.* New York: The Haworth Press, Inc.

US Department of Health and Human Services (1989). Report of the secretary's task force on youth suicide. Vol. 3: Prevention and interventions in youth suicide. Rockville, MD.

Uribe, V. (1988). The implementation of a district-wide counseling program for lesbian and gay youth: Los Angeles Unified School District-Secondary Division. Doctoral dissertation, Sierra University.

Woods, S., & Harbeck, K. (1992). Living in two worlds: The identity management strategies used by lesbian physical educators. In K. Harbeck, (Ed.), *Coming out of the classroom closet: Gay and lesbian students, teachers, and curricula.* New York: The Haworth Press, Inc.

Educators, Homosexuality, and Homosexual Students: Are Personal Feelings Related to Professional Beliefs?

James T. Sears, PhD

University of South Carolina

SUMMARY. This study is based on interviews with Southern lesbian and gay young adults and survey data from school counselors and prospective teachers living in the South. The essay explores adolescents' perceptions of the beliefs and abilities of school counselors and teachers with regard to issues of homosexuality and the treatment of gay and lesbian students. As a complement and a contrast, it also presents educators' personal beliefs about homosexuality, and how these attitudes are actualized in the schools. One major conclusion is that while school counselors and, to a lesser extent, classroom teachers often expressed the feeling that they should be more proactive and supportive as professionals committed to the welfare of all of their students, due to countervailing expressions of high levels of personal prejudice, ignorance, and fear, the realities of their professional intervention and support were negligible.

James T. Sears is Associate Professor of Curriculum in the Department of Educational Leadership and Policies at the University of South Carolina and senior research associate at the South Carolina Educational Policy Center. He is author of *Growing up Gay in the South,* upon which the data presented in this paper are based. The founder of the Lesbian and Gay Studies special interest group of the American Educational Research Association, Professor Sears is currently completing a book on sexual understandings held by members of distinct cultural communities in the United States. The author expresses special thanks to Lorin Anderson and Karen Harbeck for their helpful comments and suggestions.

29

What are educators' personal attitudes and feelings about homosexuality? How do these personal beliefs affect their everyday activities as teachers and guidance counselors? What impact do these personal beliefs and professional activities have upon students struggling with their sexual identities?

This paper will first examine the perceptions of lesbian and gay youth about educators based on data from Southern youth between 1986 and 1988 who recently graduated from high school. A purposive sample of young people representing different social classes, races, and gender were interviewed in 90-minute sessions. These interviews were taped, transcribed, and analyzed using standard qualitative methodology.[1] Participants were promised anonymity; all names used in this paper are fictitious.

The next part of this paper presents survey data gathered from school counselors and prospective teachers regarding their personal attitudes and feelings about homosexuality. The quantitative data in this paper come from surveys administered to guidance counselors and prospective teachers as South Carolina developed legislation on sexuality education (Earls, Fraser, & Sumpter, in press). In collaboration with the South Carolina Guidance Counselors' Association, 483 middle school and high school guidance counselors received a questionnaire during the spring of 1987. The questionnaire included the modified Attitudes Toward Homosexuality (ATH), a 30-item Likert-type instrument, and the Index of Homophobia (IH), a summative category partition scale of a person's reactions toward homosexual encounters and feelings toward homosexual persons (Hudson & Ricketts, 1980; MacDonald, Huggins, Young, & Swanson, 1973; Price, 1982).[2] Additionally, counselors completed a questionnaire with items related to their experiences in working with homosexual students, knowledge and beliefs about homosexuality, assessment of the school climate for homosexual-identified students; and projected professional activities relating to enhancing their knowledge and skills in working with gay youth. One hundred forty-two persons returned usable questionnaires. The typical respondent was a white, native South Carolinian female in her late thirties with a master's degree and ten years counseling experience with rural adolescents.

A second sample was 258 prospective teachers at the beginning and end points of their teacher preparation program. These students attended either a required undergraduate social foundations course or a student teaching seminar between springs of 1987 and 1988, and completed an anonymous questionnaire mid-way through their semester. Most of the study participants (n = 191) were attending a social foundations course with a nearly equal number of secondary and elementary education majors. The typical respondent was a white, unmarried female, twenty-year-old, solid "B" sophomore from rural South Carolina taking her second education course. Sixty-seven questionnaires also were completed by prospective teachers completing their student teaching. On average, these respondents had taken seven teacher education courses. The typical respondent was a white, unmarried, twenty-eight-year-old female student teaching in a secondary school setting from which she graduated eleven years ago.

The prospective teacher questionnaire included two standardized attitudinal instruments: the modified Attitudes Toward Homosexuality (ATH) and the Index of Homophobia (IH). In addition, they also completed a questionnaire with items related to their encounters with homosexual students as a high school student, knowledge about homosexuality, professional attitudes regarding homosexuality in the school curriculum, and projected professional behaviors regarding homosexual students.[3]

The third part of this paper discusses these educators' attitudes regarding their *professional* role of educators in working with lesbian and gay-identified students. As I will argue, while these educators assert their ability to bracket personal feelings in professional settings, their past and anticipated future professional behaviors make such a claim suspect.

ADOLESCENTS' PERCEPTIONS OF EDUCATORS

Everyday:
We wake up and get ready for work.
We drive our cars on the same roads,
the same highways.
We park right next to your cars.
We use the same bathrooms.
We listen to the same music.
We breathe the same air.
We live in the same society.

So, why do you abhor us when we share so many of the same things?
Okay, so we love differently!
Why does that matter?
There is really nothing to fear from us
except the pain that comes from your ignorance!

Brett, a high school student

Sexual rebels, such as Brett, spoke at length about the difficulty they faced in school as the result of the negative attitudes of educators (Sears, 1989b; Sears, 1991). Most noted that this topic was simply avoided by teachers, counselors, and administrators in their school. They viewed guidance counselors, in particular, as academic not personal advisors. A few of the participants, however, relayed stories of supportive educators who made a difference in their adolescent lives.

Franklin lives in a predominantly black South Carolina rural town. He remembers harassment from educators inside and outside the classroom:

> In high school, like the town, it was very hush-hush about homosexuality. You never talked to the students, teachers, principal, or counselors about it. They never talked to you about it. Even though I had two friends who were open and admitted it at the time, the teachers just ignored it and kept their feelings to themselves. But, the principal would always try to look out for the bad things these two were doing. He was always trying to get them for something. One day I was with my friends—when you are with them you are labelled—and this real flaming and feminine guy was telling someone off so the principal wrote him up and sent him to the "box" [in-school suspension].

Franklin also recalled an incident with his high school physics teacher:

> Mr. Jenson would usually drift away from the subject. He'd often bring up homosexuality. He mainly talked about the wrongs of it and how it was such a sin and that they should be condemned. I felt really bad.

Other participants reported similar incidents. For example, Fawn remembers one teacher who "hated me because she knew I was gay. She would fill out these forms that got me into trouble and then make comments like, 'People like you . . .'"

Only a handful of participants, including Brett, reported speaking to a guidance counselor or teacher about their homosexuality. In general, they perceived these adults to be ill-informed and unconcerned; they simply felt uncomfortable talking to them. The image of counselors communicated to the participants in this study was summed up by Kimberly: "Our counselors had never been presented to us as someone there to talk about problems other than education. They were just there for grades, signing up for classes, tests like the PSAT, and finding colleges to attend."

Similar sentiments were echoed about teachers and their unwillingness to show concern for lesbian and gay-identified students or to express their feelings about homosexuality. A senior in high school, Nathaniel, recalls a recent classroom discussion dealing with homosexuality:

> In my sociology class we were talking about AIDS. One guy said, "I think gay guys are just sick. How could they do that? It's wrong!" One of my friends who is gay asks, "Why do you think it's wrong?" Well, everyone looks over to Miss L., our teacher, for what she thinks. She says, "I have no comment. I'm not even going to get into this discussion. I'm going to keep my opinion to myself." So we lingered on this topic for awhile. I kept my mouth closed. Another guy said, "If a fag makes a move on me, I'd whip his ass." I thought to myself, "Yeah, right. We had gotten in a fight earlier and I liked dogged him out." Then two of the football players joined in. One was on each side. So, I piped up. (I had just gone into wrestling, so I was safe. The people who had been calling me gay had been coming up to me saying, "Hey man, I'm sorry for calling you queer.") So, I say "If you don't try it, you never will know what's going on. You're just going on hearsay. How can you judge these people? They're people too, just because their sexuality is different."

This detachment of teachers from personal concerns and social issues was underscored repeatedly in conversations with these sexual rebels. Carlton stated:

> Teachers seem to keep themselves so removed. In high school, teachers weren't people. They just lived in the school, went into the closet, stayed there over night, and then came out during the day, right? It was hard to think of them as real people. It was hard to interact with them. You know, a lot of the child's life is spent in school. If all that time is dealt with them through the book and not attending to any kind of personal needs, it just seems so ridiculous to me—stilted. It puts such a damper on what could be done.

Georgina's comments illustrate how quickly young people can pick up on teachers' personal detachment from their students—and how students can hide behind the role teachers expect them to assume:

Teachers don't see much of your inner self. They don't ask. It's easy to put on a face with teachers. For example, Miss Morrison wanted someone very Christian-like, a little angel. For her, I wrote in my English journal about Jesus and love all the time. Mr. Boozer was the band director. He wanted somebody with good leadership skills who could play well. He got that. Mrs. Laman, she liked slaves. So, if you volunteered for everything, like I did, she liked you. As long as you keep them happy, they think that you're well-adjusted.

Carlton is studying to become a teacher. Arguing that "a teacher is involved in growth and guidance and not simply to teach math, science or English," he asserts:

I would think that a student would be quicker to want to talk to teachers if they had been kind to them. If they had just started talking to me on a personal basis. Just to talk about interests, "Well, how's the rest of school? What do you like to do? I hear you're in chorus?" I might have more easily been able to bring it up. I remember this one woman, she was so hard. It would not have taken much for her to have asked me more personal questions. Like, "Carlton, how are you doing in school and I don't mean academically?" She possibly could have made me think about things that I hadn't even gotten up to the conscious level yet and then just leave it open for me to talk about them with her. If she'd only have said, "If you want to talk about anything, you can"—but she didn't.

Of course, being open to a student does not guarantee a response from that student. Darla, for example, was not ready to respond to teacher initiatives the way Brett and Georgina were. In ninth grade, Darla had Mrs. Taxel for sex education. "At first I hated her. All I heard throughout the whole year was that she talked about her little grandson. Sure enough, the first day of class that was the first thing she talked about, her stupid grandson." After several weeks of engaging in subtle but defiant acts in the classroom, Darla found herself confronted by Mrs. Taxel:

I got ready to walk out after class. She stopped me and slammed the door. "Sit down. We're talking," she said. "I can't understand why you dislike me so much." I said, "Frankly, because you're a bitch." Mrs. Taxel saw my cigarettes hanging out of my pocket. "Are those yours?" I told her they were. "Can I have one?" I said, "Sure." I handed her one and I got one. We just sat there smoking and talking. After that, we became good friends. I could talk to her about anything — except being gay.

Most teachers, of course, are not as open or willing to engage adolescents on their own terms — let alone to broach the subject of homosexuality. Carlton appreciates the teacher's dilemma. "Looking back, they probably were aware but afraid to talk about my homosexuality. Besides, they probably didn't know what kind of reaction they would get from me if they had tried or if they were wrong." Nevertheless, Carlton is resentful about the inability or unwillingness of educators to try to communicate with him.

> I've felt cheated by school. I felt there was so much potential, so much I could have done and we didn't nearly approach it. I've lost time, and a lot of that can't be gotten back. It was as if I was there for a prison term or they were my baby sitters without permission to do anything with me. Teachers act like they have total authority *and* that they can do nothing all at the same time!

This latter point is well illustrated by Franklin's observation of how teachers in his high school dealt with slurs. "The teachers weren't very tolerant as far as racial slurs. If a teacher heard it, she might write him up. If there was a sexual slur, like 'fag,' they would pay no attention to it. That told me they didn't feel homophobia was as important as racism." Carlton concurs:

> If a teacher got tired of hearing these derogatory remarks they would only say "stop" — never questioning as to why they were feeling that way or trying to make them think about what they were doing. Only that, "I just don't want to hear that." They would be a lot quicker to jump on other minority groups than homosexuals.

Despite the bleakness of these tales, there are educators who genuinely care about lesbian and gay-identified students and try to work with them. One of these was Laura Huggins, a counselor intern at the school where Georgina attended.

In tenth grade, Georgina's lover, Kay, began to see Miss Huggins who after a while asked to see Georgina. Georgina stopped by Miss Huggins' office for a quick chat, and found her to be pleasant and mild-mannered. "She told me to see her if I had any problems." Six weeks later, Georgina discovered that Kay was seeing another girl; a violent quarrel erupted.

Thinking that she had no one to turn to, Georgina suddenly remembered Miss Huggins' words:

> I wrote Miss Huggins a note and slipped it under her door. The next time she saw me, she said, "I know. Do you want to talk about it?" I told her all about my relationship with Kay. She acted as kind of an umpire in our fight. I remember her telling me, "You have different walls around you, Georgina. Every once in a while a wall will collapse and you'll kick it back up. Someday they will all come down and you will get hurt. You'll be tempted to put them back up again. But, don't." I really didn't quite understand what she was saying but it was a relief not to have to put on an act around somebody.

Miss Huggins helped to mend the quarrel between the twosome. Georgina continued to see Kay through her sophomore year. Georgina reminisces, "When you first fall in love, you're always caught up. Love is blind. You can't see what is really going on around you. I knew that Kay liked other people and wanted to date them along with me. She just wasn't ready to settle down." A short time later Miss Huggins completed her internship at the school. Georgina regretted her departure:

> If Miss Huggins would have stayed, I feel that I would have accepted myself a lot better. But, they didn't send anybody else. I remember after she left feeling so sad and needing to talk to somebody. All the time I kept thinking, "I can do what Patton did; I could try to kill myself." I was going to take some sleeping pills and eat them right before my mom came home. I thought, "If she catches me in time, I'll get to talk to someone." I didn't want to kill myself; I just wanted to talk to someone who knew what they were talking about.

Though Nathaniel never found an educator like Miss Huggins with whom he could speak frankly, he did receive advice early in high school from an adult working at his school. At 14, Nathaniel hadn't identified himself as gay though he knew that he enjoyed males physically as well as socially. He developed a crush on Reuben, a neighborhood boy three years his senior. The first time the two met, the older boy told Nathaniel, "'Look, I'm gay. I want you to know this if you have any problems.' I had no problems with that and we soon became real close." Nathaniel continues: "One night we got some beer and got wasted, or at least acted like we were drunk. We started feeling on each other, grabbing one another. One thing lead to another and we just kept going."

Nathaniel also had sexual fantasies about girls and enjoyed their emotional company. About this time he started to date Delta. "I was scared, I really was. I was wondering if I was going to lose my feelings for Delta, who I loved, while I still really loved Reuben." Confused about these feelings, Nathaniel "thought about talking to the counselor, but I just didn't build up enough nerve." He finally sat down in the corridor after school one day and just cried. Suddenly he felt a gentle tap on his shoulder. Looking up he saw Ol' Jessie, the school's janitor. His short grey hair stood out against his black skin. Jessie invited Nathaniel down to his "office." Once in the boiler room, the two pulled up a couple of crates and had a long talk. "He told me that I was too young to even worry about being a homosexual. 'Every man,' he said, 'has them feelings. You're going to look over at another guy in the bathroom and say, 'I'm big enough. Can I satisfy this person?' Then I sat down and thought. 'Well, if it's normal for someone to have homosexual feelings, why isn't it normal for a guy to try homosexual sex?'"

Having supportive adults such as Miss Huggins and Ol' Jessie was certainly helpful to Georgina and Nathaniel. Though most participants in this study said they would have liked to have had such educators while attending high school, some were much more reticent about such prospects. There were a variety of reasons for such caution, including unwillingness of the student to assume the initiative, lack of trust in confidentiality, the worry of losing teacher friendship, and personality differences. Audrey states, "I did not have direct counseling. I'm glad because I don't know how I would have acted. In high school if it were to get out I would have been so embarrassed. I could not have stood the peer pressure." Kimberly remembers:

> I didn't talk to counselors because they're human, too. Homosexuality is taboo. People just kind of go bonkers when they hear that word or find out that somebody is homosexual. Even the adults act like kids. They don't know how to handle it. I thought, "I can't trust anybody with this information." You know, teachers talk.

This was echoed by Franklin: "I didn't want them to know my feelings. I wasn't that trusting of them. I felt that they might tell my parents." Phillip, who enjoyed close friendship with several teachers, feared sharing his sexual feelings because it would be "like risking them not liking me."

How accurate are these students' perceptions of educators? What is the relationship between educators' personal feelings and beliefs about homosexuality and their views of their professional responsibilities to serve homosexual students? The next two sections of this paper addresses these questions.

EDUCATORS' PERSONAL ATTITUDES AND FEELINGS

Popularized by sociologist Weinberg (1972), "homophobia" originally meant an irrational fear of homosexual persons. Over the years, however, homophobia has been expanded to include disgust, anxiety, and anger (MacDonald, 1976). Further, it has come to be used not only to the reactions of heterosexuals but the internalization of negative feelings by homosexual men and women (Lehne, 1976; Malyon, 1982; Margolies, Becker, & Jackson-Brewer, 1987). Despite the methodological, conceptual, and political problems associated with "homophobia," the term is a useful benchmark for a beginning understanding of the attitudes and feelings of persons about homosexuality and the sources for these beliefs (Herek, 1984; Lehne, 1976; Sears, 1990).

One of the more extensive areas of research in lesbian and gay studies is on adult attitudes toward homosexuality or toward homosexuals. These studies often report the relationships between attitudes and personality traits or demographic variables.[4] Though such studies are not without conflicting data, Herek (1984) has summarized some consistent patterns. People with negative attitudes report less personal contact with gays and lesbians, less (if any) homosexual behavior, a more conservative religious ideology, and more traditional attitudes about sex roles than do those with less negative views. Those harboring negative attitudes about homosexuality are also more likely to have resided in the Midwest or the South, to have grown up in rural areas or in small towns, and to be male, older, and less well-educated than those expressing more positive attitudes.

Quasi-experimental research studies have demonstrated that adult males harbor more homophobic attitudes or feelings than females and are more concerned about male homosexuality than lesbianism (Aguero, Bloch, & Byrne, 1984; Braungart & Braungart, 1988; Clift, 1988; Coles & Stokes, 1985; Hong, 1983; Larsen, Reed, & Hoffman, 1980; Schatman, 1989; Young & Whertvine, 1982). Further, those with less negative feelings or attitudes are more likely to have had associations or friendships with lesbians or gay men (Anderson, 1981; Gentry, 1986a, 1986b; Maddux, 1988; Schneider & Lewis, 1984; Weiner, 1989). Conflicting data, however, have been reported using different samples or research instruments. For example, as I will document in this paper, male guidance counselors were less homophobic than their female counterparts and data from opinion polls (Irwin & Thompson, 1977; Schneider & Lewis, 1984) report no sex differences. Attributing these differences to population samples and attitudinal items, Herek (1986) in his review of this phenomenon, concludes "Males and females probably hold roughly similar positions on general questions of morality and civil liberties, but males are more homophobic in emotional reactions to homosexuality'' (p. 565).

Studies have also assessed the attitudes and feelings of people in the helping professions toward homosexuality and homosexual persons (Casas, Brady, & Poterotto, 1983; Davison & Wilson, 1973; DeCrescenzo, 1983/84; Douglas, Kalman, & Kalman, 1985; Garfinkle & Morin, 1978; Gartrell, Kraemer, & Brodie, 1974; Hochstein, 1988; Larkin, 1989; McQuoid, 1988; Pauly & Goldstein, 1970; Wisniewski & Toomey, 1987). These studies have found a heterosexual bias in these persons' professional attitudes and homophobia in their personal feelings. Only a handful of studies, however, have examined issues relating to homosexuality in the context of the public elementary or high school (Dressler, 1985; Fischer, 1982; Griffin, 1992; Price, 1982; Smith, 1985). These studies have focused on teachers, high school students, principals, and gay/lesbian teachers. For example, most school administrators would dismiss a teacher for disclosing her homosexuality to students, and one fourth of all college students preparing to teach at one institution acknowledged their inability to treat fairly a homosexual student or discuss homosexuality in the classroom. While several studies have explored this topic with counselor trainees (Clark, 1979; Glenn & Russell, 1986; Schneider & Tremble, 1986; Thompson & Fishburn, 1977), only two (Baker, 1980; Maddux, 1988) have examined the attitudes and feelings of persons preparing to be teachers and none have studied school guidance counselors' perceptions.

Most education-related articles have been normative essays discussing the special needs and problems of homosexual students (Benvenuti, 1986; Dillon, 1986; Gumaer, 1987; Krysiak, 1987; Russell, 1989; Schneider and Tremble, 1986; Scott, 1988; Sears, 1987; Sears, 1988b). The few empirical studies cited above, however, support the essayist's view that educators, in general, lack the sensitivity, knowledge, and skills to address effectively the needs of students with same-sex feelings. This following section adds to the growing empirical data in this area by focusing on the least researched groups: prospective teachers and school guidance counselors.

Prospective Teachers' Attitudes and Feelings

This section examines prospective teachers attitudes and feelings about homosexuality, their encounters with homosexuals and homosexuality while high school students, and their knowledge about homosexuality.

Eight out of ten prospective teachers surveyed harbored negative feelings toward lesbians and gay men; fully one third of these persons, using the Index of Homophobia classification, are "high grade homophobics" — nearly five times as many as classified by Hudson and Rickets (1980) in their study of college students a decade ago. Prospective teachers pursuing certification in elementary education were more likely to harbor homophobic feelings and express homo-negative attitudes than those planning to teach in the secondary schools; black prospective teachers also expressed more negative attitudes about homosexuality than their white counterparts but were no more homophobic in their feelings toward lesbians and gay men (Sears, 1989a).

Two separate instruments assessed prospective teachers *attitudes* toward homosexuality (ATH) and their *feelings* toward lesbians and gay men (IH). Since the conceptualization of "homophobia" as a research construct nearly 20 years ago, there is agreement that attitudes and feelings must be treated as separate constructs. Thus, in this study attitudes have been conceptualized as a set of cognitive beliefs about homosexuals and homosexuality whereas feelings are defined as a set of deep-rooted emotive reactions to homosexual situations or persons. Examples of attitudinal survey items are: "Homosexuality is unnatural," "Homosexual marriage should be made legal," and "I would not want homosexuals to live near me"; examples of items which tap respondents' feelings are: "I would feel nervous being in a group of homosexuals," "If I saw two men holding hands in public, I would feel disgusted," and "I would feel comfortable if I learned that my best friend of my same sex was homosexual."[5]

Given the uni-dimensionality of the Attitudes Toward Homosexuality (ATH) and the Index of Homophobia (IH), respondents' summative scores were computed for each (Sears, 1988b). These adjusted scores could range from 0 (most positive) to 100 (most negative). Students' scores on the ATH ranged from 0 to 98, with a mean score of 45, and a standard deviation of 18. Students' scores on the IH yielded more negative results. The scores ranged from 2 to 99, with a mean score of 65 and a standard deviation of 19. The relationship between these two scores are depicted in Figure 1.

As indicated in Figure 1, the distribution of students' attitudes toward homosexuality (ATH) falls much more closer to the classic bell-shaped curve than do those for their feelings toward lesbians and gay men (IH). For example, one quarter of the sample scored between the ninth and tenth decile on feelings toward homosexual persons whereas less than 3 percent of the students scored in this range on the attitudes toward homosexuality.

In order to provide a point of reference for interpreting these scores,

Figure 1
Distribution By Decile
of Preservice Teachers Attitudes Toward Homosexuality
and Feelings About Homosexual Persons

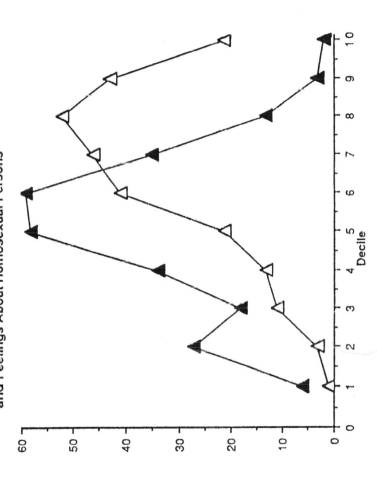

41

data from other studies using the IH and the ATH are summarized in Tables 1 and 2.

According to the authors of the Index of Homophobia scale (Hudson & Ricketts, 1980, p. 360), scores of less than 25 evidence "high grade non-homophobics," and those who score between 25 and 50 are considered "low grade non-homophobics." Persons who scores lies between 50 and 75 are regarded as "low grade homophobics," and "high grade homophobics" score above 75. As Table 1 indicates, eight out of ten prospective teachers harbor negative feelings toward lesbian and gay men; fully one-third of these persons are high grade homophobics. This represents five times the number of high grade homophobics found in Hudson and Ricketts' study a decade ago in Hawaii.

Given difference in geographic region and time, a more useful comparison is the sample of South Carolina guidance counselors surveyed at about the same time as these prospective teachers. As noted in Table 1, both the mean scores of these two groups and the proportion scoring above 50 are similar. The prospective teacher sample, however, is composed of half again the number of "high grade homophobics."

Attitudes about homosexuality among students and educators also have been assessed by several researchers. As shown in Table 2, prospective students' attitudes toward homosexuality, though less negative than a sample of Ohio high school students, is considerably less positive than a group of North Carolina teachers. Prospective teachers in this study scored identical to a sample of college students.

Table 3 depicts the relationship between prospective teachers' attitudes about homosexuality and feelings toward lesbian and gay men vis-à-vis

TABLE 1

Percentage Distribution of
Index of Homophobia Scores
Among Various Populations

Population	<25	25-50	51-75	>75	N	$\overline{X}$
PRESERVICE TEACHERS	.03	.16	.44	.37	252	65
College Students (Hudson & Ricketts, 1980)	.04	.33	.56	.07	300	53
Guidance Counselors (Sears, 1988a)	.01	.26	.50	.22	141	61

TABLE 2

Comparison of
Attitudes Toward Homosexuality
Among Various Groups

Population	$\overline{X}$ Score	N
PRESERVICE TEACHERS	56	255
Teachers (Fischer, 1982)	42	255
High School Students (Price, 1982)	60	278
College Students (Goldberg, 1982)	56	131
Guidance Counselors (Sears, 1988a)	53	141

their race, gender, area of certification, and point in the teacher education curriculum using multiple t-tests.

As Table 3 indicates, the point at which prospective teachers are at in their professional program of studies is not significantly related to either their attitudes toward homosexuality or their feelings toward lesbians and gay men. Further, unlike studies of other populations, no differences on attitudes or feelings were found with respect to gender. African-American prospective teachers were more likely to express negative attitudes toward homosexuality than Anglo students. There was no relationship between respondent's race and feelings he or she expressed toward lesbians and gay men. The area of certification was the only factor that discriminated on respondents' attitudes and feelings. In both cases, students intending to teach at the elementary level evidenced more negative scores.

To explore the relative effects of race, gender, program status, and certification area, these four categorical factors together with age, marital status, college grade point average, and type of home community were entered into a multiple regression analysis using either student attitudes about homosexuality scores (ATH) or their scores on feelings toward lesbian and gay men (IH) as the dependent variable. The results of these analyses with the Beta weights appear in Table 4.

These eight variables explain only 11 percent of the variance on prospective teachers' attitudes toward homosexuality and 13 percent of the variance on their feelings toward lesbians and gay men. Two or three variables, however, account for the majority of this variance. Using a step-

TABLE 3

Prospective Teachers'
Attitudes About Homosexuality and
Feelings Toward Lesbians and Gay Men
According to Respondents'
Gender, Race, Certification Area & Program Status

Demographic	ATH $\overline{X}$	ATH SD	t	df	IH $\overline{X}$	IH SD	t	df
Gender								
Male	45	18	- .16	192	64	18	-.49	113
Female	45	17			65	20		
Race								
White	45	18	-2.16	33*	65	20	-.70	34
Black	52	16			67	15		
Certification Area								
Elementary	50	17	3.18	208*	73	18	4.73	196*
Secondary	43	18			62	18		
Point in Professional Studies								
Early	45	19	.17	122	65	20	.47	142
Late	45	17			64	16		

* p <.001

wise multiple regression analysis, certification area, home community, and point in professional studies explain slightly less than seven percent of the reported prospective teachers' variance on their attitudes toward homosexuality; area of certification explaining one-third of that variance. With respect to prospective teachers' feelings, area of certification and point in the teacher education curriculum explained more than ten percent of the variance with area of certification representing 95 percent of that variation.

Prospective teachers were also asked questions regarding their encounters with homosexuality as a high school student. About six years had elapsed since respondents in this study graduated from high school. The actual range was 1 to 41 years. However, nearly two-thirds of the sample had left high school within the past four years; about one in ten respondents had graduated from high school 15 or more years ago. Students at the early point in their professional studies had completed high school, on

TABLE 4

Multiple Regression (Betas) of Categoric/Demographic
Variables onto Prospective Teachers' Scores on
Attitudes About Homosexuality and
Feelings Toward Homosexual Persons

Factor	ATH	IH
Age	-.12	-.16
Gender	-.06	-.09
Certification Area	-.26*	-.36*
Point in Professional Studies	.18*	.18*
Race	0	-.06
Home Community	-.15*	-.03
GPA	.10	.01
Marital	.06	.02

* Regression coefficient greater than twice its standard error

average, four years earlier; students completing their student teaching and participating in the MAT program had completed high school eleven years ago. This section examines respondents' exposure to homosexuality and homosexual students while attending high school. Further, the relationships between prospective teachers' present attitudes and feelings regarding homosexuality and lesbians and gay men and their exposure to this topic or acquaintance with lesbian and gay students during their high school years are explored.

Four questions were posed regarding prospective teachers' acquaintance with lesbian and gay students during their high school experience. These questions and the distribution of responses are presented in Table 5.

Table 5 indicates that nearly one half of the respondents suspected a fellow high school student of having a homosexual orientation, and more than one quarter knew such a student, yet fewer than one out of five acknowledged being friends with a lesbian or gay student during high school.

Comparison of prospective teachers' current feelings toward lesbians and gay men and attitudes about homosexuality were examined in light of

TABLE 5

Respondents Association with
Lesbian and Gay Students
While Attending High School

Relationship	No	Yes
Suspected another student of having a homosexual orientation	.55 (143)	.45 (115)
Knew a student who had a homosexual orientation	.72 (186)	.28 (72)
Suspected a friend of having a homosexual orientation	.74 (190)	.26 (68)
Knew a friend who had a homosexual orientation	.82 (212)	.18 (46)

these high school experiences. Prospective teachers who, as high school students, knew a homosexual student or were friends with a person they knew or suspected was lesbian or gay evidenced less negative feelings toward homosexual persons and less negative attitudes about homosexuality. In an absolute sense, however, these feelings were still in the "low grade homophobic" range. These data are depicted in Tables 6 and 7.

Respondents addressed nine questions relating to their exposure to homosexuality during their high school years. One question asked them to assess the adequacy and accuracy of information about homosexuality provided to them during high school. Three fourths of the sample (n = 191) did *not* believe such information was accurate or adequate. Students who reported that they were provided with accurate and adequate information, however, harbored less negative attitudes about homosexuality (Provided $\overline{X}$ = 52, Not Provided $\overline{X}$ = 58; df = 110, t = 2.4; p < .001) and exhibited less negative feelings toward lesbians and gay men (Provided $\overline{X}$ = 60, Not Provided $\overline{X}$ = 67; df = 97, t = 2.4; p < .001).

Prospective teachers also assessed the extent to which their fellow high school students and educators were knowledgeable about homosexuality and the degree of acceptance exhibited toward it. The frequency distributions of these responses appear in Table 8.

There are several interesting findings to highlight in this table. First, as evidenced by the large proportion of the sample responding "don't know" to items on educators, homosexuality was not an issue on which most educators had taken a public position. A substantial number of respondents simply were unaware of educators' knowledge about homosex-

TABLE 6

Prospective Teachers' Feelings
Toward Homosexual Persons
According to Their Association with
Lesbian and Gay Students
While Attending High School

Relationship	IH $\overline{X}$		IH SD		t	df
	No	Yes	No	Yes		
Suspected another student of a homosexual orientation	66	64	17	22	.69	208
Knew a student who had a homosexual orientation	66	62	19	21	1.35	117*
Suspected a friend of a homosexual orientation	67	58	19	21	2.5	60*
Knew a friend who had a homosexual orientation	68	53	18	22	4.44	58*

* p <.001

TABLE 7

Prospective Teachers' Feelings
Toward Homosexual Persons
According to Their Association with
Lesbian and Gay Students
While Attending High School

Relationship	ATH $\overline{X}$		ATH SD		t	df
	No	Yes	No	Yes		
Suspected another student of a homosexual orientation	57	56	14	15	.5	228
Knew a student who had a homosexual orientation	57	54	14	17	1.4	109*
Suspected a friend of a homosexual orientation	58	50	14	16	3.1	60*
Knew a friend who had a homosexual orientation	58	46	13	16	4.9	59*

*p <.001

TABLE 8

Respondents' Assessments of
Fellow High School Students
and Their High School Educators
Knowledge and Acceptance of Homosexuality

Group Characteristic	Approximate Size of Group[1]					
	All	Most	Some	Few	None	Don't Know
Students knowledgeable about homosexuality	.11 (28)	.36 (94)	.26 (67)	.20 (51)	.02 (4)	.04 (14)
Teachers knowledgeable about homosexuality	.14 (37)	.27 (69)	.21 (54)	.15 (39)	.02 (4)	.21(55)
Counselors well informed about homosexuality	.09 (23)	.12 (32)	.12 (30)	.14 (35)	.13 (34)	.40(104)
Students displaying negative attitudes about homosexuality	.11 (28)	.73 (187)	.09 (24)	.02 (5)	.02 (4)	.04 (10)
Teachers supportive of homosexual students	----	----	.05 (14)	.19 (48)	.29 (74)	.47 (126)
Students considering homosexuality an alternative lifestyle	.01 (2)	.02 (6)	.07 (17)	.54 (190)	.22 (56)	.14 (37)
Teachers considering homosexuality an alternative lifestyle	----	.02 (5)	.09 (24)	.34 (88)	.21 (55)	.33(86)
Teachers discuss homosexuality in the classroom	----	.02 (4)	.06 (15)	.39 (100)	.48 (124)	.16(15)

[1]Percentages rounded to nearest decimal point

uality or the degree of support they accorded to homosexual students or
gay rights. The absence of classroom discussion in all but a few classrooms may explain why so few respondents could assess the position of
their teachers.

Second, when asked if all or most of the school's faculty were knowledgeable about homosexuality, respondents rated twice as many of the
teaching faculty (.41) than the counseling staff (.21) as knowledgeable. A
very large percentage (.40) of these prospective teachers, however, simply reported no basis for assessing their counselors' knowledge while attending high school. Interestingly, respondents generally rated their fellow high school students, as a group, more knowledgeable about the
subject than the faculty. This may reflect the willingness of each of these
groups to express their ideas about homosexuality.

Third, while respondents considered many of their fellow students relatively knowledgeable about homosexuality, these same students, they reported, were very likely to display negative attitudes on this topic. Eight
out of ten prospective teachers noted that most if not all of their fellow
students in high school harbored homo-negative attitudes. And, like their
teachers, few or none considered homosexuality an alternative lifestyle.

Another dimension on which this sample of prospective teachers were
examined was their current knowledge about homosexuality. A 14-item
test was developed that included questions from the natural and behavioral
sciences. A majority of the prospective teachers answered 10 of the 14
questions correctly. These responses are arranged in order of correct frequency in Table 9.

Items which had the most correct responses included those that directly
dealt with childhood sexuality. Most respondents correctly noted that, according to most authorities, homosexuality is not a phase which children
outgrow and that sexual orientation is established at an early age. Relatively few prospective teachers, however, were aware that most men and
women engage in homosexual and heterosexual behaviors during their
lifetime or that same-sex activities occur in many animal species.

Individual scores from this 14-item test were calculated yielding a Homosexuality Knowledge Index (HKI) which ranged from 0 (lowest possible score) to 100 (perfect score). The distribution of prospective teachers
on this index in pictured in Figure 2.

These scores roughly conformed to a normal bell-shaped curve. The
mean score was 57.5 with a range of 0 to 92 and a standard deviation of
19.5. One third of the respondents scored at or above the 60th percentile.
There were no significant differences on these scores between prospective
teachers who were at the early point in their professional studies and those

TABLE 9

"Correct" Response Percentages
on Knowledge about Homosexuality

Item	Correct Response	% Correct Response
Homosexuality is a phase which children outgrow	False	81
There is a good chance of changing homosexual persons into heterosexual men and women	False	77
Most homosexuals want to be members of the opposite sex	False	76
Some church denominations have condemned the legal and social discrimination of homosexual men and women	True	76
Sexual orientation is established at an early age	True	72
According to the American Psychological Association, homosexuality is an illness	False	64
Homosexual males are more likely to seduce young boys than heterosexual males are likely to seduce young girls	False	58
Gay men are at least four times likely to be victims of criminal violence as members of the general public	True	54
A majority of homosexuals were seduced in adolescence by a person of the same sex, usually several years older	False	53
Sixty percent of pre-adolescent males report at least one homosexual experience	True	52
A person become a homosexual (develops a homosexual orientation) because he/she chooses to do so	False	46
Homosexual activity occurs in many animals	True	40
Most adults engage in neither exclusive homosexual or heterosexual behavior	True	29
Sexual relations between two people of the same sex is a criminal act in most states, including SC	False	28

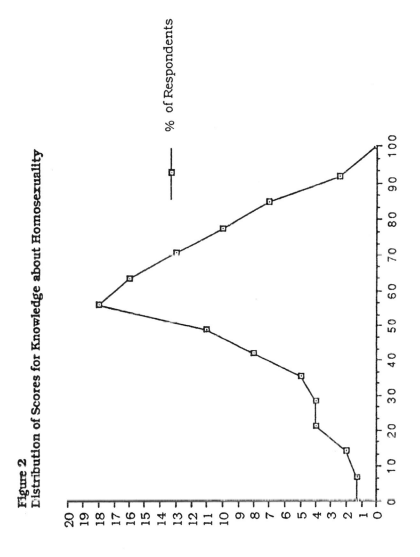

Figure 2
Distribution of Scores for Knowledge about Homosexuality

who were completing their teacher education curriculum. However, relationships existed between the other three demographic factors. African-American prospective teachers were less knowledgeable about homosexuality than their white counterparts (Black $\overline{X}$ = 50, White $\overline{X}$ = 58; df = 31, t = 2.0; p < .001). Similarly, females evidenced less knowledge than males (Females $\overline{X}$ = 56, Male $\overline{X}$ = 61; df = 110, t = 1.6; p < .001). Finally, prospective teachers pursuing certification in elementary education were less knowledgeable than their secondary education cohorts (Elementary $\overline{X}$ = 55, Secondary $\overline{X}$ = 59.2; df = 208, t = -1.7; p < .001).

The scores on the 14-item knowledge test were correlated with the respondents' scores on the Attitudes Toward Homosexuality Scale and the Index of Homophobia scale. In both cases, negative correlations were found (ATH r = -.34; IH r = -.26). That is, the more knowledgeable the student, as measured on the Homosexual Knowledge Index, the less negative attitudes toward homosexuality and feelings toward lesbians and gay men were evidenced.

In order to discern this pattern more fully, prospective teachers scoring one standard deviation above or below the mean on the Homosexual Knowledge Index were selected. The t-test results are presented in Table 10.

There were significant differences between most knowledgeable/least knowledgeable students and their attitudes about homosexuality and their feelings toward lesbians and gay men. Those demonstrating the least knowledge harbored the most negative attitudes and were the most homophobic.

Summary. In this sample of Southern prospective teachers, most ex-

TABLE 10

Knowledgeable and Not Knowledgeable
Prospective Teachers' Scores on
Attitudes About Homosexuality
and Feelings Toward Lesbians and Gay Men

Knowledge Index	ATH $\overline{X}$	ATH SD	t	df	IH $\overline{X}$	IH SD	t	df
Low Scorers	65	10	6.7	85*	75	16	4.69	84*
High Scorers	48	14			57	21		

* p < .001

pressed negative attitudes about homosexuality and harbored homophobic feelings toward lesbians and gay men. In comparison with other populations, these prospective teachers held much more negative feelings. They were five times more likely to be classified as "high grade homophobics" than a group of college students surveyed a decade ago (Hudson & Ricketts, 1980). Further, in comparison with a recently sampled group of Southern guidance counselors, they also were more likely to express negative feelings toward lesbians and gay men. For example, less noticeable differences were found among these prospective teachers and other professional or student groups with respect to attitudes about homosexuality. In all cases, the scores were moderately negative.

Some clear differences with respect to the four demographic variables were found. Most importantly, prospective teachers pursuing certification in elementary education were more likely to harbor homophobic feelings and express homo-negative attitudes than those planning to teach in the secondary schools. Black prospective teachers also expressed more negative attitudes about homosexuality than their white counterparts but were not any more homophobic in their feelings toward lesbians and gay men.

Two or three factors account for most of the variance discerned in prospective teachers attitudes and feelings. In no case, however, was more than 15 percent of the variance explained. The type of home community, level in professional program, and certification area accounted for the majority of the variance on prospective teachers' attitudes about homosexuality. These two later factors accounted for the vast majority of the variation in prospective teachers' feelings toward lesbians and gay men. Interestingly, race, age, and gender exerted little influence on prospective teachers' attitudes or feelings vis-à-vis the three aforementioned variables.

Regarding prospective teachers' encounters with homosexuality, about one in four of the respondents in this study knew a student who had a homosexual orientation or suspected one of their friends was lesbian or gay during their high school years. One in five had a homosexual friend during high school. Prospective teachers who had one or more of these associations during high school exhibited less negative attitudes about homosexuality and held less homophobic feelings toward lesbians and gay men than those who lacked such associations. Having a homosexual friend in high school was the most significant factor that discriminated between those prospective teachers harboring relatively low or high homophobic attitudes and feelings.

Exposure to homosexuality was another dimension of these prospective teachers' high school experiences. Most reported that the information provided about this topic was neither accurate nor adequate. Nevertheless, those (about one quarter of the sample) who were exposed to the topic of homosexuality during high school scored lower on the two scales assessing attitudes and feelings about homosexuality.

There are two caveats in interpreting these data. First, while prior (high school) association with lesbians and gay persons was related significantly to less negative attitudes and feelings, the scores of these students were still in a moderately high range. That is, simply knowing a friend who is lesbian or gay or receiving accurate information about homosexuality in high school does not correlate with *positive* attitudes about homosexuality or feelings toward homosexual persons. Generally, though, the relationship is one in which their feelings and attitudes are less negative. Second, within the limits of this study it is not possible to determine the causal relationship, if any, which exists between encounters with homosexual persons or exposure to homosexuality and the less homophobic feelings or homo-negative attitudes expressed by such persons.

A substantial number of prospective teachers could not assess the knowledge or attitudes of their high school teachers or counselors with respect to homosexuality. Classroom discussion about homosexuality was conducted by few or none of their teachers. Though these respondents rated their fellow high school students more knowledgeable about this topic than their educators, a vast majority reported that all or most of these students displayed negative attitudes about homosexuality.

Finally, prospective teacher's cumulative knowledge about homosexuality was minimal. Though they were more likely to correctly understand the psychosexual dynamics of childhood than the legal or biological aspects of homosexuality, most would have failed the knowledge "test" if passing would have been set at 60 percent. Women, African-Americans, and elementary education majors evidenced less knowledge than their male, Anglo, and secondary education cohorts.

The question of the relationship between prospective teachers' knowledge and their attitudes/feelings regarding homosexuality yielded noteworthy results. The more knowledgeable the student the less negative attitudes toward homosexuality and feelings toward lesbians and gay men were evidenced. Even when comparing the extreme groups on their knowledge about homosexuality, however, the absolute scores for both groups were still high.

Thus, like high school associations, adequate and accurate knowledge about homosexuality lessened prospective teachers' negative attitudes and feelings; they did not eliminate them. The importance of this point is evident when exploring their professional attitudes and expected behaviors relating to homosexuality or lesbian/gay students.

Guidance Counselors' Attitudes and Feelings

In absolute terms, nearly two thirds of the school counselors surveyed in this study expressed negative attitudes and feelings about homosexuality and homosexual persons. Like prospective teachers, their feelings against homosexuality (e.g., feeling uncomfortable with the prospect of a gay or lesbian sibling) and reactions to homosexual situations (e.g., personal sexual advances) were more negative than their attitudes against homosexuality (e.g., the criminalization of homosexuality). For example, about one third of the attitudinal statements reflect positive support for homosexuals and an understanding of homosexuality and only two statements in the 30-item survey drew negative responses. Few counselors expressed positive feelings toward homosexuals or indicated positive reactions to situations wherein they might personally confront homosexuality. Moreover, many counselors were much more likely to express ambivalence on attitudinal items (e.g., the nature of sexual pleasure between members of the same sex) than they were to have ambivalent feelings about homosexuality or being in homosexual situations.[6]

Overall, the school counselors' scores were slightly less homophobic and homo-negative that those of the prospective teachers. Counselors working in administrative areas or in testing and evaluating students were more likely to express homo-negative attitudes than those who devoted more time to counseling students. Further, guidance counselors were much more likely to adopt liberal positions on civil rights issues (e.g., decriminalization of consenting adult homosexual relationships) but to hold a conservative moral view (e.g., homosexuality is a sin) and fear personal contact (being uncomfortable around lesbians or gay men). These patterns have been found in other studies (Gentry, 1986a; Irwin & Thompson, 1977) leading one set of researchers to conclude, "[M]any people separate their moral censure of homosexuality per se and attitudes about the civil rights of homosexuals" (Irwin & Thompson, 1977:118).

In addition to comparing summative counselors' scores with those of prospective teachers and other samples (see Tables 1 & 2, above), the relative effects of seven factors on the ATH and IH scores are indicated by the Beta weights appearing in Table 11.

Two conclusions are warranted from an examination of these data. First, almost none of the categoric-demographic variables exerts any significant influence on counselors' attitudes or feelings about homosexuality. Second, the only variable having a consistent and moderate effect on

TABLE 11

Step-wise Multiple Regression (Betas) of Categoric Demographic
Variables onto IH and MATH Scores

Variable	IH	ATH
Age	.15	.15
Gender	.19*	.11
Race	-.01	.16*
Education	-.28*	-.30*
Experience	-.01	-.13
Childhood Background	.03	-.04
School Site	.02	.04

* Regression coefficient greater than twice its standard error

both of these factors is the level of education of the respondent. Even this variable's effect, though, is limited since in no case does it account for more than seven percent of the variance in these measures. The gender and race of the respondent modestly contributed, respectively, to the variance of scores on these two scales. The marginal effect which these demographic variables have on counselors' attitudes and feelings about homosexuality suggest the existence of other, more powerful factors not included in this regression analysis.

Further data analyses explored the modest relationships of gender, race, and education on counselors' attitudes and feelings about homosexuality. Parametric t-tests were used to determine the nature of these differences. These data are summarized in Table 12.

Attitudes toward homosexuality vary significantly according to a counselor's gender, race, and educational background. Specifically, counselors who are males, white or who have earned a degree beyond the master's have more positive attitudes toward homosexuality. With respect to counselors' feelings about homosexuals or reactions to homosexual situations, gender and education were discriminating demographic vari-

TABLE 12

Means and Standard Deviations of the
IH and MATH Scores According to
Counselor's Gender and Race

Demographic	IH $\overline{X}$	IH SD	t	df	MATH $\overline{X}$	MATH SD	t	df
Gender								
Male	54.3*	21.2	-2.27	137	73.0*	22.2	-1.57	139
Female	62.3	15.8			79.4	18.9		
Race								
White	60.5	18.3	-0.11	137	76.3*	20.3	-1.84	139
Black	60.8	14.3			83.4	17.3		
Education								
BS/MS	62.7*	16.0	2.56	137	81.3*	18.5	3.44	139
Spec/ Ph.D.	54.2	19.7			68.6	20.6		

* p < .001

ables. Again, males were likely to harbor more *positive* feelings in this area as were those who had extensive graduate education. Consistent with studies of other segments of the population (Baker, 1980; Irwin & Thompson, 1977; Nyberg & Alston, 1977), racial minorities and those with less education expressed more negative attitudes or feelings about homosexuality and toward homosexual persons. Unlike these other studies, however, the males in this sample were more supportive than their female counterparts.

In addition to examining the relationship between aggregate scores and these demographic variables, multiple regression was used to determine what items on each of these scales contributed the greatest variance to these three demographic factors. Table 13 reveals the results.

Using multiple regression in which gender served as the dependent vari-

TABLE 13

Most Discriminating Items on the MATH and IH
According to Gender, Race, and Education

Scale	Item #	Beta	Group 1 $\bar{X}$	Group 2 $\bar{X}$
IH				
Gender			Male (30)	Female (112)
	19*	-.52	3.27	2.83
	20	.22	2.70	3.29
	25	.42	2.40	3.04
Education			BS/MS (103)	Spec/Ph.D. (35)
	24*	-.29	3.67	2.94
MATH				
Race			White (106)	Black (36)
	2	-.23	2.02	2.11
	4	.35	1.55	2.19
	7	.15	2.72	3.19
Education			BS/MS (103)	Spec/Ph.D. (35)
	7	-.16	3.07	2.25
	12	.17	2.74	2.44
	15	-.25	2.56	1.78
	24	-.19	2.61	2.23

* Reverse-coded items (5 = Strongly Agree, 4 = Agree, etc.)

able and the 25 items on the IH scale were predictive variables revealed
that the scale accounted for 36 percent of the total variance of gender;
three of these items comprised 22 percent of the total variance: "I'd feel
comfortable if I learned that my boss was homosexual" (#19); "It would
not bother me to walk through a predominantly gay section of town"
(#20); "I would feel comfortable working closely with a female homo-

sexual'' (#24). When education served as the dependent variable and the predictive variables were items on the IH, the scale accounted for 26 percent of the total variance of educational level with one item accounting for one third of this total variance: "I would feel uncomfortable knowing that my son's teacher was a male homosexual.''

Using multiple regression in which race served as the dependent variable and the 30 items on the ATH were predictive variables revealed that this scale accounted for 22 percent of the total variance of race. Three items accounted for one half of this total variance: "Homosexuals should not be allowed to hold important positions'' (#2); "Homosexuals should be locked up and not released until cured'' (#4); and, "Homosexuality is a sin'' (#7). When education served as the dependent variable with the same set of predictive variables, ATH accounted for 30 percent of the variance with four items comprising 16 percent of this variance: "Homosexuality is a sin'' (#7); "If homosexuality is allowed to increase it will destroy our society'' (#12); "I find it hard to believe that homosexuals can really love each other'' (#15); and, "Homosexuals are very unhappy people who wish they could be like everyone else'' (#24).

The items which most clearly discriminated between males' and females' attitudes and feelings about homosexuality, and between blacks' and whites' attitudes are also indicated in Table 9 as is the relationship between these attitudes and feelings and one's educational level. For example, religious and civil rights attitudes vis-à-vis homosexuality were the best discriminators between white and black counselors. Whites were more willing for gay and lesbians to hold important positions, more likely to object to the detention and "curing'' of homosexuals, and more certain that homosexuality was not sinful.

Summary. School guidance counselors, like prospective teachers and professionals surveyed by other researchers, harbor negative attitudes and feelings about homosexuality. The feelings of these school counselors (e.g., "I would feel uncomfortable knowing that my son's teacher was a male homosexual," "I would feel uncomfortable if I learned that my boss was homosexual.") are much more pronounced than their beliefs (e.g., "Homosexuals should never be allowed to teach school or supervise children," "It would be a mistake to ever have homosexuals for bosses and leaders over other people.")—which are often rooted in belief about civil rights and the right of privacy. Situations that place school counselors in direct contact with homosexual men and women create among many intensely negative feelings. Significantly, it is in personal situations (e.g., counseling a homosexual student, meeting with lesbian parents) that these professionals must apply their knowledge, experience, and skills. The degree to which their personal feelings and beliefs affect their ability to enter into such relationships is discussed in the next section.

In reflecting upon data presented in this part of the paper, what is most disturbing is the high degree of negativism expressed by school guidance counselors and prospective teachers whose principal responsibility it is to educate and advise young adults—some of whom will identify themselves as lesbian, gay, or bisexual; all of whom will deal with issues related to homosexuality. Attitudes and feelings, of course, are subject to change. Several researchers have reported on the positive impact which seminars, employing lectures, guest speakers, films, debate, and dialogue, have had on reducing homo-negativism (e.g., Anderson, 1981; Goldberg, 1982; Greenberg, 1975; Rudolph, 1988a; Taylor, 1983). Yet, as these data indicate, for such efforts to be effective they must be directed at the level of affect, not cognition. Feelings of discomfort, fear, and hatred are more pervasive than these educators' attitudes about lesbian and gay civil rights. Sadly, few workshops—particularly in teacher preparation or staff development seminars—focus on the emotions.

Homophobia educators need to borrow from the work, experience, and knowledge of those involved in anti-racism workshops who engage persons in three to five day workshops. There has been a tendency for those engaged in homophobia education not to collaborate with those engaged in other types of anti-oppression work, such as racism and sexism. This lack of communication contributes to splintering of educational efforts to end prejudice and violence directed at lesbians, gay men, and bisexuals. One such group that has recognized the need to explore the interrelationship of oppressions based on race, gender, social class, and sexual identity is the Campaign to End Homophobia. This group insists that its leaders participate in an intensive workshop in which participants engage in one-on-one and small group activities that strip away the socially acceptable facade of toleration and open up long-held feelings rooted in childhood experiences and translated into powerful life scripts. Through the use of a "social identity development model," workshop leaders of VISIONS, a multi-racial collective based in North Carolina, uses a form of transactional analysis to return participants to their earliest childhood racial memories (Batts, 1982; Batts, 1989; Jackson & Hardiman, n.d.). Once a person has disclosed this event, members of the group work the person to "unlearn" cognitive and affective misinformation acquired in childhood and covered up through years of adult socialization.

Shifts in a person's attitudes and feelings, however, does not mean there will be a concomitant shift in behavior. There may be a gap between attitudes professed on a survey and the everyday behaviors practiced in the school. Many educators surveyed in this study also posited the belief in their ability to distance one's personal attitudes and feelings from the professional responsibilities of their jobs. In the next section, I will examine their effectiveness in accomplishing this task.

PROFESSIONAL ATTITUDES AND PROJECTED ACTIVITIES IN THE SCHOOLS

As "professionals," educators often assert that personal beliefs and community values do not interfere with the delivery of professional services to students. In reality, of course, students' race, social class, and gender have a significant impact on how they are perceived by peers, evaluated by teachers, and tracked by school counselors (Oakes, 1985; Rist, 1973; Rosenbaum, 1976; Willis, 1977). With the rise of Christian Fundamentalism and the spiraling number of HIV-cases, homosexuality and the homosexual became the "new Nigger" of the 1980s. No longer a taboo topic, persons who acknowledged their same-sex feelings were prime targets for night club comics, skin-heads, rock-and-roll bands, and television evangelists.

The South, perhaps more than other regions of the United States, openly practices one of the few remaining forms of socially accepted bigotry: homophobia. From the enforcement of sodomy laws in Georgia's *Hardwick* case to the venomous attacks of North Carolina's senator Jesse Helms on the Mapplethorpe collection funded by the National Endowment for the Arts, to the banning of references to homosexuality in South Carolina's state approved sexuality texts, the South is a lonely place for a boy or girl blossoming into adulthood as a lesbian, bisexual, or gay man.

Educators significantly influence the experiences of these boys and girls in school. It is the educator who chooses *how* to teach the prescribed sexuality curriculum; it is the educator who challenges or winks at homophobic comments or jokes among students; it is the educator who comforts or ignores a student suffering from the heterosexist tirades of peers or doubts about her sexual identity; it is the educator who fosters dialogue among fellow professionals about the penalties *all* pay in a heterosexual-mandated society. Thus, it is to educators—prospective teachers and school counselors—and their beliefs and values to which we look for a reduction of heterosexual hegemony.

Professional Attitudes of Future Teachers

As detailed in the previous section, seldom in these prospective teachers' own K-12 experiences was sexuality discussed in the formal curriculum; when sexuality was discussed, homosexuality was generally ignored or reproved. Only *six* of these Southern youth ever talked with a teacher about sexuality. Three fourths of the participants reported that their high school teachers had negative attitudes about homosexuality and more than 80 percent reported few or none of their high school teachers considered homosexuality an alternative lifestyle or that classroom discussion included this topic.

These prospective teachers were asked how they would respond as teachers to situations relating to homosexuality in classroom interaction, counseling, student harassment, fellow teachers, and human rights. The proportion of students responding affirmatively to statements within each of these categories are indicated in Table 14.

As indicated in Table 14, despite the sample's generally negative personal feelings and attitudes, prospective teachers expressed a professional regard for homosexual students in a variety of areas and instances. For example, a substantial majority of prospective teachers expected to take appropriate action in situations involving the harassment of students due to their actual or perceived homosexuality. Further, nearly three fourths of the prospective teachers did not believe they would have difficulty treating an openly gay student fairly.

On the other hand, prospective teachers were most reticent about assuming proactive counseling or teaching roles, working with an openly homosexual teacher, or striving to end discrimination against lesbians, bisexuals, and gay men in their community. About one half of the sample thought it would be appropriate for *another* teacher to provide supportive materials to a lesbian, bisexual, or gay student but less than one third felt personally comfortable speaking with a student about his or her same-sex feelings or discussing homosexuality in the classroom. Further, four of ten future teachers thought it acceptable to transfer a homosexual student to another class on the request of a homophobic teacher.

Another method for examining how personal feelings and attitudes translate into professional activity is to ask prospective teachers their specific response to the following classroom situation.

Assume that you are teaching at your grade level within a public school in this state. You are leading a discussion about current events. Today's topic is AIDS. After several minutes of give-and-take discussion among students in the class, the following dialogue occurs:

TABLE 14
Prospective Teachers' Attitudes and Behaviors Relating to Homosexuality in the School

Statement	% Agree	N (n=258)
Classroom Interaction		
Teachers who regard homosexuality in a negative way should be able to request a homosexual student to enroll in another class	37	93
I would discuss homosexuality in the classroom	29	70
It would be difficult for me to deal fairly with an avowed homosexual student	24	62
Counseling		
Providing a homosexual high school students with supportive materials is appropriate for a teacher	49	121
I would feel comfortable if a student talked with me about his or her sexual orientation	36	93
Student Harassment		
I would discipline a student for harassing another student suspected of having a homosexual orientation	86	219
I would openly disagree with a faculty member who made a disparaging comment about a suspected homosexual student	64	162
I would discipline a student for making a derogatory remark about homosexuals	64	159
I would ignore student jokes about homosexuals	42	107
Homosexual Teachers		
I would feel uncomfortable if my school hired an openly gay or lesbian teacher	52	132
Homosexual persons should not be allowed to teach in the public schools	26	63
Adolescents who know several homosexual teachers will be strongly influenced to be homosexual	22	36
Human Rights		
A teacher must work in school to lessen prejudicial attitudes about homosexuality	62	157
I would work in my community to bar discrimination against homosexual men and women	32	80

Mary: I think it's too bad that all these people are so sick and are going to die. I just think . . .

Paul (interrupting): Those fags get what they deserve. What makes me mad is that we're spending money trying to find a cure. If we just let God and Nature take its course, I won't have to worry about any queer bothering me.

Mary: I never thought about it that way before.
Mary then faces you and asks, "What do you think about Paul's com-
ments?" Briefly state how you would most likely respond.

Seven percent of the respondents to this scenario agreed with Paul. One
wrote, "Once homosexuals have AIDS and know they're going to die,
they want to spread it. Our tax money should not be spent. I agree with
Paul." Another wrote, "I feel that if someone does get AIDS because
they are homosexual—hell! Let them die."

Two thirds of the respondents chose to address Paul's statements about
AIDS. Most of these persons chose to battle with Paul on logical or factual
grounds: "If AIDS is God's punishment from God and Nature, what
about cancer?" "A cure is for all society, no one deserves to die." Several who used logic to counter Paul's arguments, reflected their homo-negative feelings. For example, "It's true that homosexual contract AIDS, but
think of the unfortunate people who are not homosexual who contact
AIDS. It is not fair to let those unfortunate people be sick and die."
Another wrote, "We must find a cure to prevent the spread of AIDS
among the innocent." A third said, "Look, asshole, AIDS affects everybody. If it was just restricted to queers that would be another story."

Others chose a more factual approach: "Paul, your statement is not
accurate. You should watch the news more often"; "Homosexuals are not
a high risk group for AIDS, people who engage in high-risk behavior are
at risk"; "AIDS affects more than gay people."

A handful chose (6%) to personalize the situation or to ridicule Paul:
"How would you feel if you were condemned to die because you fell in
love with Lucy and she got pregnant?" "What if someone in your family
got AIDS?" and, "You're narrow-minded and insensitive." A few (2%),
branding Paul for his un-Southernly rudeness in public, wrote such comments as: "It wasn't polite for him to say those things."

Eight percent asked Paul for tolerance and compassion: "You have a
point, Paul. But people are different and what you think is 'normal,' others think is 'abnormal.' You must learn to face life and see it for what it
really is." "Gays are human beings; they shouldn't be treated as ani-
mals." Four confessed ambivalence or the desire to allow everyone to
hold their own opinion: "I'm not sure. I haven't thought much about it. I
believe we need to find a cure for AIDS but we cannot condone a lifestyle." "Each person has the right to their own opinion. School is not a
place to have such discussions." "I wouldn't try to change Paul's or
Mary's attitudes, that isn't up to me."

These prospective teachers' responses reflect an understanding of
AIDS, a cognitive orientation to dealing with the classroom issue, and a
desire to ignore the inherent homo-negativism of the dialogues. Given the

multiple levels on which a teacher could respond, it is noteworthy that almost all of the prospective teachers focused on the anti-AIDS comment and chose to ignore its homophobic content or to discuss homosexuality in class.

Six of the persons who responded directly to Paul's homophobic comments expressed those of their own: "There needs to be a cure because the homos and bisexuals are giving it to us. I really think God is trying to tell us to get back to morals." Another stated, "Homosexuality is a sin and AIDS is God's way of warning us that it is a sin, but God loves everyone. We should help to change their lifestyle."

Despite the fact that two thirds of the respondents indicated that they would discipline a student for making a derogatory comment about homosexuality, only 6 percent actually did so when provided the opportunity: Five chose to provide Paul with a short lecture: "'Fags' aren't the only people dying from AIDS. Homosexuals are people, too. People don't choose to be gay, they can't help it if they don't go along with societal norms." Another wrote, "First teach him that 'fag' is crude and explain that homosexuals do not choose their lifestyles." Two chose punishment: "I would punish Paul for his rude and opinionated comments."

Given the aforementioned discussion on the division between attitudes and feelings, it is also noteworthy that the predominant response was at the *cognitive* level. Only a couple of respondents explored Paul's feelings. One wrote, "I would have a discussion with this young man to find out why he feels so hostile toward homosexuals." Clearly, as this scenario illustrates, there is a significant gap between attitudes regarding appropriate professional responses to homosexual-related issues in the school and actual professional behavior. School situations which require teachers to *react* to homophobia are clearly influenced by personal feelings and attitudes. To what degree are these personal beliefs and feelings related to prospective teachers' willingness to assume *proactive* roles in the school and community vis-à-vis homosexual issues?

In order to better understand the constellation of factors that contribute to prospective teachers' attitudes and feelings the 14 items in Table 14 were aggregated to form a Professional Attitudes Index Scale.[7] The lower the score, the less supportive professionally a person is regarding homosexual persons and issues in the school. Prospective teachers who were at the student teaching point of their professional studies exhibited statistically significant *lower* scores on this index than those early in their program. Further, students pursuing an elementary certificate at the early point of their teacher education curriculum scored significantly lower on this Index than their secondary cohorts; white prospective teachers scored significantly higher than their black peers.

Responses to these statements resulted in the adoption of seemingly paradoxical positions. First, despite their personal abhorrence of homosexuality and the homosexual, most prospective teachers professed a willingness to protect the homosexual student from harassment and to treat that student fairly. Second, though only one quarter of these prospective teachers believed that homosexual adults should not teach in public schools, most would feel uncomfortable if an openly lesbian or gay teacher worked at their school. Third, though these college students agreed that teachers must work in the school to lessen prejudicial attitudes about homosexuality, fewer than one third indicated a willingness to work toward such an end within their communities.

Many of these prospective teachers made a distinction between "the sin and the sinner." That is, while believing in the wrongness of homosexuality and expressing negative feelings in encounters with homosexuals, these students assumed a professional demeanor in treating homosexual students fairly and with respect—expecting similar behaviors from students. Those persons who were nearing the end of their professional preparation, however, were less likely to profess these attitudes.

In order to explore the relationship between personal beliefs and feelings and their professional attitudes, the students' scores on the Professional Attitude Index were correlated with those of the Homosexual Knowledge Index, the Attitudes Toward Homosexuality scale, and the Index of Homophobia scale. Prospective teachers' professional attitudes showed only a mild correlation with their knowledge of homosexuality (.25). However, the degree of the negative correlation between their professional attitudes and the attitudes about homosexuality ($-.76$) and feelings toward lesbians and gay men ($-.66$) was powerful.

Exploring this relationship further, prospective teachers scoring one standard deviation above or below the mean on the Professional Attitude Index were selected. T-tests discerned the margin of difference among these more extreme groups vis-à-vis their attitudes about homosexuality and feelings toward lesbians and gay men.

As illustrated in Table 15, students who expressed low professional regard, as measured on the Professional Attitudes Index, for issues relating to homosexuality in the schools, fit within the domain of "high grade homophobics" while those who expressed a high professional regard were within the "low grade non-homophobics" domain. Similarly, a 50 point spread on attitudes toward homosexuality separated those who expressed a high regard for addressing homosexual issues in the school compared with those whose regard was low.

Clearly, the degree to which prospective teachers assume a proactive role in meeting the needs of homosexual and bisexual students and creat-

TABLE 15

High and Low Professional Attitudes of
Prospective Teachers Scores on
Attitudes About Homosexuality
and Feelings Toward Lesbians and Gay Men

Attitude Index	ATH $\overline{X}$	ATH SD	t	df	III $\overline{X}$	III SD	t	df
Low Scorers	64	11	16	36*	81	12	9.4	23*
High Scorers	13	10			35	18		

* p <.001

ing an environment of respect and support for them is related to the teachers' personal feelings and beliefs. At best, teachers who are knowledgeable about the social, medical, and legal issues related to homosexuality will more likely treat those students suspected of sexual difference fairly and with respect. Deep-seated personal beliefs and feelings about this issue — generally not the level on which staff development workshops are directed — govern the type of personal involvement that these soon-to-be professionals expect to have with homosexuality and the homosexual. Expecting these teachers to be supportive of the hiring of an openly gay or lesbian teacher, discussing homosexuality in the classroom, or talking with a student about his or her sexual identity is not reasonable.

Finally, prospective teachers checked those proactive activities in which they *might* participate as a professional. These activities, arranged in order of frequency of occurrence, are listed in Table 16.

With the exception of attending a school sponsored workshop on strategies dealing with lesbian and gay students, only a minority of this sample expected to engage in professional activities relating to homosexuality. Further, those activities which required the greatest risk or visibility — encouraging classroom discussion on homosexuality, integrating homosexual themes into the curriculum, or meeting with homosexual adults — were the least selected activities. Prospective teachers coming from rural backgrounds were least likely to express a willingness to meet with homosexual adults to discuss the special needs of sexual minority students. Those students completing their student teaching were less likely than those at the early stage of their professional studies to desire to integrate homosexual issues or themes into the curriculum or to encourage the discussion of homosexuality in their classrooms. Finally, females were less likely than males to seek such curricular integration.

Table 16

Distribution of Agreement About
Expected Professional Activities
Among Prospective Teachers

Professional Activity	% Agreed	N
1) Attend school sponsored workshop on strategies in working with gay students	75	185
2) Prepare educational materials for students interested in homosexuality	31	77
3) Assemble resource packet on homosexuality for teachers in the school	29	72
4) Discuss concerns of gay students at faculty meeting	26	64
5) Engage in dialogue with parents about homosexuality at a school sponsored program	26	64
6) Meet with homosexual adults to learn more about gay students special needs	23	56
7) Encourage classroom discussion about homosexuality	23	56
8) Integrate homosexual themes and issues into the curriculum	15	37

The relationships between prospective teachers' attitudes about homosexuality, feelings toward lesbians and gay men, knowledge about homosexuality, and professional attitudes about homosexuality are explicated in Table 17.

Without exception, prospective teachers' scores on three of the scales — the Attitudes About Homosexuality Scale, the Index of Homophobia, and the Professional Attitudes About Homosexuality Index — were related in the expected manner. That is, prospective teachers who expressed less negative attitudes about homosexuality or harbored less homophobic feelings toward lesbians and gay men were more likely to indicate a willingness to engage in such professional activities. Further, those who expressed more supportive professional attitudes regarding homosexual issues were also more likely to hold an expectation for participating in these activities.

The expressed willingness of prospective teachers to address homosex-

TABLE 17

Distribution of Prospective Teachers' Scores
on Four Instruments According to Their
Expectation of Engaging in
Supportive Activities*

Activity	IH	ATH	HKI	PAI
1) Attend Workshop				
YES	65	56	---	39
NO	68	59	---	37
2) Student Educational Materials				
YES	60	50	60	41
NO	68	56	59	37
3) Teacher Resource Packet				
YES	60	53	---	40
NO	67	58	---	38
4) Faculty Meeting				
YES	59	50	---	42
NO	68	59	---	37
5) Parent Dialogue				
YES	61	52	---	41
NO	67	58	---	37
6) Homosexual Adults Meeting				
YES	54	47	---	43
NO	69	59	---	37
7) Encourage Classroom Discussion				
YES	54	48	62	43
NO	69	59	56	37
8) Integrate into Curriculum				
YES	54	48	---	43
NO	68	58	---	38

* all data are significant with $p < .001$

ual-related issues in the schools is highly correlated with their attitudes about homosexuality and their feelings toward lesbians and gay men. This relationship is most clearly seen in comparing low and high respondents' scores on the Professional Attitudes Index with their scores on the Attitudes Toward Homosexuality and the Index of Homophobia scales. Those who were most willing to adopt a proactive role in the schools were classified as non-homophobic and expressed tolerant attitudes regarding homosexuality. Those who were not willing to assume such a proactive role tended to be more advanced in their professional studies. Those who were at the early point in their teacher education curriculum, those who were white, or who were majoring in secondary education evidenced a more proactive position than their counterparts.

In summary, though *most* students proclaimed their ability to treat homosexual students fairly as well as to establish a climate of respect among all students, *few* of them were willing to become personally involved in meeting the special needs or concerns of lesbian, gay, and bisexual students. With the exception of attending a school-sponsored workshop on strategies for working with lesbian and gay students, only a minority expected to participate in any other activity. Those activities most directly related to teaching, classroom discussion and curriculum integration, were the least chosen areas of projected activity. Their woefully inadequate knowledge and homophobic attitudes and feelings means that relatively few of these prospective teachers believe that this group of largely invisible, at-risk students merit special attention or assistance.

Professional Attitudes of School Counselors

Counselors were asked to assess the school climate for homosexual students and the discussion of homosexual-related issues. The vast majority of counselors observed that few, if any, of their school's teachers were supportive of gay and lesbian students, discussed homosexuality in the classroom, or considered it an alternative lifestyle. Further, slightly less than one third of these professionals indicated that their building level administrators even viewed homosexual concerns as legitimate topics for counselors to discuss with their school-age clients. Those working in rural schools or at the middle school level reported less receptivity on the part of the school administration or the teaching staff to address this issue.

Given this homo-negative environment, it is noteworthy that four out of ten counselors have discussed homosexuality and homosexual-related issues among their counseling staff or have counseled students about their homosexual orientation. Those working with high school juniors and seniors were most likely to report discussing these issues.

Like the prospective teachers, school counselors indicated their willingness to participate in a variety of professional activities during the next year. Their responses are listed in Table 18.

Clearly, situations in which the counselor would be more personally involved were less appealing. Counselors were more willing to discuss concerns of homosexual students within a faculty setting if they had known such a student and had attended workshops about counseling homosexual-identified students.

Table 18
Expectation of Engaging in
Supportive Activities
by Prospective Teachers

Activity	Percentage Planning to Participate
Workshop on AIDS	72
Workshop on Homosexual Youth	68
Reading Professional Materials about Homosexuality	51
Preparing educational materials about homosexuality for teachers	40
Assembling a counseling packet for concerned students	32
Meeting with homosexual adults	25
Discussing concerns of homosexual students at faculty meeting	17
Dialogue with parents on homosexuality in a school-sponsored program	12

Most guidance counselors also reported knowing at least one homosexual student during their professional career. Few felt prepared to work with this at-risk population. Despite their inadequate preparation and these personal contacts, less than one fifth of these counselors indicated that they had participated in programs to expand their knowledge about homosexuality.

A strong relationship existed between the likelihood of counselors engaging in these activities and their personal attitudes toward homosexuality and feelings toward homosexual-identified women and men (Sears, 1988a). Counselors working below the high school level were three to six times less likely to attend such workshop or to engage in any other activities (e.g., reading professional materials) to enhance their professional knowledge in counseling homosexual-identified students. There is a powerful relationship between participating in such workshops and providing materials to teachers or counseling of gay students.

Of course, one cannot determine whether this willingness is due to prior participation in such workshops or to confronting this issue with a client at an earlier point in time. It is interesting to note that those who have suspected students of having a homosexual identity expressed a greater willingness to participate in workshops to expand their knowledge about homosexuality. Further, those willing to participate in these workshops also expressed less negative attitudes and less negative feelings about homosexuality.

Most of the young Southerners interviewed in *Growing Up Gay in the South* (Sears, 1991) perceived these counselors to be ill-informed and unconcerned ; these students felt uncomfortable talking to them. These students' image of counselors was summed up by one lesbian adolescent: "Our counselors had never been presented to us as someone there to talk about problems other than education. They were just there for grades, signing up for classes, tests like the PSAT, and finding colleges to attend."

Though most homosexual-identified youth in my study wanted a supportive adult counselor while attending high school, some were more reticent. The reasons for their caution included students' unwillingness to assume the initiative, lack of trust in confidentiality, fear of losing teacher friendship, and personality differences. One homosexual student comments:

> I didn't talk to counselors because they're human, too. Homosexuality is taboo. People just kind of go bonkers when they hear that word or find out that somebody is homosexual. Even the adults act like kids. They don't know how to handle it. I thought, "I can't trust anybody with this information." You know, teachers talk.

Precisely what role should school counselors assume when working with a homosexual-identified student? What professional responsibilities do counselors believe that they have in dealing with homosexuality in the school? Most school counselors proclaim that a non-judgmental role should be adopted when dealing with homosexual students or the issue of homosexuality in the school curriculum. For example, the vast majority believed that sexual concerns of students were legitimate topics for discussion; few expected homosexual students to overcome their same-sex feelings. Most believed it acceptable for counselors to work in school to lessen prejudicial attitudes about homosexuality.

Like the prospective teachers, these counselors claim an ability to set aside personal prejudices and assume a professional relationship with their gay or lesbian clients. As expected, however, their professional expectations correlated with counselors' attitudes toward homosexuality and feelings about homosexual persons. For example, on the Index of Homophobia Scale, those who were categorized as "low grade non-homophobics" were three times more likely to believe that counselors should lessen prejudicial attitudes in the school and six times more likely to disagree that a counselor should help students overcome their homosexual feelings than those classified as "high grade homophobics." Further, counselors with less formal education, less counseling experience, and coming from African-descent were more likely to expect the student to overcome his/her homosexual feelings.

Despite the apparent liberal, professional model adopted by many of these school counselors, less than one quarter have chosen to counsel such students about homosexuality although nearly two thirds of the counselors knew students who have a homosexual orientation. Those counselors working with older students and having more professional experience and formal education were most willing to work with sexual minority youth. Those spending a greater proportion of their time in administrative tasks such as testing and evaluating students expressed more negative attitudes and were less interested in the concerns of this special population. Consistent with studies of other segments of the population, counselors belonging to racial minorities and those with less education expressed more negative attitudes or feelings about homosexuality and toward homosexual persons (Baker, 1980; Irwin & Thompson, 1977; Nyberg & Alston, 1977). In contrast to the respondents in these other studies, however, male counselors were more tolerant than their female counterparts.

These counselors, like the prospective teachers, adopted a variety of paradoxical perspectives. For example, the professed professional roles of working with homosexual students stands in stark contrast to the relatively few who have actually counseled such persons—although most admit to knowing these students. Rudolph (1988b, p. 167), discussing the consistency of research on counselors' paradoxical beliefs about homosexuality, writes "The counselor is torn. He or she is formally told one thing about homosexuality from the profession (i.e., "homosexuality is okay"), and more informally, but no less pervasively, quite another from the society-at-large ("homosexuality is not okay"). . . . Although the admittedly homophobic or heterosexist counselor can clearly be harmful to a gay client, a greater risk of danger may lie with the homophobic or heterosexist counselor who is not aware of his or her prejudicial sentiment."

These attitudes are similar to those of the white liberal who proclaims herself supportive of black civil rights and "color blind," but has no black friends and associates in almost all-white (except for the few token minorities) professional and personal settings. Clearly, it is easier to proclaim socially acceptable attitudes which have little direct bearing on one's everyday activities, than to examine how heterosexist scripts and institutional homophobia—embedded in the air we breathe and the rain that falls—affects each of us.

CONCLUSIONS

On the surface, it would appear that many educators, though personally bothered by homosexuality, adopt a professional, non-judgmental demeanor in the school. Treating a student equally, however, is not necessarily treating that student fairly or equitably. For example, educators' willingness to curtail verbal harassment or to attend school-sponsored workshops related to homosexual students is noteworthy. However, their unwillingness to assume a proactive role in the school means that the special needs of these homosexual students will remain unmet. As a largely invisible part of the student body, gay, lesbian, and bisexual students have few allies outside the school to speak on their behalf. Consequently, aside from reacting to blatant homophobic situations in the school or attending one-shot, school-sponsored workshops, educators indicate little willingness to help create an environment that will facilitate the intellectual and social growth of these at-risk students.

This benign neglect by professionals reinforces the heterosexual curriculum. Lacking formal sexuality education classes which dispel the myths associated with homosexuality, educators become silent conspirators in sexual oppression (Sears, in press). The absence of visible support from educators conveys to *all* students the legitimacy and desirability of the heterosexual standard. This absence creates a climate of isolation, guilt, and fear for students confronting same-sex feelings — which, in adolescence, may be the majority of a school's population.

NOTES

1. For a discussion of the methodology and more detailed data on the participants and their responses, see Sears, 1991.

2. For more specific information about these instruments, including issues of validity and reliability as well as the individual items, see Sears, 1988a.

3. For more specific information about these instruments, including issues of validity and reliability as well as the individual items, see Sears, 1988a.

4. For a summary of many of these studies, see Fyfe, 1983; Herek, 1984; Larsen, Reed, & Hoffman, 1980; Morin & Garfinkle, 1978; Taylor, 1983.

5. The complete survey questions as well as the responses to these questions from guidance counselors are reported in Sears, 1988a.

6. For an item-by-item analysis of counselors' scores on these attitudinal instruments, see Sears, 1988a.

7. A summative score for this 14-item questionnaire was computed by reversing the codes of positively worded statements and assigning 1 through 4 points on the basis of participants' item responses. The possible range of this summative score, the Professional Attitude Index (PAI), is from 14 (low) to 56 (high); the

actual range was 17 to 55 with a mean of 38 and a standard deviation of 6. For specific details on the statistical results of the findings reported in this section, see Sears, 1989a.

REFERENCES

Aguero, J., Bloch, L., & Byrne, D. (1984). The relationships among sexual beliefs, attitudes, experience, and homophobia. *Journal of Homosexuality, 10*(1/2), 95-107.

Anderson, C. (1981). The effect of a workshop on attitudes of female nursing students toward male homosexuality. *Journal of Homosexuality, 7*(1), 57-69.

Baker, D. (1980). *A survey of attitudes and knowledge about homosexuality among secondary school teachers in training.* Unpublished master's thesis, Southern Methodist University, Dallas, TX. ERIC No. ED204693.

Batts, V. (1982). Modern racism: A TA perspective. *Transactional Analysis Journal, 12*(3), 207-209.

Batts, V. (1989). Modern racism: New melody for the same old tune. Unpublished manuscript. Rocky Mount, NC: VISIONS.

Benvenuti, A. (1986). *Assessing and addressing the special challenge of gay and lesbian students for high school counseling programs.* Paper presented at the Annual Meeting of the California Educational Research Association: ERIC Document No. ED 279958.

Braungart, R., & Braungart, M. (1988). From yippies to yuppies: Twenty years of freshman attitudes. *Public Opinion, 11*(3), 53-57.

Casas, J., Brady, S., & Ponterotto, J. (1983). Sexual preference biases in counseling: An information processing approach. *Journal of Counseling Psychology, 30,* 139-145.

Clift, S. (1988). Lesbian and gay issues in education: A study of the attitudes of first-year students in a college of higher education. *British Educational Research Journal, 14*(1), 31-50.

Coles, R., & Stokes, G. (1985). *Sex and the American teenager.* New York: Harper & Row.

Clark, M. (1979). *Attitudes, information and behavior of counselors toward homosexual clients.* Unpublished doctoral dissertation, Wayne State University. *(Dissertation Abstracts International,* 40, 5729A), Detroit, MI.

Davison, G., & Wilson, G. (1973). Attitudes of behavior therapists toward homosexuality. *Behavior Therapy, 4*(5), 686-696.

DeCrescenzo, T. (1983-84). Homophobia: A study of the attitudes of mental health professionals toward homosexuality. *Journal of Social Work and Human Sexuality, 2*(2-3), 115-136.

Dillon, C. (1986). Preparing college health professionals to deliver gay-affirmative services. *Journal of American College Health, 35*(1), 36-40.

Douglas, C., Kalman, C., & Kalman, T. (1985). Homophobia among physicians and nurses: An empirical study. *Hospital and Community Psychiatry, 36*(12), 1309-1311.

Dressler, J. (1985). Survey of school principals regarding alleged homosexual teachers in the classroom: How likely (really) is discharge? *University of Dayton Law Review, 10*(3), 599-620.

Earls, R., Fraser, J., & Sumpter, B. (in press). Sexuality education in the South: In whose interests? In J. Sears (Ed.), *Sexuality and the curriculum.* New York: Teachers College Press.

Fischer, T. (1982). *A study of educators' attitudes toward homosexuality.* Unpublished doctoral dissertation, University of Virginia, Charlottesville, VA. (Dissertation Abstracts International, 43, 10, 3294A).

Fyfe, B. (1983). "Homophobia" or homosexual bias reconsidered. *Archives of Sexual Behavior, 12*(6), 549-554.

Garfinkle, E., & Morin, S. (1978). Psychologists' attitudes toward homosexual psychotherapy clients. *Journal of Social Issues, 34*(3), 101-112.

Gartrell, N., Kraemer, H., & Brodie, H. (1974). Psychiatrists' attitudes toward female homosexuality. *Journal of Nervous and Mental Diseases, 159*(2), 141-144.

Gentry, C. (1986a). Social distance regarding male and female homosexuals. *Journal of Social Psychology, 127*(2), 199-208.

Gentry, C. (1986b). Development of scales measuring social distance toward male and female homosexuals. *Journal of Homosexuality, 13*(1), 75-82.

Glenn, A., & Russell, R. (1986). Heterosexual bias among counselor trainees. *Counselor Education and Supervision, 25*(3), 222-229.

Goldberg, R. (1982). Attitude change among college students toward homosexuality. *Journal of American College Health, 3*(3), 260-267.

Greenberg, J. (1975). A study of personality change associated with the conducting of a high school unit on homosexuality. *Journal of School Health, 45*(7), 394-398.

Griffin, P. (1992). From hiding out to coming out: Empowering lesbian and gay educators. *Journal of Homosexuality, 22*(3/4).

Gumaer, J. (1987). Understanding and counseling gay men: A developmental perspective. *Journal of Counseling and Development, 66*(3), 144-146.

Herek, G. (1984). Beyond "homophobia": A social psychological perspective on attitudes toward lesbians and gay men. *Journal of Homosexuality, 10*(1/2), 1-18.

Herek, G. (1986). On heterosexual masculinity: Some physical consequences of the social construction of gender and sexuality. *American Behavioral Scientist, 29*(5), 563-577.

Hochstein, L. (1986). Pastoral counselors: Their attitudes toward gay and lesbian clients. *Journal of Pastoral Care, 40*(2), 158-165.

Hong, S. (1983). Sex, religion and factor analytically derived attitudes towards homosexuality. *Australian Journal of Sex, Marriage, and Family, 4*(3), 142-150.

Hudson, W., & Ricketts, W. (1980). A strategy for the measurement of homophobia. *Journal of Homosexuality, 5*(4), 357-372.

Irwin, P., & Thompson, N. (1977). Acceptance of the rights of homosexuals: A social profile. *Journal of Homosexuality, 3*(2), 107-121.

Jackson, B., & Hardiman, R. (n.d.). Social identity development model. Unpublished manuscript. Rocky Mount, NC: VISIONS.

Krysiak, G. (1987). Very silent and gay minority. *School Counselor, 34*(4), 304-307.

Lance, L. (1987). The effects of interaction with gay persons on attitudes toward homosexuality. *Human Relations, 40*(6), 329-336.

Larkin, F. (1989). Attitudes of female registered nurses toward homosexual men. Unpublished master's thesis, University of Lowell, Lowell, MA. *(Masters Abstracts International* 28, 1, 110).

Larsen, K., Reed, M., & Hoffman, S. (1980). Attitudes of heterosexuals toward homosexuality: A Likert type scale and construct validity. *Journal of Sex Research, 16*(3), 245-257.

Lehne, G. (1976). Homophobia among men. In D. David & R. Brannon (Eds.), *The forty-nine percent majority: The male sex role* (pp. 66-88). Reading, MA: Addison-Wesley.

MacDonald, A. (1976). Homophobia: Its roots and meanings. *Homosexual Counseling Journal, 3*(1), 23-33.

MacDonald, A., Huggins, J., Young, S., & Swanson, R. (1973). Attitudes toward homosexuality: Preservation of sex morality or the double standard? *Journal of Counseling and Clinical Psychology, 40*(1), 161.

Maddux, J. (1988). *The homophobic attitudes of preservice teachers.* Unpublished doctoral dissertation, University of Cincinnati, Cincinnati, OH. *(Dissertation Abstracts International* 49, 8, 2091A).

Malyon, A. (1982). Psychotherapeutic implications of internalized homophobia in gay men. In J. Gonsiorek (Ed.), *Homosexuality and psychotherapy: A practitioner's handbook of affirmative models* (pp. 59-69). New York: The Haworth Press, Inc.

Margolies, L., Becker, M., & Jackson-Brewer, K. (1987). Internalized homophobia. Identifying and treating the oppressor within. In Boston Lesbian Psychologies Collective (Ed.), *Lesbian psychologies: Explorations and challenges* (pp. 229-241). Urbana: University of Illinois Press.

McQuoid, D. (1988). *Attitudes toward homosexuality: Implications for responsible psychotherapy.* Unpublished doctoral research paper. LaMirada, CA: Biola University. ERIC Document No. 298397.

Morin, S., & Garfinkle, E. (1978). Male homophobia. *Journal of Social Issues, 34*(1), 29-47.

Nyberg, K., & Alston, J. (1977). Homosexual labeling by university youths. *Adolescence, 12*(48), 541-546.

Oakes, J. (1985). Keeping track: How schools structure inequality. New Haven, CT: Yale University Press.

Pauly, I., & Goldstein, S. (1970). Physicians' attitudes in treating male homosexuals. *Medical Aspects of Human Sexuality, 4*, 26-45.

Price, J. (1982). High school students' attitudes toward homosexuality. *Journal of School Health, 52*(8), 469-474.

Rist, R. (1973). The urban school: A factory of failure. Cambridge: MIT Press.

Rosenbaum, J. (1976). Making inequality: The hidden curriculum of high school tracking. New York: Wiley.

Rudolph, J. (1988a). *The effects of a multimodal seminar on mental health practitioners' attitudes toward homosexuality, authoritarianism, and counseling effectiveness.* Unpublished doctoral dissertation, Lehigh University, Bethlehem, PA. (Dissertation Abstracts International 49, 7, 2873B).

Rudolph, J. (1988b). Counselors' attitudes toward homosexuality: A selective review of the literature. *Journal of Counseling and Development, 67*(3), 165-168.

Russell, T. (1989). AIDS education, homosexuality, and the counselor's role. *School Counselor, 36*(5), 333-337.

Schatman, M. (1989). *The prediction of homophobic attitudes among college students.* Unpublished doctoral dissertation, University of North Texas, Denton, TX. *(Dissertation Abstracts International 50, 10, 4820B).*

Schneider, W., & Lewis, I. (1984). The straight story on homosexuality and gay rights. *Public Opinion, 7*(1), 16-20, 59-60.

Schneider, M., & Tremble, B. (1986). Training service providers to work with gay or lesbian adolescents: A workshop. *Journal of Counseling and Development, 65*(2), 98-99.

Scott, D. (1988). Working with gay and lesbian students. *Association of College Unions-International Bulletin, 56*(2), 22-25.

Sears, J. (1987). Peering into the well of loneliness: The responsibility of educators to gay and lesbian youth. In Alex Molnar (Ed.), *Social issues and education: Challenge and responsibility* (pp. 79-100). Alexandria, VA: Association for Supervision & Curriculum Development.

Sears, J. (1988a). Paper presented at the American Educational Research Association. *Attitudes, experiences, and feelings of guidance counselors about working with homosexual students.* New Orleans. ERIC Document No. 296210.

Sears, J. (1988b). Growing up gay: Is anyone there to listen? *American School Counselors Association Newsletter, 26,* 8-9.

Sears, J. (1989a). Paper presented at the 1989 American Educational Research Association. *Personal feelings and professional attitudes of prospective teachers toward homosexuality and homosexual students: Research findings and curriculum recommendations.* San Francisco. ERIC No. 312222.

Sears, J. (1989b). The impact of gender and race on growing up lesbian and gay in the South. *NWSA Journal, 1*(3), 422-457.

Sears, J. (1990). Problems and possibilities in "Homophobia" education. *Empathy, 2*(2), 61.

Sears, J. (1991). *Growing up gay in the South: Race, gender, and journeys of the spirit.* New York: The Haworth Press, Inc.

Sears, J. (in press). The impact of culture and ideology on the construction of gender and sexual identities: Developing a critically-based sexuality curriculum. In J. Sears (Ed.), *Sexuality and the curriculum.* New York: Teachers College Press.

Smith, D. (1985). *An ethnographic interview study of homosexual teachers' perspectives.* Unpublished doctoral dissertation, State University of New York at Albany, Albany, NY. *(Dissertation Abstracts International 46, 1, 66A).*

Taylor, A. (1983). Conceptions of masculinity and femininity as a basis for stereotypes of male and female homosexuals. *Journal of Homosexuality, 9*(1), 37-53.

Thompson, G., & Fishburn, W. (1977). Attitudes toward homosexuality among graduate counseling students. *Counselor Education & Supervision, 17*(2), 121-130.

Weinberg, G. (1972). *Society and the healthy homosexual.* New York: St. Martin's Press.

Weiner, A. (1989). *Racist, sexist, and homophobic attitudes among undergraduate social work students and their effects on assessments of client vignettes.* Unpublished doctoral dissertation, Rutgers University, New Brunswick, NJ. *(Dissertation Abstracts International 50, 11, 3741A).*

Willis, P. (1977). Learning to labour: How working class kids get working class jobs. Westmead, England: Saxon House.

Wisniewski, J., & Toomey, B. (1987). Are social workers homophobic? *Social Work, 32*(5), 454-455.

Young, M., & Whertvine, J. (1982). Attitudes of heterosexual students toward homosexual behavior. *Psychological Reports, 51*(2), 673-674.

Liberal Attitudes and Homophobic Acts: The Paradoxes of Homosexual Experience in a Liberal Institution

William P. Norris, PhD

Oberlin College

SUMMARY. Rates of victimization of and attitudes towards lesbians, gay men, and bisexuals at a well-known national liberal arts college were reported and compared to other institutions. Based on two campus-wide surveys of employees and students respectively, differences in degree of exclusion, isolation, sexual harassment, needing to deny one's sexuality, self-censorship, and other factors were found among employees and students, people with varying sexualities, people of color, and whites. The paradoxical finding of extensive attitudinal support and widespread victimization was explored. The explanation suggested for the paradox drew on institutional characteristics, culture, and priorities. Based on the configuration of these, I suggested that the paradox resulted from two competing values, a liberal ethos focused on equal rights, and a heterosexual orthodoxy, and that many people were pulled between the two. Theoretical implications, counter-explanations, and implications were briefly explored.

Dr. Norris is Professor and Chair of Sociology at Oberlin College. He has his PhD from Harvard and has done research and published on comparative poverty and grassroots organizing in Brazil and the U.S. He wishes to thank Jan Cooper and Michael Zimmerman for reading and commenting on countless drafts, George Langeler for his support, and Clayton Koppes for his generous and good-humored advice. He also thanks all other committee members listed in note 1. Correspondence and requests for reprints may be addressed to him at the Sociology Department, Oberlin College, Oberlin, OH 44074-1095.

81

Increasing levels of violence and discrimination against lesbians, gay men, and bisexuals (LGBs) have led colleges and universities to attempt to document the problem on campus. This paper details the research done at Oberlin College,[1] a nationally known, highly selective liberal arts college, and compares it to some other institutions.

The research at Oberlin addressed the diversity of LGBs and the campus — differences of class, race/ethnicity, gender — in several ways. The entire campus community was surveyed, thus providing information on employees as well as students. The study explored the experiences of heterosexuals, some of whom are sometimes perceived to be LGBs and suffer problems because of it. Race, ethnicity, and gender differences were treated extensively in the separate analysis of people of·color and whites, lesbians, gay men, and bisexuals. This analysis revealed important differences in patterns of victimization, attitudes, and experiences of these various groups at the college.

The research also revealed a puzzling paradox between strong positive attitudes expressed towards LGBs and the widespread victimization experienced by LGBs and others. Two Oberlins seemed to emerge from the data. On the one hand employees and students of all race/ethnic groups and sexualities expressed strong positive attitudes towards LGBs. Not only is their presence on campus positively regarded, but respondents manifested strong support for working, studying, socializing, and living with them. In the other Oberlin, LGB individuals were confronted with many instances of direct discrimination, ranging from verbal abuse to physical attacks, violent intolerant language, and the sense that there was no place to turn in order to seek help when attacked or discriminated against. When apprised of this outcome of the research, people have typically asked how this could happen at a progressive place like Oberlin. This paper also explores and essays a preliminary explanation of the two Oberlins.

The paradox exists at the collective level, not the individual. The situation at Oberlin cannot be reduced to individuals who are both expressing positive attitudes and discriminating against LGBs. Rather it appears that the victimization goes on within their dorms and workplaces without their involvement, but also without their active disapprobation. Furthermore, if the problem is seen only as an aggregation of individual actions, important interactive and institutional components will be ignored. Thus the two Oberlins coexist in the same space and are shaped by collective and institutional factors. The question for the paper can be restated — what are the aspects of Oberlin as an institution, a community, and a culture which lead to this paradoxical outcome?

The posing of the problem as one of institutional culture suggests the theoretical significance of this issue. It is an attempt to begin to specify the dimensions of difference among institutions of higher education which contribute to variation in the situation (victimization, attitudes, degree of integration) of LGBs at those institutions.

I will argue that several dimensions of Oberlin life and history combine to account for this paradox. One is its progressive tradition with a strong commitment to equal rights. The College was the first co-educational institution of higher education in the United States (1833) as well as the first to admit African Americans to degree programs on an equal basis (1835). In the 1950s and 1960s, many students and some faculty were actively involved in civil rights and anti-war activities. Oberlin Gay Liberation, the first student LGB organization, was founded in 1971, and LGBs have been a strong campus presence from the 1960s. Another component of this orientation is the large numbers of students who go into human service careers.

However, equal rights for LGBs has not been an institutional priority. While among the first colleges and universities to include sexual orientation in its anti-discrimination statement (1973), implementation of the clause, as well as serious concern in most quarters for the situation of LGBs, has been lacking. Even so, institutional inaction is a necessary, but not sufficient contributor to this situation.

Public discussion of sexuality issues has not been legitimated. Sexuality brings to the fore discussion about an issue that is often deemed inappropriate. Sexual activity is private behavior, and as such, what one does in one's bedroom may be protected — or ignored — but should not be the subject of public discussion. As one person said when confronted with this survey, "Why did a nice person like him bring this up?" Privacy on the one hand is a right, supporting LGBs, on the other a problem, challenging such processes as coming out (Thomas, 1986) and impeding progress on LGB rights in general (Caserio, 1989).

Religion permeates Oberlin institutional culture. Founded by religious leaders, it became an abolitionist center. The school maintained a theological seminary until the 1960s. The Anti-Saloon League was founded in the town. Religious strictures against homosexuality underlie some opposition. On the other hand, reform and religion have gone hand-in-hand there, thus religion leads some individuals and groups to be very supportive of LGBs.

These factors — progressivism, institutional priorities, appropriateness of discussion of LGB issues, religion — are affected or formed by U.S.

society. However, at Oberlin, they receive different emphases and relationships among them are reconfigured.

The structures and geography of community play important roles. Oberlin is a residential college, and is located in the small town (8000 population) of the same name where most of the faculty and staff reside. It is located on the western edge of the Cleveland metropolitan area and has a student population of about 2700 of which 500 are students in the music conservatory. Churches play an important role in community formation. Many of the lower-level staff and service employees have a small-town background, and growing up in a small town has been shown to correlate with intolerance towards LGBs (Greenberg, 1988). Faculty and upper-level staff, while drawn from across the country and reflecting changing demographic patterns, still focus much activity around traditionally-structured family life. Traditional gender roles which assume heterosexuality are the norm. These elements of an explanation are explored below in the data and discussions.

OTHER CAMPUS STUDIES

Before turning to the data, questions of comparability of Oberlin and this study to other institutions and studies need elaboration. Oberlin is always compared to, and competes for students with a stratum of national liberal arts colleges and some research universities.[2]

Many studies at other institutions differ from this one because they utilize convenience (non-representative) samples rather than sampling or surveying the entire campus population as was done at Oberlin. Thus, they typically ask LGBs only, and they find them by giving out surveys at LGB meetings or events. The Oberlin study surveyed everyone on campus and asked them to identify themselves according to sexuality. Berrill (1990) summarized other studies' findings in the following paragraph:

> In studies of anti-gay violence and harassment at Yale (Herek, 1986), Rutgers (Cavin, 1987), and Penn State (D'Augelli, 1989), approximately 5% of the respondents had been punched, hit, kicked, or beaten at some point in their college careers; 16% to 26% had been threatened with physical violence, and 55% to 76% had been verbally harassed. Similar rates of victimization were documented at the University of Massachusetts at Amherst (Yeske, 1985) and at the University of Illinois at Urbana-Champagne (O'Shaughnessey, 1987). Among the gay, lesbian, and bisexual students surveyed at the University of Massachusetts (N = 174), 45% had been verbally

threatened or harassed, and 21% had been physically confronted or assaulted. Rates of such abuse at the University of Illinois (N = 92) were 58% and 15%, respectively.

As is evident, almost all of the studies have been conducted at state universities.[3] The conclusions of the New York Governor's Task Force on Bias Related Violence which surveyed state campuses stated "while evidence shows serious problems for many groups, the most severe hostilities are directed at lesbians and gay men" (Berrill, 1990, p. 285).

Several universities have conducted sample surveys of their student bodies. University of California at Santa Cruz (Nelson & Baker, 1990) utilized several questionnaire items similar to ones used in this research. The Oberlin results are compared below to the Yale, Penn State, and Rutgers victimization studies, and the Santa Cruz research on other dimensions.

THE OBERLIN STUDY: ORIGIN AND METHOD

Discriminatory incidents in the spring of 1988 led LGBs — students, staff and faculty — to insist that the problems facing LGBs on campus had to be confronted. A committee was created which organized this study. Committee members included lesbians and gay men, heterosexual men and women, people of color and white people, students, faculty, and staff.

We developed and distributed by mail two questionnaires — one to all students and one to all employees — late in the spring of 1989. The two surveys were in recognition of the differing situations (age, work, family status) of the two groups. We selected three areas for investigation for both groups — victimization, attitudes towards LGBs, and services for LGBs. Although the format of the survey was fixed response, comments, examples, and anecdotes were encouraged. Some items were drawn from questionnaires used at other schools, in particular Herek's victimization list (1986).[4] The questionnaires were only distributed one time; no second mailings were utilized because, in an attempt to convince the respondents that this was anonymous, the first mailing had no respondent-specific identification on it.

Self identification rather than behavior was used as the means of categorizing people. It was felt that identity resonated more clearly with the social interaction issues at the core of the study. The behavioral approach has been used in important studies such as Kinsey et al. (1948); (see Stein, 1989, for discussion). Respondents were asked in which of several cate-

gories they would place themselves. We employed the following categories: heterosexual, lesbian, gay man, bisexual, and questioning. The latter
refers to someone who is literally questioning their heterosexual identity.
As far as I know, no one in this study employed it to suggest questioning
their LGB orientation. Questioning should not be understood to presage
an inevitable change in orientation.

THE EMPLOYEE SURVEY

Demographic Characteristics of Respondents
Compared to All Employees

The employee respondents were representative of employees as a
whole. The proportion of each employee group responding to the questionnaire was:

Faculty	111 respondents out of a total of 279 or 39.8%
A&PS	89 respondents out of a total of 212 or 42.0%
Admin Asst	66 respondents out of a total of 205 or 32.2%
Service	11 respondents out of a total of 201 or 5.5%

Thus, more than two of every five faculty and A&PS (Administrative and
Professional Staff), and almost one of three administrative assistants (predominantly secretarial positions) responded to the survey. The response of
Service employees was much lower than that of the other three groups; the
reasons for this are not clear.

Among the faculty, respondents were similar to the overall faculty[5] in
proportions of men and women. On the other hand, proportionately fewer
people of color responded. Subdividing the faculty according to employment status (tenured, untenured tenure-line, and temporary) provided evidence that somewhat fewer temporary faculty and somewhat more tenured
faculty responded. Proportionately fewer men and people of color among
A&PS and administrative assistants responded to the survey.

Sexual Orientation

A larger proportion of men employees identified themselves as gay or
bisexual than women as lesbian or bisexual. The self-identified sexual
orientation of employees was, among women: heterosexual women
93.5% (143), lesbians 2.6% (4), bisexual women 2.6% (4), and questioning women 1.3% (2); and among men: heterosexual men 81.3% (109), gay
men 8.2% (11), bisexual men 6.0% (8), and questioning men 4.5% (6).

These had to be combined into a smaller number of categories to protect the anonymity of respondents. This led me to place the questioning individuals with the heterosexuals in one category, lesbians with bisexual women (5.2% of all women), and gay men with bisexual men (14.2% of all men). Anonymity and concerns with consistency led to the creation of two race/ethnic categories — white and people of color. The small number of LGBs of color forced combination of all lesbians and bisexual women of color and white lesbian and bisexual women into one category and all gay and bisexual men of color and white gay and bisexual men into another category.

The result was six categories of employees: heterosexual women of color, heterosexual men of color, heterosexual white women, heterosexual white men, all lesbians and bisexual women, all gay and bisexual men. Their proportions are presented in Table 1.

Knowledge of Lesbians, Gays, and Bisexuals

A large proportion of heterosexual employees were at least acquainted with LGBs and almost 40% knew at least one quite well. Considering only heterosexuals, the proportions responding that they were acquainted with or knew well an LGB person were: 89% women of color, 84% white men, 77% white women, and 70% men of color.

Knowledge about LGB concerns, history, and culture was not quite so widespread. About 8.1% of heterosexual respondents said they knew a great deal, and another 55% said they had some knowledge. Among

Table 1. Sexual Orientation by Race/Ethnicity and Sex

Sex	Heterosexual		Lesbian, Gay, Bisexual	Total
	People of Color	White		
Female	15 (9.8)	130 (85.0)	8 (5.2)	153 (100.0)
Male	9 (6.7)	106 (79.1)	19 (14.2)	134 (100.0)
Total	24 (8.4)	236 (82.2)	27 (9.4)	287 (100.0)

these, women of color (77.8%) indicated the most knowledge and men of color (50%) reported the least. Many employees — 55% — expressed some to great interest in learning more about LGB concerns, history, and culture. This response among heterosexual individuals ranged from 53.6% (white women) to 61.1% (women of color).

Stereotypical or Degrading Comments and Graffiti

The large number of derogatory or stereotypical comments about LGBs — almost 60% of all respondents had heard them — is one part of the puzzle. Slightly over half (51.2%) had observed stereotypical or degrading graffiti. A common graffiti was "kill all faggots." A heterosexual woman (A&PS) described conditions in her workplace, where "there are frequent jokes about homosexuality among the top-level, but not the lower-level, people. These range from blatant practical jokes to finger-pointing at heterosexual members of the staff suggesting that they are gay." A heterosexual man (tenured faculty) recounted the following incident: "I was talking with a friend of mine on a bench in front of the Oberlin Inn one Sunday at 12 or 1 when some [unclear] drove nearby on Main Street calling us faggots, with no apparent cause or provocation."

Employee Victimization

Victimization experiences provide direct evidence of one aspect of the paradox. Between one and eight Oberlin employees reported having been the target of every non-violent form of discrimination listed on the survey.

The problems most frequently reported were social ostracism (4 out of 19 or 21% of gay and bisexual men), accusations of being LGB (6 of 27 or 22.2% of LGBs), verbal insults (5 of 27 or 18.5% of LGBs), and threats to expose the individual (5 of 27 or 18.5% of LGBs) — the latter three problems were divided between men and women. In addition, heterosexual individuals also experienced victimization of which 6 incidents were reported: being ostracized, threatened with exposure as a lesbian, verbally insulted, and accused of being LGB. Anecdotal examples included the report of a gay man (tenured faculty) that "after it became known on campus that I was gay, I found I was no longer invited to certain places." A lesbian employee recounted an incident in which gossip about her sexuality was spread by a co-worker. As a result she found, "It hurt my reputation, and I lost a few friends (so-called). It is very hard for me now, since the whole department knows . . . this one person actually MADE ME 'come out' with no choice. I am now looking for other employment." Most of those who responded said that they had not reported the incidents citing fear of more victimization (4) or expecting that nothing would be done (4).

The people surveyed were asked if they knew of victimization of others. Their answers indicated that physical violence and property damage had occurred. The discriminatory acts most frequently reported were social ostracism or exclusion (23 or 8% of all respondents), verbal insults (33 or 11.5%), and accusations of being lesbian, gay, or bisexual (17 or 5.9%). Denials of promotion (10 or 3.5%) and threats of exposure (10 or 3.5%) were also reported. Seven people (2.4%) reported being followed/chased and a similar number reported being sexually harassed. A heterosexual woman wrote, "Some gay men and a woman were verbally harassed by young males. They didn't report it to the police because the police seem to find such incidents understandable!" A heterosexual woman said, "An applicant for a faculty position was passed over although in judgment of many was best qualified, because he seemed effeminate." A gay man characterized what he had felt or observed in the following ways:

> Denied salary raises — Salary reviews have been written which call attention to certain characteristics in such a way that it undermines an otherwise positive review, e.g., men's way of dressing.

> Denied promotion and/or tenure — While no one has been denied either only for this, there is a pervasive belief, and enough people had problems to suggest that being a lesbian or gay leads to a much harder look than others get.

These incidents were not reported by about three quarters of the respondents (33/45). Those victimized did not expect any results from reporting (23) or did not expect the incident to be taken seriously. For example, a heterosexual woman who had observed frequent derogatory language in her workplace wrote:

> I find this behavior very offensive, and in fact become depressed when it occurs because it makes me very uncomfortable. After much consideration, however, I decided not to report it to [the responsible committee], because it would be difficult to protect my identity if that committee should try to do anything about it. Everyone else in this office seems to take it all in stride. I feel like the oddball, because I choose not to participate.

ATTITUDES ABOUT LESBIANS, GAY MEN, AND BISEXUAL INDIVIDUALS

Attitudes represented the other side of the paradox. The majority of answers to all the questions were positive or supportive, although the degree varied. Similar responses were elicited by workplace questions about hiring, working with, or socializing with lesbians, gays, or bisexuals (see Table 2). All respondent groups strongly agreed that they supported hiring, working, and socializing with LGBs.

Two other questions—on AIDS and on whether one is assumed to be LGB if interested in their issues—had more complicated responses. Respondents in general indicated overwhelmingly that they did not fear contact with gays because of AIDS and that they did not assume that a person

Table 2. Employee Attitudes towards Lesbian, Gay, and Bisexual Employees

Question	Strongly Agree	Agree	Neutral	Disagree	Strongly Disagree	Totals
Respondent Would oppose hiring LGB	7 (2.4)	5 (1.7)	20 (7.0)	51 (17.8)	203 (71.0)	286
Respondent avoids work with LGBs	4 (1.4)	4 (1.4)	20 (7.0)	53 (18.5)	206 (72.0)	286
Respondent feels comfortable including an LGB in social occasion	169 (59.1)	60 (21.0)	16 (5.6)	11 (3.8)	30 (10.5)	286
Respondent afraid of contact with gays because of AIDS	10 (3.5)	12 (4.2)	33 (11.5)	77 (26.9)	154 (53.8)	286
When someone talks about LGB issues Respondent assumes that s/he probably is LGB	6 (3.5)	21 (7.4)	51 (17.9)	93 (32.6)	114 (40.0)	285

was lesbian, gay, or bisexual because she or he was interested in their issues. However, interpreting contact in a more physical way, some gay and bisexual men responded that they did fear contact with other gay and bisexual men because of AIDS. By the same token, when asked what they would assume about someone who knew details about certain issues, some LGBs agreed that they did sometimes assume that the individual was probably gay. Women heterosexuals expressed more ambivalence than men about contact with gay men because of AIDS.

The questions about political expression by LGBs and about self-censorship displayed the most diverse responses (Table 3). Slightly over 53% of the heterosexual individuals disagreed to some extent with the statement that "LGBs push their demands too forcefully." Almost one in five

Table 3. Detailed Responses to Political and Self-Censorship Questions

Question and Group Membership	Strongly Agree	Agree	Neutral	Disagree	Strongly Disagree	Totals
Lesbians and gay men push their demands too forcefully						
Heterosexual						
Male of color	1 (11.1)	1 (22.2)	1 (11.1)	3 (33.3)	2 (22.2)	9
Female of color	2 (13.3)	1 (6.7)	7 (46.7)	3 (20.0)	2 (13.3)	15
Male white	3 (2.8)	17 (16.0)	32 (30.2)	28 (26.4)	26 (24.5)	106
Female white	10 (7.8)	14 (10.9)	31 (24.0)	42 (32.6)	32 (24.8)	129
Lesbians, Gays, Bisexuals						
Female	--	--	--	3 (37.5)	5 (62.5)	8
Male	--	--	5 (26.3)	3 (15.8)	11 (57.9)	19
Total	16 (5.6)	34 (11.9)	76 (26.6)	82 (28.7)	78 (27.3)	286

Table 3 (cont). Detailed Responses to Political and Self-Censorship Questions

Question and Group Membership	Strongly Agree	Agree	Neutral	Disagree	Strongly Disagree	Totals
Respondent has felt the need to censor self when addressing LGB issues in his/her work at OC						
Heterosexuals						
Male of color	1 (11.1)	2 (22.2)	2 (22.2)	2 (22.2)	2 (22.2)	9
Female of color	1 (6.7)	2 (13.3)	1 (6.7)	7 (46.7)	4 (26.7)	15
Male white	5 (5.0)	20 (19.8)	20 (19.8)	19 (18.8)	37 (36.6)	101
Female white	6 (4.8)	16 (12.7)	26 (20.6)	36 (28.6)	42 (33.3)	126
Lesbians, Gays, Bisexuals						
Female	1 (12.5)	3 (37.5)	1 (12.5)	1 (12.5)	2 (25.0)	8
Male	3 (15.8)	5 (26.3)	1 (5.3)	5 (26.3)	5 (26.3)	19
Total	17 (6.1)	48 (17.2)	51 (18.3)	70 (25.1)	92 (33.0)	279

agreed to some extent with this statement, and over 27% were neutral. Among LGBs, 81.5% disagreed to some extent and 18.5% were neutral. None agreed. Heterosexuals differed among themselves—white women were most supportive (about 57%) and women of color least supportive (about 33%), while almost exactly one-half of the men did not indicate that the LGBs were being too forceful.

The responses to the question about self-censorship in Table 3 revealed a striking pattern. All groups had felt the need to exercise self-censorship. This ranged from 17.5% of the white heterosexual women to 42.1% of gay and bisexual men and 50% of the lesbian and bisexual women. Given the strong supportive pattern of responses to many of the other attitude questions, it is reasonable to assume that much of this censorship by heterosexual individuals was due to anxiety about being seen as too pro-LGB. On the other hand, we should not ignore the fact that an overall majority reported that they did not feel the need to restrict their comments. The following quotations from comments written by respondents on the survey illustrate some the range of attitudes on this issue:

(heterosexual man, tenured faculty): I'm not sure that "censor" is the right word for what I've felt, but this may be the place to mention it. I teach one course in which issues of sexual identity enter naturally. My own reticence on sexual matters, along with my own sexual orientation ("straight"), make it difficult for me to discuss these issues in a natural way.

(heterosexual woman, non-tenured faculty): Only because of the hyper-sensitive atmosphere I perceive, I'm careful because I feel that remarks may be easily misunderstood.

(heterosexual woman, A&PS): I have never lived or worked any place where people are as supersensitive as they are in Oberlin about issues such as sexual identity. I resent the fact that administrative committees constantly tell me what I should think, how I should act, and what is moral and immoral. The assumption is always that the majority is heterosexist, racist, etc., and that the minority is oppressed, virtuous, correct, and without prejudices. I believe that all people have prejudices. The difference between people we categorize as prejudiced and those we categorize as believing in equality is simply this—those who believe in equality recognize their own prejudices and work to counter them.

(heterosexual woman, A&PS): I mean this to say that I know I would be fired if I expressed my position as a Christian that non-heterosexual relationships (and any sexual relationship outside of marriage) is sexual sin. I can be fired for my religious beliefs, but someone else could not be fired for conduct associated with their sexual preference.

(heterosexual man, A&PS): Although I have a few gay friends, I don't feel as though I've become sensitive to their needs well enough to know when they might be slighted. I know that they are more easily insulted than I am and probably with good reason.

A different set of questions explored perceptual differences about the degree of inclusion of LGB concerns in the life of the institution. Benefits were singled out by LGBs as a problem area. A lesbian wrote "I as a lesbian in a long-term relationship with a full-time position with the college could not list my partner on a health insurance policy. Though she and I had joint everything else. She was not recognized as family/spouse."

Another area of perceptual difference regarded the extent of reporting of campus LGB events and information about LGBs. While virtually no material of any sort about LGBs was included in the two main publicity organs of the institution (the administrative newspaper and the alumni magazine) many heterosexuals believed that some coverage existed.

CHARACTERISTICS AND ATTITUDES OF LESBIAN, GAY MALE, AND BISEXUAL EMPLOYEES

Lesbians, gay men, and bisexuals were asked how "out" they were to various members of their social network. Women tended to be somewhat more open to family, friends, students, and supervisors than men. Neither were very open to neighbors or health-care providers.

Both women (lesbians and bisexuals) and men (gays and bisexuals) employees were most open to friends. About three quarters of each group indicated that they were out to at least some friends, and a large portion of the rest indicated all friends. About three quarters of women and slightly fewer men indicated they had told some members of their families and some co-workers about their sexual orientation.

Relationships with students also tended to be open at least in some cases for 75% of women and 58% of the men; about 25% of each indicated that they were not out to any students. An example of one lesbian employee's attitude about being open with students was the following:

> I am *out*. I do not keep my sexual orientation a secret but I am also very ethical. I do not flaunt my orientation. If someone asks I tell them the truth. I used to be concerned about students telling parents about my sexual orientation but I grew to realize that the students don't care about it. They are here to be students. This was especially a concern in my first job, not Oberlin, but I was very at ease here from the start on.

Employees were less open with their supervisors. Among women, 37.5% indicated that no supervisor knew their sexual orientation. This was true of an even larger proportion (42.1%) of men. Most of the rest of both sexes indicated that some supervisors knew.

The two groups with whom LGBs were least open were health providers and neighbors. Over one half of the men and three quarters of the women said they had not revealed their sexual identities to any such individuals.

Gender differences were also evident in responses from employee LGBs about interaction with heterosexuals at the college. One question asked if they felt isolated from others because of their sexual orientation to which about one third of the women and men responded yes. One lesbian employee described her sense of isolation in this way: "I feel forced into the closet and I guess I 'accept' that plight."

When queried if they thought that it would be easier to make friends if they were *not* LGB about 37.5% of the women and 19% of the men agreed that it would be easier.

Two questions probed fear of discrimination from supervisors or co-workers. A majority of men and women did not fear discrimination or harassment because of sexual orientation. Fear was expressed by one quarter of the women and 15% of the men. On the other hand a majority of the women feared harassment or discrimination from their co-workers. One quarter of the men indicated such fear.

The last question asked about coming out—"If I were to come out it would negatively affect my friendships with others." A majority of women (62.5%) agreed that coming out would have a negative effect; substantially fewer men (35%) agreed.

To summarize this section, women indicated more fears than men about friendships and relations with co-workers and supervisors.

THE STUDENT SURVEY

Demographic Characteristics of Student Respondents
Compared to All Students

Slightly less than one third of the student body (869 or 31.4%) answered the questionnaire. This was lower than the response rate of the three employee groups reported above.

The students who responded to the questionnaire differed proportionately in sex and college division from students in general.[6] While 52% of the student body are women, 60.4% of the respondents were women. Similarly, the Conservatory is under represented in this survey—while 11.7% of all students were enrolled in the Conservatory, only 6.2% of the respondents were from that division. Regarding race and ethnicity, people of color made up 18.3% of the student body and 15.7% responded to the questionnaire. Non-U.S. citizens were 2.8% of all students and respondents. The comparison of class rank of undergraduates in general and respondents also showed a reasonably comparable distribution. The differences between respondents and all students suggest that one should be careful interpreting and generalizing the findings, especially for male and Conservatory students, but that, in general, the study is representative of racial/ethnic divisions and class year.

Student Sexual Orientation and Racial/Ethnic/Citizenship Characteristics

Students were asked to identify their sexual orientation by choosing among heterosexual, gay and lesbian, bisexual, or questioning categories. Among women students, 73.7% said that their sexual orientation was heterosexual. Of the remaining 26.3% women, lesbians constituted 5.7%, bisexual women 8.2%, and questioning women 12.4%.

The proportions of men choosing the various categories differed from women. More said that they were heterosexual (84.3%) and gay (6.4%), and fewer indicated that they were bisexual (5.2%) or questioning (4.2%). Thus, 15.7% of the men students indicated they were gay, bisexual, or questioning.

The much larger number of student respondents reduced problems of maintaining anonymity and allowed the use of more refined categories. In that regard questioning individuals could be treated separately. Small numbers forced the continued combination of bisexuals with lesbians and gay men respectively. Thus, six sex/sexuality subdivisions were used — heterosexual men, heterosexual women, lesbian and bisexual women, gay and bisexual men, questioning women, and questioning men.

A separate category of non-US citizens was provided for respondents in the race/ethnic question. It was utilized because of our expectation that those born and socialized in other countries would have different attitudes towards LGBs. The small numbers of lesbian, gay, bisexual, and questioning people among the various US minorities, mixed race and non-US citizens led to the creation of two categories: people of color and MRNUS (mixed race and non-US citizens). The survey indicated that both the mixed race and non-US citizens groups were very heterogeneous, thus MRNUS is a very heterogeneous group. In conclusion the student analysis employs three group subdivisions — whites, people of color, and MRNUS.

The proportions of people identifying with a given sexual orientation varied by group (see Table 4). Thus, people of color had higher propor-

Table 4. Student Sexual Orientation by Racial/Ethnic Characteristics[3]

	People of Color[1]		White[2]		MRNUS[4]	
	Women	Men	Women	Men	Women	Men
Heterosexual	49 (87.5)	35 (85.4)	313 (71.8)	225 (84.9)	22 (73.3)	25 (80.6)
Lesbian & Bisexual Women	4 (7.1)	--	65 (14.9)	--	4 (13.3)	--
Gay & Bisexual Men	--	4 (9.8)	--	31 (11.7)	--	3 (9.7)
Questioning Women	3 (5.4)	2 (4.9)	58 (13.3)	9 (3.4)	4 (13.3)	3 (9.7)

1. Includes Asian and Pacific Islander, African-American, Latino, and Native American.
2. Includes Jewish, German American, Northern Italian, Russian Jew.
3. All percentages refer to their respective columns.
4. Combines mixed race and non-U.S. citizens.

97

tions of heterosexual women than the whites or MRNUS groups. Lesbian and bisexual and questioning women were disproportionately found among whites. Gay and bisexual men were distributed rather evenly in the groups while a slightly higher proportion of the MRNUS category consists of questioning men.

Note that the small number of individuals who are lesbian, gay men, bisexual, or questioning among the people of color and MRNUS means that care must be taken in generalizing the findings about them.

Knowledge of Lesbian, Gay Male, and Bisexual Students and Their Concerns

A majority of each group knew LGBs. A large majority of white students (58.7%) reported that they knew a LGB individual very well. The other groups evidenced more acquaintance relationships with LGBs. The major difference among the groups was the response of women. While more white heterosexual women reported great or some knowledge of LGBs, fewer women than men among the women of color and MRNUS categories, had great, or some knowledge of LGBs.

When asked about their knowledge of LGB history and culture, over half of the MRNUS and white respondents said that they knew at least something about these topics. On the other hand, only about 40% of the people of color had some knowledge of LGB history.

The question about whether courses on LGB issues should be offered received broad and deep support. Over 90% of each of the three groups indicated they believed such courses should be offered. About 60% of white and MRNUS students and 50% of students of color indicated they would take such a course if offered.

Comments and Graffiti: Everyday Life

Graffiti and comments contributed to a hostile climate towards LGBs. Large numbers of students had overheard stereotypical or derogatory comments about lesbians, gay men, or bisexuals. Eighty-two (87.3%) people of color, 595 whites (88.1%), and 45 (78%) from the MRNUS group answered yes. In general, heterosexual, lesbian, gay, bisexual, and questioning individuals all heard these comments to an equal extent.

Comments frequently reported were, referring to lesbians, "all she needs is a good fuck," and referring to gay men, "they should be shot;" "don't bend over in the shower around —;" and "AIDS is God's way of eliminating gay men." A heterosexual white woman provided other typical comments which she had heard: "Lesbians cut their hair short to deny femininity. Lesbians lust after all women. Lesbians are athletically inclined. Females who are athletic are gay. Lesbians are violent. Gay men are not masculine. Gay men are weak. Gay men like to do 'traditional' female things like cook." A woman of color responded, "PLENTY. Mimicking of effeminate behavior supposedly that of 'fags'. *LOTS* of AIDS jokes, a commentary by a professor to the effect that all male dancers are gay (presented as a well-known 'fact'), etc. . . . " One white heterosexual woman said, "I have heard persons say they fear that a gay/lesbian/bisexual would make a pass at them and fear being touched by them."

Respondents were also asked if they had seen graffiti degrading or stereotyping LGBs and roughly three quarters of all respondents answered yes — 70.7% of people of color, 79.4% of whites, 76.3% of MRNUS. Very common graffiti were "kill fags" and "lesbians be dead." Others included "spermeaters deserve to get AIDS and die"; "She's ugly, no wonder she's a lesbian"; "Try sucking cock you dykes"; "Gay power = AIDS power." Beyond that, we were told that the bathrooms in the library and classroom building were places where one could see all the graffiti one wanted.

Student Victimization

The extent of victimization was surprising considering positive attitudes expressed. Students experienced every kind of victimization listed — violent and non-violent. Some students wrote general comments about discrimination. A white lesbian/bisexual woman reported, "In this environment the pressures I have felt have been academic and social, a combination of being female *and* gay. The obvious forms of harassment — articles in [student newspaper], graffiti in the bathrooms [and elsewhere] have an effect, but are easier to cope with than: fear of not being taken seriously by academic professors and peers; labelled 'trendy' or 'strident'; social pressure to not be too political; or verbal harassment from men who think you're 'too pretty to be a dyke' or 'an ugly dyke.'"

Both anecdotal and quantitative data indicated that heterosexuals as well as LGBs felt they received different treatment because they were being identified as homosexual. For example, a white heterosexual man wrote: "Some people think I'm gay and treat me accordingly. Usually I let them think so, because it's their problem. But it has helped me understand what gays and lesbians go through all the time." A white heterosexual woman reported, "I was called a lesbian for holding hands with another female," and another reported being harassed because she was walking with a woman. On the other hand, some students did not believe that this kind of biased treatment was in fact bias at all. Instead, as a heterosexual white male put it, "You get what you deserve."

The forms of victimization experienced most frequently were "felt the necessity of denying that s/he was LGB," 15.2% (132), and "received verbal insults," 13.6% (118). Among those who had to deny that they were LGB (Table 5, Part I), heterosexuals were least often affected, and LGBs most often affected. LGBs, people of color, and white women had proportionately more problems with this issue. Considering gay and bisexual men, all (4) men of color and two thirds (21) of white men had denied their sexual orientation. Three quarters (3) of the lesbian and bisexual women of color, over two thirds (45) of the white lesbian and bisexual women, and half (2) of the MRNUS lesbian and bisexual women had the same experience. One person summed up why she concealed her sexual identity. It was because of "fear of my peers (including some good friends) finding out and being alienated."

Students of all groups and sexualities received verbal insults (Table 5, Part II). LGBs, men of color, and white women were most likely to be insulted; white men indicated somewhat fewer but still extensive numbers of insults. One (25%) woman of color, 28 (43.1%) white women, and 2 (50.0%) MRNUS women had been treated in this way. High proportions of gay and bisexual men suffered the same problem, that is 3 (75.0%) men of color and 10 (32.3%) white men. A white lesbian woman wrote extensively about the whole environment of distrust and disrespect that she felt verbal abuse had created around her:

> Part of the problem stems from dealing with loving in a small, midwest town w[h]ere gay men/lesbians/bisexuals are still considered immoral if not child molesters. I feel that tension on the job . . . and knew that coming out would probably seriously jeopardize my relationships with my supervisors and with other employees. My immediate superiors have made comments about hair length and political involvement—homophobic, yes, but not personally threatening.

> A good number of professors have openly questioned the validity of my views solely because I am a woman, or a lesbian—general idea being theirs (as straight men) are normal, therefore correct. Many have been uncomfortable with the entire subject. I often feel like a freak in the department, and, talking with the 1 or 2 other out students I know I am not alone in that feeling.

> Still, much of the tension comes from fellow students—I've lost a good number of "friends" and acquaintances by coming out, been avoided in the dorm; my roommate made uncomfortable by assump-

Table 5. STUDENT EXPERIENCES OF DISCRIMINATION AT OBERLIN COLLEGE BY SUBDIVISIONS
==
Part I: Need to Deny LGB Status

Q. "Felt the necessity of denying that I was gay/lesbian/bisexual."
==

	People of Color		
	Yes	No Answer	Total
Hetero Woman	--	49 (100.0)	49
Hetero Man	4 (11.4)	31 (88.6)	35
Les Bi Woman	3 (75.0)	1 (25.0)	4
Gay Bi Man	4 (100.0)	--	4
Quest Woman	--	3 (100.0)	3
Quest Man	1 (50.0)	1 (50.0)	2
	12 (12.4)	85 (87.6)	97 (100.0)

	White		
	Yes	No Answer	Total
Hetero Woman	14 (4.5)	299 (95.6)	313
Hetero Man	16 (7.1)	209 (92.8)	225
Les Bi Woman	45 (69.2)	20 (30.7)	65
Gay Bi Man	21 (67.7)	10 (32.2)	31
Quest Woman	15 (25.9)	43 (74.1)	58
Quest Man	2 (22.2)	7 (77.8)	9
	113 (16.1)	588 (83.9)	701 (100.0)

	MRNUS		
	Yes	No Answer	Total
Hetero Woman	1 (4.5)	21 (95.5)	22
Hetero Man	3 (12.0)	22 (88.0)	25
Les Bi Woman	2 (50.0)	2 (50.0)	4
Gay Bi Man	--	3 (100.0)	3
Quest Woman	--	4 (100.0)	4
Quest Man	1 (33.3)	2 (66.7)	3
	7 (11.5)	54 (88.5)	61 (100.0)

TABLE 5 (continued)

```
===========================================================================
```
Part II: Received Verbal Insults at Oberlin College

Q. "Received verbal insults (because I am or perceived to be
    lesbian/gay/bisexual)."
```
===========================================================================
```

	People of Color		
	Yes	No Answer	Total
Hetero Woman	--	49 (100.0)	49
Hetero Man	5 (14.3)	30 (85.7)	35
Les Bi Woman	1 (25.0)	3 (75.0)	4
Gay Bi Man	3 (75.0)	1 (25.0)	4
Quest Woman	1 (33.3)	2 (66.7)	3
Quest Man	1 (50.0)	1 (50.0)	2
	11 (11.3)	86 (87.6)	97 (100.0)

	White		
	Yes	No Answer	Total
Hetero Woman	24 (7.7)	289 (92.4)	313
Hetero Man	18 (8.0)	207 (92.0)	225
Les Bi Woman	28 (43.1)	37 (56.9)	65
Gay Bi Man	10 (32.3)	21 (67.8)	31 (4.4)
Quest Woman	19 (32.8)	39 (67.2)	58
Quest Man	1 (11.1)	8 (88.9)	9
	100 (14.3)	576 (82.2)	701 (100.0)

	MRNUS		
	Yes	No Answer	Total
Hetero Woman	1 (4.5)	21 (95.5)	22
Hetero Man	1 (4.0)	24 (96.0)	25
Les Bi Woman	2 (50.0)	2 (50.0)	4
Gay Bi Man	1 (33.3)	2 (66.7)	3
Quest Woman	1 (25.0)	3 (75.0)	4
Quest Man	1 (33.3)	2 (66.7)	3
	7 (11.5)	54 (88.5)	61 (100.0)

tions or statements made about her. On general principle I avoid places (dorms/activities) on this campus which I perceive would be threatening to me . . . anywhere where the assumption is 'straight function' (i.e., anywhere or time that's not specifically designated as a Lesbian/Gay dance or party).

I have yet to be attacked by another student — physically attacked, but who knows? It would not surprise me if someone tried it.

Thus, in all groups, substantial numbers of the lesbians, gays, and bisexuals had encountered situations in which they had to deny they were LGB and/or were verbally insulted about their sexual orientation. Questioning individuals in smaller numbers had been victimized in the same way and even heterosexual students were not immune.

In order to have some indication of the total proportion of students experiencing victimization, I combined the responses for the two questions above. A total of 184 (or 21.4%) of the student respondents reported experiencing one or both of these problems. Thus, 21.4% of *all* Oberlin students who answered the survey either needed to deny that they were LGB or were verbally insulted for being (or being perceived to be) LGB.

These responses were then subdivided by sexual orientation of the respondents. The numbers below refer to the number experiencing the problem, the total number of the group, and the proportion:

lesbian and bisexual women	57/73	78.1%
gay and bisexual men	27/38	71.1%
questioning women	30/65	46.2%
questioning men	5/14	35.7%
heterosexual women	35/384	9.1%
heterosexual men	30/275	10.9%

Thus, 80% of the lesbian and bisexual women, and over 70% of gay and bisexual men, had experienced one of these two experiences. That, coupled with the relatively high proportions of questioning and heterosexual individuals indicating they also had these experiences point to a pervasive problem on campus. It seems fair to conclude that a climate of discrimination exists which affects almost all lesbians, gays, and bisexuals as well as large numbers of the rest of the student body.

Sexual harassment or assault because of being or being perceived to be LGB had happened to 3.3% (29) of all students. White lesbian/bisexual women and gay/bisexual men were most frequently targets — respectively

20% (13) of the women and 16.1% (5) of the men. A white lesbian woman reported:

> I have been harassed by male dorm mates in a large dorm. I received rape threats through a closed door from them. 'That dyke just needs a good fuck. Who's going to give it to her' and the like. Lots of subtle harassment too—people left the bathroom when I came in, wrote on my door. Last year several males attempted to sexually harass and one began to assault me, [he was] threatened by my 'out' lesbianism and said as much.

Social exclusion was reported by 2.9% (26) of all students. Among heterosexuals two men of color (5.7%) and 3 white men (1.3%) experienced this, as did two white questioning women (3.5%). It was more common among lesbians, gay men, and bisexual individuals where half of the people of color, 10.8% of white women, 19.4% of white men, and 1 MRNUS woman (25.0%) and 1 MRNUS man (33.3%) reported being excluded.

Property damage was sustained by seven individuals, most of whom were white. Three gay and bisexual white men (9.7% of all gay and bisexual white men) and three lesbian/bisexual women (4.6%) indicated that this had happened to them.

Eleven white students said that they had been penalized in a work situation. Seven of these were lesbian/bisexual women.

When asked if they had been threatened with exposure as a lesbian, gay man, or bisexual individual, fifteen people answered yes. Of these, twelve were white; six of the twelve were lesbian/bisexual women (9.2%) and three were gay/bisexual men (9.7%).

Some students experienced direct violence in varying degrees. Eleven individuals had had objects thrown at them. Almost all of them were white, and all sexual orientations were represented (1 heterosexual woman, 3 heterosexual men (1.3%), 3 lesbian/bisexual women (4.6%), 2 gay/bisexual men (6.5%), and 1 questioning woman).

When asked if they had been followed or chased, twenty individuals responded yes. Half of those reporting this were white lesbian/bisexual women. Most of rest were white and included 5 heterosexuals (3 women and 2 men).

Five people indicated that they had been spat on. Three people, all white, said that they had been punched, hit, or beaten. One person indicated that she had been physically assaulted/wounded.

In spite of these experiences, a relatively small number of students said they expected further problems at Oberlin. Twenty-four responded yes.

Of these, three were MRNUS. Of the 21 whites, 11 were lesbian/bisexual women (16.9%) and 4 gay/bisexual men (12.9%)

In sum, the number and variety of victimization experiences was disturbing. Significant acts of violence were reported, and by fairly large numbers of people. Lesbians and bisexual women, especially whites, reported more experiences than other groups, but all groups, including large numbers of heterosexuals had suffered sexuality-related victimization.

Student Reporting of Incidents of Discrimination

Lack of student reporting of incidents compounded the victimization, because most felt that their experiences were regarded as frivolous by administrative officers and staff. Of the 213 students who experienced incidents, 93.9% of them did not report them. Students of color, white students, and MRNUS gave similar reasons for not reporting — the incidents would not be taken seriously. Smaller numbers of students of color and MRNUS students said they did not know where to report the incidences or did not trust the authorities to protect their identity.

Some white students stated that they believed that the administration was not concerned about discrimination against LGBs, or in the words of a white lesbian woman, "I have *never* heard, officially stated, in a house meeting or classroom that harassment of Lesbians/Gay men/Bisexuals is unacceptable and will not be tolerated." Another reason was the expectation that nothing would be done anyway. A white questioning woman commented on this: "I know another man who was verbally insulted [and] brought charges against the person who insulted him through judicial board — judicial board in turn seemed completely insensitive and essentially swept the whole case under the carpet in the name of preserving a 'sense of community' at Oberlin."

The students were also asked if they knew of other students who had experienced discrimination because they were or were perceived to be LGB. Verbal insults had been heard about by about 40% of the sample and most of the LGBs. Large numbers had heard about someone being followed or chased, being punched, hit or beaten, and being penalized at work. In each of these cases, proportionately more LGBs were aware of these incidents than heterosexual or questioning individuals.[7]

More than one half of respondents in all groups and sex/sexuality categories had heard of people being gossiped about in a derogatory way. For example, one white heterosexual woman reported: "This usually consists of joking about stereotypic behaviors of persons — speech patterns or mannerisms . . . imitation or making fun of these things, or just laughing at them." Few had heard of incidents of sexual harassment. A white lesbian/

bisexual woman recounted: "I knew a woman who lived in [a dorm] who received verbal and written insults about her sexuality. Males living in the dorm would leave graphic pictures of male genitalia on her door along with written insults. They would also knock on her door and when she answered say things like, 'Does this mean you won't suck my dick?'" Some isolated instances of LGBs harassing other LGBs were also reported, mainly by exposing their sexual orientation.

It appears that incidents of a more violent nature or which have the potential to threaten others are more often known about than those which are verbal interactions between individuals. One bisexual white student eloquently expressed the hopelessness she and many others felt about the situation, "they [the insults and harassment] become a part of everyday life, nothing can really be done about them."

Attitudes About Lesbian, Gay Male, and Bisexual Students

Attitude questions showed evidence of a high degree of support and tolerance. Students overwhelmingly supported the presence of lesbian, gay, and bisexual students on campus—93% of the respondents of color, 94% of the MRNUS group, and 96% of the whites agreed. Students evinced similar overwhelming support for the presence of lesbian, gay, and bisexual staff and faculty; although a heterosexual woman of color commented, "I never knew there were any." One white lesbian woman supported their presence because, "they offer visible support for projects and groups," and another said, "It's hard to be an aspiring lesbian academician with no role models." Opposing their presence were about 5% of the students of color and 4% of the white students. In this regard a white heterosexual male said:

> I really don't feel that we should encourage homosexual behavior in any way. I don't think that homosexuals should be able to adopt children, and homosexual teachers, role models for many, are not a good idea.

However, students who supported LGBs sometimes had to hide their support. In particular higher proportions of men than women in all groups answered the question indicating that they felt they had to hide their support. Between 20-25% of all heterosexual men had concealed their support (23.6% of men of color, 19.1% of whites, and 20% of MRNUS) and the proportions were even higher among questioning men (50% of men of color, 33.3% of whites, and 66.7% of MRNUS), and gay and bisexual men (50% of men of color, 32.3% of whites).

Lower proportions of the women students had concealed their support (12.2% of women of color, 9.4% of whites, and 9.1% of MRNUS). More women, all of whom were white, reported hiding their support among the other sexuality categories (questioning women 12.1% and lesbian and bisexual women 24.6%). A white heterosexual woman commented that she often had "to make it clear that I am heterosexual." Thus, this was a general problem for men of all groups and sexual orientations, and for some white women.

Another question concerned whether people who talked about lesbian or gay issues were perceived to be lesbian or gay. About two thirds of the students disagreed with this question. Talking about LGB issues was perceived to result in being labeled an LGB by proportionately more men than women in all sex/sexuality categories among white and MRNUS students. The highest percentage was among gay or bisexual men 22.6%, and MRNUS gay or bisexual men 33.3%. On the other hand, equal proportions (14.3%) of heterosexual men and women said that someone who discussed LGB issues probably was LGB.

Whether the AIDS epidemic had made the respondent afraid of contact with gay men (Table 6) was the subject of one question. Overall, no more than 10.3% of any group of respondents agreed that the epidemic had led to greater fear. On the other hand, gay or bisexual white men and men of color disproportionately responded that they were more afraid than before of contact with other gay men. As one gay man said, "sex with men is scary with AIDS around."

Students were asked their attitude toward LGB political actions in the question "lesbians and gays push their demands too forcefully." Altogether, almost 80% of the students disagreed with the statement. On the other hand, heterosexuals were the only ones agreeing with the statement except among whites — one third of the whites agreeing with the statement were LGBs. A common response was, "I don't think they should advertize it." A white heterosexual man explained this sentiment further:

> If homosexuals would be 'as' loud as the norm and not set themselves apart, they would not be set apart by society. The only time I get mad is when I am forced to see their graffiti, their demands, their protests, like they were the only ones discriminated against in some way.

Another heterosexual white man wrote:

Table 6. Attitudes about Lesbians, Gays, and Bisexuals on Campus by Student Respondents -- Selected Questions

Question and Group	Responses					
	Strong Agree	Agree	Neutral	Disagree	Strong Disagree	Total
AIDS - *"The AIDS epidemic has made me afraid of contact with gay men"*						
People of Color	4	6	8	25	54	97
	(4.1)	(6.2)	(8.2)	(25.8)	(55.7)	(100.0)
White	13	28	40	191	421	693
	(1.9)	(4.0)	(5.8)	(27.6)	(60.8)	(100.0)
MRNUS	1	5	3	18	34	61
	(1.6)	(8.2)	(4.9)	(29.5)	(55.7)	(99.9)
Politics - *"Lesbians and gays push their demands too forcefully"*						
People of Color	9	13	22	38	14	96
	(9.4)	(13.5)	(22.9)	(39.6)	(14.6)	(100.0)
White	34	107	147	202	206	696
	(4.9)	(15.4)	(21.1)	(29.0)	(29.6)	(100.0)
MRNUS	3	13	15	15	12	58
	(5.2)	(22.4)	(25.9)	(25.9)	(20.7)	(110.0)
Housing - *"I would refuse to live with an LGB person"*						
People of Color	6	8	10	12	59	95
	(6.3)	(8.4)	(10.5)	(12.6)	(62.1)	(100.0)
White	12	20	45	115	506	698
	(1.7)	(2.9)	(6.4)	(16.5)	(72.5)	(100.0)
MRNUS	--	2	5	15	39	61
		(3.3)	(8.2)	(24.6)	(63.9)	(100.0)
Interaction - *"I have a negative response to LGBs"*						
People of Color	2	11	15	26	41	95
	(2.1)	(11.6)	(15.8)	(27.4)	(43.2)	(100.0)
White	7	26	65	218	380	696
	(1.0)	(3.7)	(9.3)	(31.3)	(54.6)	(100.0)
MRNUS	--	--	9	25	27	61
			(14.8)	(41.0)	(44.3)	(100.1)
Self-Censorship - *"I have felt the need to censor myself in speech, writing, or actions in my academic life in addressing LGB issues"*						
People of Color	10	19	26	22	17	94
	(10.6)	(20.2)	(27.7)	(23.4)	(18.1)	(100.0)
White	45	138	161	205	134	683
	(6.6)	(20.2)	(23.6)	(30.0)	(19.6)	(100.0)
MRNUS	4	15	14	16	10	59
	(6.8)	(25.4)	(23.7)	(27.1)	(16.9)	(99.9)

I agree that, outside Oberlin, there is the need to be forceful and vocal, that need is not as great here. To be blunt, I'm on the side of gay rights, and yet because I'm heterosexual I feel I should feel guilty for my orientation . . . that by the very fact that I am heterosexual I am heterosexist. If anything, this forcefulness has served to distance me from supporting these issues.

A white heterosexual woman responded:

I am sometimes irritated by the fact that I cannot go into the bathroom stall without being confronted by advertisements for lesbian activities, etc. I understand the need to voice their feelings, but I don't always enjoy having their personal sexual desires shoved in my face.

Two questions concerned living or interacting with LGB students (Table 6). When asked if they would refuse to live with an LGB person, 94.6% of all students disagreed. Students of color agreed somewhat more than the other groups—14.7% (14) of respondents of color agreed, as opposed to 4.6% (32) of the whites and 3.3% (2) of the MRNUS group. One way a white heterosexual male explained his attitude was: "I might object if it were just a two-person dorm room but not a house." A second question concerned interaction—"I have a negative response to LGBs." The response pattern was almost identical—94.7% disagreed.

The final question asked whether the respondent felt the need to censor him/herself in speech, writing, or actions in his/her academic life in addressing LGB issues. About 30% of each group exercised self-censorship (30.8% of people of color, 26.8% of whites , and 32.2% of MRNUS). Self-censorship was Janus-faced. For instance, a heterosexual MRNUS woman said, "because no one is allowed to open their mouth about [LGB issues] if they don't have the 100% PC opinion (or else *they* will be harassed)." On the other hand, more LGBs engaged in self-censorship than the others—over one half of lesbian and bisexual women and over 43% of gay and bisexual men said they had censored themselves. A white bisexual woman gave an example of how fear of affecting recommendations from professors influenced her self-censorship at Oberlin.

My future vocation is to teach. I feel, since I can appear heterosexual, that its best not to let anyone involved in my education know. Because of this I have to limit my relationships with women and must generally keep them quiet when they occur. Though I don't know for sure, I would guess that open bisexuality would be strongly discouraged in . . . department, because as teachers we must be role models. I fear that if my . . . teachers knew I was bi, they would doubt my ability to be a good role model.

Treatment Received by LGBs at Various Campus Work Units

Another set of questions investigated the perceptions of students regarding how LGBs were treated (same, better, worse than any other individual) when dealing with various campus entities. Choices included deans' offices, library, clinic, campus security, gym/physical education/teams, various specific student services, psychological services, and faculty advising. Three work units were singled out by respondents as places where LGB students were perceived to receive worse treatment than other students — gym/physical education/teams, the clinic, and campus security.

Over 1/3 (35.9%) of all students perceived the gym/physical education/ teams as a locale of unequal treatment of LGBs. The perception was widespread across the groups and sex/sexuality subdivisions. For instance, 33% of all white students and 47.4% of all students of color perceived the treatment to be worse. While LGBs consistently indicated this to be a problem more often than heterosexual or questioning students (all gay and bisexual MRNUS men, 46.2% of white lesbian and bisexual women, 75% of gay and bisexual students of color, 38.7% of white gay and bisexual men), relatively high proportions of heterosexual and questioning students also saw this as a problem (48.6% heterosexual men of color, 27.8% white heterosexual women, 32% MRNUS heterosexual men).

More than 20% of students in each of the three groups indicated that they expected LGBs to be treated worse than other students by campus security. Within each of those groups, more lesbians, gays, and bisexual women expected worse treatment than other members of the groups, and LGBs of color and MRNUS had the highest proportions of all.

The student clinic was perceived to offer worse treatment to LGBs than other students by about 17.5% of all respondents. Among all students, those of color indicated that about 22% perceived worse treatment, and 16.5% among white students and 23% among MRNUS students agreed. These proportions were fairly stable within each group, although somewhat more LGBs perceived worse treatment.

The other entities and faculty advising were given high marks overall although specific groups disagreed. Thus the library and psychological services were regarded as discriminating against lesbian and bisexual women of all three groups while student residential services and faculty advising were perceived by large minorities of LGBs (about 1/3) of all groups to not offer equal treatment. Lesbian and bisexual MRNUS and women of color consistently demonstrated the highest proportion of students perceiving unequal treatment.

Thinking About One's Sexual Orientation

All students were asked to whom they would turn if they had concerns about their sexual orientation. The majority of students mentioned more than one source of advice, e.g., friends and family (see Table 7). Friends were most often indicated. Psychological services (15.6%) and student organizations (21.1%) were indicated fairly frequently in addition to some other source of help. Whites more frequently mentioned psychological services than the other two groups. On the other hand, students would seldom turn to family, off-campus counselors, LGB students, and chaplains/priests.

Table 7. Whom Do Students Turn to with Questions about Their Sexual Orientation*

Type of Source	Only Source	One of at least two or more sources
Friends	288 (33.1)	356 (40.9)
Psychological Services	19 (2.2)	117 (13.4)
Student Organizations**	12 (1.4)	172 (19.7)
Family	11 (1.3)	52 (6.0)
Self	11 (1.3)	9 (1.1)
Non-OC Counsellors	6 (0.7)	70 (8.0)
Lesbian, Gay and Bisexual Students	5 (0.6)	22 (2.5)
Chaplains/Priests	1 (0.1)	19 (2.3)
No Problems	22 (2.6)	--

* More than one source and some very idiosyncratic answers mean that these figures will not total 871. However, the proportions are calculated with the total number of respondets, i.e. 871.

** Includes LGBU, SIC, Lesbians be Loud, and 7th Sense.

How "Out" Are LGB Students?

Several questions investigated how open LGBs were about their sexual orientation. Students were asked about their relationships with friends, family, dorm residents, staff, and faculty.

A large majority of lesbians and bisexual women of color (75%) and almost half of the white women (49.2%) had told some of their family about their sexual orientation, and 14.3% of the white women had told everyone. Half of the gay and bisexual men of color and 57% of the white men had told no one in their family. The MRNUS students exhibited very diverse patterns.

All groups and sexes were more open with their friends than their family. And, women were more open than men, with more women indicating that they were out to all friends than any other response (62.5% of MRNUS women, 75% of women of color, and almost 50% of white women). For the men, one half of men of color and two thirds of the MRNUS men and about 1/3 of white men were open to all friends.

Whites of both sexes tended to be more open than others to fellow dormitory residents or housemates, and more whites said that they were out to everyone in their residence.

Fewer responded that they were out to college staff persons. Women in each group split very evenly, half saying they were out to no staff and half saying they were out to some. Somewhat more men were out than women in each group.

When asked whether they were out to faculty, lesbian and bisexual women in all groups were less open than gay and bisexual men students, and whites were more open than people in the other two groups.

In sum, the trend was for women of all groups to be more open with friends and family, while men were somewhat more open with staff and faculty. Among the groups, students of color and MRNUS students tended to be more out to family and friends and less out to faculty and staff, although the differences were not dramatic.

Lesbian, Gay, and Bisexual Students' Attitudes

The LGB students' responses about feeling isolated and excluded provided another counterpoint to the positive attitudes expressed. LGB attitudes varied by gender and race/ethnicity. All LGB students of color felt isolated, and a majority felt excluded, because of both sexual orientation and other reasons. Gay and bisexual men of color indicated that they feared harassment or discrimination for sexual orientation while women did not. Three quarters of LGBs said they feared harassment or discrimination from professors.

White lesbian, gay, and bisexual students also indicated feelings of isolation, with more (50%) blaming their sexual orientation than other reasons (16%). More women felt isolated than did men. On the other hand, a majority did not feel excluded for either reason. Close to one half indicated fear of harassment because of sexual orientation—fewer feared harassment in general. More lesbian and bisexual women (42%) reported fear of harassment or discrimination from professors than gay and bisexual men (30%).

Most MRNUS students did not feel isolated. Lesbian and bisexual women reported more feelings of exclusion than did men. Neither feared harassment to any extent. Three quarters of the women and none of the men said they feared harassment or discrimination from their professors.

THE OBERLIN SURVEY RESULTS COMPARED TO OTHER INSTITUTIONS

Comparisons of these results are difficult. Many studies have resorted to non-representative (convenience) samples because of the difficulties of studying this population and the lack of institutional support. Those studies which use random samples seldom utilize identical questionnaire items. Below are presented some comparisons from other institutions.

Oberlin victimization rates (Table 8) are generally lower than the three universities discussed by Berrill (1990). The Oberlin LGB group is based on a survey of the population; the others are convenience samples. Oberlin LGBs experience proportionately more sexual harassment than LGBs at the other three institutions; are more likely to be spat upon than LGBs at two of the other institutions; and have rates of being assaulted/wounded similar to the other three. Non-reporting of incidents is comparable.

Certain responses from the study at the University of California at Santa Cruz (UCSC) which utilized a random survey can be compared to the Oberlin study. The sexual orientation of UCSC students was lesbian (8% of women), gay man (9% of men), and bisexual (6% of all students). Oberlin proportions were lesbians (5.7% of women), gay men (6.4% of men), and bisexuals (7% of all students). Fairly comparable items were concealment of sexual orientation among LGBs (UCSC 20%; Oberlin 68%), self-censorship (UCSC, 50%; Oberlin, 47%); verbal harassment at UCSC 40%, verbal insults at Oberlin 40%. More than 90% of Oberlin students would room with a LGB person; about 80% of UCSC students said they would be comfortable with a LGB roommate.

Table 8. Oberlin Rates of Victimization of LGBs Compared to Three Other Institutions[*] in Percentages

	Oberlin (n=111)	Yale (n=166)	Rutgers (n=141)	Penn State (n=125)
Verbal insults	40	65	55	76
Overheard anti-gay remark	84	98	90	NA
Property damaged or destroyed	5	10	6	17
Objects thrown at	5	19	12	12
Followed or chased	14	25	18	27
Spat upon	5	3	1	5
Assaulted/wounded	1	1	2	1
Punched, hit, kicked	3	5	4	5
Sexually harassed	18	12	8	NA
Non-reporting of incident	>90	90	88	94

Source: Yale (Herek, 1986), Rutgers (Gavin, 1987), Penn State (D'Augelli, 1989) reported in Berrill, 1990.

[*]All 3 are non-representative (convenience) samples.

DISCUSSION

Compared to the other institutions for which data was available, Oberlin appears to have more positive attitudes expressed towards LGBs, and lower levels of victimization (compared to Yale, Rutgers, and Penn State), except in the areas of sexual harassment and being spat upon and assaulted/wounded. Concealment of sexual orientation was much higher at Oberlin than UCSC, while the two institutions had nearly identical proportions of self-censorship and verbal insults. Proportionately more Oberlin students (more than 90%) were willing to room with LGBs than UCSC students (about 80%). Although the lack of comparable methods and questionnaire items made conclusions difficult, the Oberlin situation appeared to be most comparable to UC Santa Cruz.

The variety of experiences of LGBs at Oberlin was shaped by gender, race/ethnicity, and employee/student status. Women in general faced more problems than men with co-workers and supervisors (staff) and faculty. Gender was an important source of difference within the employee and student group. Women employees reported more self-censorship and more fear of negative consequences of being out to co-workers, supervisors, and friends than did men. Women students also reported more verbal insults, sexual harassment, and at work penalties. They were less open to staff and faculty, felt more isolated, and feared more harassment from students and professors than did men. They censored themselves and had to contend with harassment more than men employees and white male students. Men employees reported more ostracism and men students reported higher levels of self-censorship and hiding their support for LGB issues.

Looking at race/ethnicity differences among students revealed that LGBs of color had to deal with proportionately more problems of exclusion than whites. People of color were more open to their family and friends, but less open to staff and faculty than whites. People of color felt more isolated and excluded than whites both because of their sexual orientation and for other reasons. They also reported more fear of harassment from professors.

Other distinctions resulted from the combination of race and gender. Men students of color faced some of the same problems that women did, and women students of color faced those problems more acutely. Gay and bisexual men of color experienced proportionately the most verbal insults of any group. White lesbian and bisexual women reported the most instances of being chased and being penalized at work.

In conclusion, lesbian and bisexual women confronted in a more extreme fashion some of the problems of women in general. These included needing to conceal their identity—and hence being isolated—and fearing harassment from co-workers and supervisors among employees and from staff among students. Both expressed anxiety about friendships.

People of color faced problems of exclusion and of isolation. Specific problems were encountered by white lesbian and bisexual women (sexual harassment, being chased, work problems, and a sense of isolation because of sexual orientation). Gay and bisexual men of color dealt with high levels of verbal insults and harassment. This is not to understate the situation of white gay and bisexual men. Unlike white men in general, they had to conceal their sexual identity and faced high proportions of sexual harassment plus high rates of the other problems of victimization mentioned.

Further research is required to clarify these differences, especially given the small numbers of LGBs of color. Questions which could not be answered by this data included the differences in treatment of LGBs of color by people of color and whites, and possible differences in the construction of sexuality by people of color.[8]

The paradox of the two Oberlins emerged in the data. On the one hand great support and tolerance existed and was expressed in many ways — support for working, studying, socializing, and living with LGBs. Many responses were emphatically positive. On the other hand, problems of discrimination (exclusion, verbal harassment, and veiled threats) existed at all levels of the institution and among all segments of the population, no matter what one's sexual orientation. In this Oberlin there existed a climate of intolerance around issues of sexuality.

The paradox appeared to result from two competing sets of values. One focused on equal rights, the other on a kind of heterosexual orthodoxy. Some people at Oberlin emphasized one or the other, some were caught in the middle.

The equal rights dimension is deeply grounded in Oberlin history and is expressed in answers to all the attitude questions, especially those supporting working, socializing, and living with LGBs. This liberal ethos is widespread and underlay recent votes to organize an LGB alumni group, the formation of the ad hoc committee which supervised this research, and most recently the creation of a standing committee on LGB concerns. The ethos draws on the religious basis of the college as well, emphasizing equality, understanding, and toleration.

However, the drive for rights for homosexuals and the religious strictures are Janus-faced, because they are also found in the other dimension of the enforcement of heterosexual orthodoxy. The evidence of a heterosexual orthodoxy is straightforward. A segment of the Oberlin employees and students (certainly not all and probably not even half) do not approve of homosexuality, do not want it discussed, and harass and insult LGBs or people perceived in some way to be sympathetic to or interested in their issues.

However, other evidence is equally telling. The graffiti and stereotypical comments, besides their violent discourse, emphasized strong disapprobation of deviation from the approved male and female roles. It is impossible for the writers or speakers to conceive of a feminine lesbian or a masculine gay male. Men have to hide their support for LGBs, men and women experience insults, and women experience harassment. Perhaps most telling, this attempt to maintain a heterosexual orthodoxy is directed at heterosexuals as well as LGBs — about 10% of male and female heterosexuals had either denied being LGB or been verbally insulted for being LGB. The fact that LGBs were perceived as being accorded less equal treatment at the gym and Physical Education reinforces the point.

Anecdotes from those opposing political actions of LGBs provide further insight. The overwhelming emphasis of the anecdotes was on the inappropriateness of public discussion or manifestation of homosexuality. Respondents saw sexuality as a private matter, analogous to the privacy defense constructed to protect homosexual rights (see Caserio, 1989). They also emphasized religious proscriptions against the behavior, characterizing it as unnatural and sinful. The only natural behavior is heterosexual. This orthodoxy implicitly links heterosexuality to job performance, student roles, athletic performance, and community participation.

The community emphasis on family and heterosexual roles acts to effectively exclude LGBs. The reinforcement of this emphasis on heterosexuality by many of the churches means that LGBs are excluded from the religious-based community as well.

The argument so far would suggest that a neat division exists between those professing equal rights and those enforcing heterosexual orthodoxy, and that the equal rightists are responsible for the positive attitudes and the heterosexists responsible for the victimization. This is not the case—the situation is much more complicated because, I suspect, a high proportion of people are pulled between the two.

While the research on disjunctures between attitudes and behavior in individuals does not directly apply here, one explanation—competing values—is useful. An example of competing values was the response of some LGBs to the question about the political activity of LGBs on campus. One third of those expressing lack of support for LGB political work were LGBs. While supporting equal rights, they may not want to publicly espouse their position—they prefer the protection of privacy and are threatened by the organizing and insistence on openness by others. Other examples would be the following. While someone may express strong support for LGB rights in the abstract, she may balk at having a lesbian roommate (because of gossip), he may not include gay colleagues in either work or neighborhood socializing (he or they would not feel comfortable), and she will not intervene in any kind of verbal stereotyping or harassment (because of fear of being seen as one of them).

The institution itself expresses ambivalence about these values. While Oberlin was among the first institutions of higher education to adopt non-discrimination clauses for sexual orientation, implementation has been spotty. Many LGBs at different levels of the institution are convinced that being too out would lead to harassment. For some employees without tenure and students holding jobs this could (and has in the past) led to being fired. Some segments of the administration have been in the vanguard of dealing with these issues while others have been notably silent. The inability of the institution to legitimate discussion of sexuality and the situation of LGBs prevents an open airing of issues and concerns. Discussion of these issues has been discouraged. The large number of unreported discrimination experiences on campus indicates a recognition of the institutional position as well as lack of confidence in campus entities concerning these issues.

These structural concerns, combined with the strong emphasis on heterosexual orthodoxy among some, means, I suspect, that lesbian and gay rights, when in conflict with these values, must take second place.

This explanation accounts, in a rough way, for the paradox. One alternative to the above interpretation requires consideration. Some of the differences among or within sexualities or race/ethnic groups may be due to individual variation in identity. Some may identify more or less strongly, and others may have competing identifications with those sexuality and/or race/ethnic groups. This explanation also does not fully account for differences among race/ethnic groups.

CONCLUSIONS

This explanation indicates two competing dimensions—the progressive emphasis on equal rights and the valuation of traditional gender roles—within Oberlin institutional culture which shape the situation of LGBs. The explanation draws on a range of structural and cultural components which have been identified in many other studies as affecting LGBs—religion, heterosexism, equal rights, community, locality, race, and gender. The explanation turns on how each is configured and their relative weight in an institutional (or other) culture.

Lesbians, gay men, and bisexuals in an institution like Oberlin thus face another puzzle—how to appeal to the people across these two competing value dimensions between respect for LGB rights and enforcement of heterosexual orthodoxy. The benefit of being in an institution with a strong liberal ethos is that LGBs can organize around equal rights issues with some hope of success. While sometimes a perilous course, it may be the only alternative in such a setting.

NOTES

1. This paper draws heavily on The Report to the General Faculty of Oberlin College by the Ad Hoc Committee on Lesbian, Gay, and Bisexual Concern, which I wrote as chair of the committee. I thank the following committee participants for all their hard work and advice — Regina Airey, Mary Andes, John Anderson, Jennifer Dryfoos, Elizabeth Gregg, Eric Mader, Rod McCoy, Kevin McLaughlin, Glen Mimura, Luella Penserga, Debbie Plummer, and Emily Wilcox. In addition, Pat Day and William Hood commented on a long summary. I was also responsible for all data analysis of the report.

2. Oberlin competes for students with colleges such as Amherst, Carleton, Colgate, Grinnell, Haverford, Middlebury, Pomona, Swarthmore, Vassar, Wesleyan, and Williams. Universities include Brandeis, Brown, Chicago, Duke, Northwestern, Pennsylvania, Stanford, and Yale.

3. This is not to disparage these landmark studies. Oberlin is much smaller and conditions were right for this kind of approach.

4. The victimization questions used were: verbal insults; overheard anti-gay remarks; threats of physical violence; property damaged/destroyed; objects thrown; followed or chased; spat upon; assaulted/wounded with a weapon; punched, hit, kicked, beaten; sexually harassed/assaulted; anticipate future victimization; fear for safety; know others who have been victimized; nonreporting of at least one incident.

5. Based on the 1988-1989 Affirmative Action report.

6. Based on the Registrar's Report, 1988-89, for spring 1989.

7. On the other hand, stories of certain incidents seemed to be passed around quickly — 20 incidents were reported of someone being followed or chased, which 103 students reported hearing about. Only 3 people had been punched, hit, or beaten, but 71 had heard of this kind of incident, and 4 were penalized at work, but 75 had heard of such incidents. In each of these cases, proportionately more LGBs were aware of these incidents than heterosexual or questioning individuals.

8. Some research (John Bush, personal communication) and the experience of people working with AIDS in the various communities suggests this.

REFERENCES

Berrill, K. (1990). Anti-gay violence and victimization in the United States: An overview. *Journal of Interpersonal Violence,* 5(3), 274-94.

Caserio, R. L. (1989). Supreme Court discourse vs. homosexual fiction. *The South Atlantic Quarterly, 88,* (1), 267-299.

Cavin, S. (1989). Rutgers sexual orientation survey: A report on the experiences of the lesbian, gay and bisexual members of the Rutgers community. Unpublished manuscript.

D'Augelli, A. R. (1989). Lesbians' and gay men's experiences of discrimination and harassment in a university community. *American Journal of Community Psychology, 17*, 317-321.

Greenberg, D. F. (1988). *The construction of homosexuality.* Chicago: University of Chicago.

Herek, G. M. (1986). Sexual orientation and prejudice at Yale: A report on the experiences of lesbian, gay and bisexual members of the Yale community. Unpublished manuscript.

Kinsey, A., Pomeroy, W. B., & Martin, C. E. (1948). *Sexual behavior in the human male.* Philadelphia: W. B. Saunders.

Nelson, R., & Baker, H. (1990). The educational climate for gay, lesbian, and bisexual students at the University of California at Santa Cruz, report from the Gay, Lesbian, Bisexual Community Concerns Advisory Committee, UCSC. Unpublished report.

Stein, A. (1989). Three models of sexuality: Drives, identities and practices. *Sociological Theory, 7* (1), 1-13.

Thomas, D. J. (1986). The gay quest for equality in San Francisco. In J. K. Bowles (Ed.), *The egalitarian city: Issues of rights, distribution, access, and power* (pp. 27-41). New York: Praeger.

Gay and Lesbian Educators:
Past History/Future Prospects

Karen M. Harbeck, PhD, JD

Clark University and University of Massachusetts, Boston

SUMMARY. Although lesbians and gay men in education have been an invisible population, modern computer information retrieval techniques provided a mechanism to investigate the history of case law on gay and lesbian teacher dismissal and credential revocation. This legal framework was then augmented by social history gathered from newspapers and articles, and interviews with the parties involved in the legal or political debates. After presenting a history of the emergence of legal rights and political influence, the author discusses current trends in the employment rights and personal freedoms of gay and lesbian educators.

Although society has been confronted with the issue of the homosexual school teacher since Socrates educated the youth of Greece, little is known about this often invisible but highly emotionally arousing educational/social concern. Prior to World War II, numerous cultural, legal, and educational factors combined to support the power of school administrators in the firing of a lesbian or gay teacher. Homosexuality was considered to be innately evil; teachers were required to be role models of exemplary behavior; school administrators had almost unrestricted power in hiring and

Karen M. Harbeck holds a PhD from Stanford University's School of Education, a JD from the University of Santa Clara, and two master's degrees. She is currently a Fellow at the University of Massachusetts' New England Resource Center for Higher Education and a Lecturer at Clark University, where she teaches a course on lesbian and gay issues in education. She also has a private law practice throughout Massachusetts, specializing in the legal needs of lesbian and gay clients. The author wishes to express her appreciation to Dr. Jodie L. Wigren and Carol C. Barnes. Correspondence should be addressed to the author at: P.O. Box 1809, Brookline, MA 02146.

retention decisions; and the cost of litigation was prohibitive to the individual who might have considered rising above their own condemnation and that of society to argue his or her right to remain an educator. Since the late 1940s, however, social and legal consensus on the definition of "immoral" conduct has broken down in the face of changing sexual mores, expanding personal freedoms, and the emerging political identity of lesbians and gay men. Through the collective power of teachers' unions, special interest litigation organizations, and the gay and lesbian rights movement, a challenge has emerged within a debate that one California gubernatorial candidate characterized as "the hottest social issue since Reconstruction."[1] This paper is a brief summary of my 550-page book on the legal, social, educational, and political history of lesbian and gay teachers in American society from colonial times to the present.[2]

With the advent of computer data retrieval, it was possible to go back through the legal case law archives from the 1700s to the present and gather hitherto "lost" determinations of litigation concerning homosexual educators (approximately fifty cases) employed in all levels of instruction, elementary through university. A framework emerged of changing social and legal attitudes about homosexuality and teachers' rights that serves as the backbone of this historical interpretation. These legal opinions, however, were devoid of any contemporaneous community action or political controversy that might have been the catalyst of the legal struggle. For example, none of the opinions on homosexual teachers since 1969 mention the birth of the lesbian and gay rights movement, despite a very evident attitudinal change by the judiciary towards homosexuality. In an attempt to resolve these deficiencies, I corresponded with as many attorneys and clients involved in the litigation as was possible from the 1950s to the present. The documentation and recollections gathered from these men and women added a rich texture to the stories prejudicially detailed in the case law.[3] Furthermore, through an analysis of newspapers, articles, and interviews with politicians, political advocates, teachers' union leaders, and school personnel, the legal framework could be interwoven with a social history of specific community events and attitudes. Three major political campaigns were the major focus: Anita Bryant's "Save Our Children" campaign in Florida (1977), California's "Proposition Six" Initiative (1978), and the Oklahoma State law (1978-85) that prohibited homosexual conduct, activity, or advocacy by school employees. Each of these conservative campaigns was a reaction to the increased legal and social acceptance of the homosexual educator that has occurred since 1969.

The impetus for this research was my personal quest as a lesbian educator, attorney, and social historian, to address the meager but overwhelmingly negative information about our history and our legal rights.[4] Although the addition of case law information provided in this study is significant, possibly the larger contribution rests in its interdisciplinary analysis of social events that occurred in concert with the litigation.[5] This newly integrated information provides a rather radical departure from the previously invisible, often depressing history of gay and lesbian educators. It stands as a documentation, and a declaration, of remarkable advances made by lesbians and gay men in the past twenty years. Resources, such as this study, become mechanisms for educating ourselves, so that each of us in our differing roles as school administrators, teachers, attorneys, legislators, judges, parents, and students, can bring greater clarity and fairness into our social policy considerations.

PAST HISTORY

At present, there are approximately 2,724,000 teachers employed in the United States in public and private elementary and secondary settings alone.[6] Using Kinsey's often quoted estimate of 10 percent, there are at least 272,400 homosexual educators currently employed in schools around the nation—a number equal to the entire teaching staff of the States of California and Minnesota combined.[7] Another way to look at this figure is to realize that if the national average of number of teachers in every school is 24.8, then it is statistically likely that two or more educators per school are homosexuals.[8] In fact, the numbers may be much higher in light of the lesbian and gay rights movement that occurred after the original 1948 estimate of the homosexual population, and because teaching is an occupation that historically has attracted single women and non-traditional men.[9]

Although the number of lesbians and gay men in American education has been numerically significant, the details of their professional and personal experiences remain relatively unknown. For example, all of the historical contemporaneous critiques of the institutional role of homosexuality in education were from other cultures. Xenophon discussed pederasty in ancient Sparta's educational system,[10] and eighteenth century legal theorists, Montesquieu and Beccaria, argued that the death penalty was too severe a punishment for an activity that was fostered by educational systems that segregated boys in same sex schools.[11] Similar critiques of the British boarding school system are available from the early 1800s to the present.[12]

In terms of an individual's experience, we do know that since colonial times the most common scenario is one of a person living an exemplary life in fear of discovery. In that rare instance when his or her homosexual orientation became known, the teacher quietly resigned or quickly left town, since the potential consequences of challenging the system alone were extreme. At various times in history, homosexuality has been perceived as a sin, a mental disorder, and/or a criminal activity. Numerous social and legal restrictions have been placed on homosexual behavior, and the consequences of infractions at times have been as severe as execution or imprisonment. Furthermore, having been socialized in this culture, lesbian and gay persons often have incorporated a negative self-image. Thus, remaining invisible and not challenging the status quo were reasonable responses in the face of personal danger and financial ruin.

One highly promising method of information retrieval involved cross-referencing book details on notable American teachers with those on homosexuals in history.[13] Preliminary research suggests that the mid-nineteenth century American transcendentalists provide a rich point of departure. Margaret Fuller, Ralph Waldo Emerson, Elizabeth Peabody, Henry David Thoreau, Amos Bronson Alcott, Herman Melville, and Walt Whitman all seem to have been educators with strong same-sex affiliations, although little material is available concerning a nexus between their same-sex commitments and their careers in teaching. The most direct evidence to date concerns Amos Bronson Alcott, father of the writer Louisa May Alcott, who apparently was involved with the British educator, Charles Lane.[14] Unfortunately, this focus on notable Americans fails to address the life experiences of "average" individuals who comprise the vast number of homosexual men and women in the teaching profession and about whom we currently lack oral or written history.

Similar information is missing from the case law context because homosexuality historically has been referred to in English and American law as a "crime against nature not to be named among Christians."[15] Thus, it often has fallen under vague criminal statutes concerning "open and gross lewd conduct" or "lewd vagrancy," and the specific case details have been obfuscated. Since computer informational retrieval relies on word recognition, this total lack of references to homosexuality (or "gay," "lesbian," "same-sex," etc.) make it difficult to retrieve cases prior to World War II. By the mid-1940s, however, social/legal conflict over homosexuality begins to emerge from the closet as lesbians and gay men gravitate towards cities and establish increasingly visible communities, and as school administrators struggle to control the definition of immorality in a changing society.

In his excellent book on the history of the emergent gay and lesbian political identity, John D'Emilio provides an extensive discussion on post-World War II America's response to homosexuality.[16] Increased prosecutions for consensual homosexual conduct, police raids, surveillance of gay bars and private homes, blackmail, and postal authority investigations, suggest a heightened concern about an increasingly visible social phenomena. Furthermore, Senator Joseph McCarthy's witch-hunting tactics successfully linked homosexuality and Communism in the minds of most Americans.

On the other hand, there are hints of changing social mores, as evidenced by the American Law Institute's 1955 Model Penal Code recommendation that all forms of sexual activity between consenting adults be legalized.[17] Although all of the states initially rejected the Model Penal Code reforms, there seems to have been increased concern for the procedural rights of criminals, and a growing sympathy towards persons accused of victimless crimes. I would argue that this heightened social conflict very quickly entered the educational realm, and that for the first time in American social history the judiciary broke with educational policy concerning immorality, criminal conduct, and the extent to which someone should be punished for consenting sexual activity outside of marriage. Because of increased judicial leniency and concern for procedural protections for nonviolent criminals, school administrators faced the loss of one of their most reliable mechanisms for gathering information about the private behavior of teachers. Since any criminal conviction had served previously as the basis for dismissal on grounds of immoral conduct and unfitness to teach, the judiciary's change of attitude threatened to upset the balance of power for school administrators.

In response to these changes, lobbyists in California in the early 1950s successfully sponsored two new pieces of legislation designed to crack down on teachers treated leniently in the criminal justice system. Penal Code Section 291 required police officials to notify local boards of education whenever a teacher was detained or arrested in a criminal matter. Education Code Section 12756 permitted the immediate suspension of teaching credentials if an educator was convicted of any one of several statutes pertaining to sex and morality. This presumption of guilt streamlined the administrative process in the educational setting by automatically providing the grounds for teacher dismissal. It also set the stage for legal conflict between increasing criminal protections and constricting educational employment rights. Thus, the typical case scenario concerning a homosexual educator from the 1940s to the late 1960s involved a male school teacher arrested in a public restroom for lewd acts. After successfully defending himself in the criminal sphere, he nevertheless faced dismissal from his teaching position because the illegally gathered information could be used against him, or because merely being involved in a criminal situation served as sufficient evidence of a tainted reputation and loss of credibility as an effective role model and educator. Since homosexuality remained a criminal offense, and since the state legislatures of at least California and Florida had specifically empowered school officials to abrogate personal employment rights for the welfare of the children, school boards still enjoyed extensive power over hiring and retention. Nevertheless, persons accused of criminal homosexual activity were successful in their job retention challenges if they were able to demonstrate some unconstitutional infringement on their procedural rights. For example, in the *Fountain* and *Lerner* cases it was successfully argued that the 1954 California reporting statute could not be applied retroactively against persons who had come under scrutiny for criminal behavior in the late 1940s.[18] Similarly, the Florida cases involving the McCarthy-like witch-hunt for lesbian and gay teachers upheld state teacher dismissal procedural protections, even though the State Board of Education was instructed to remove the allegedly homosexual educators through legal means.[19]

By 1969 the case law on homosexual educators demonstrates a clear recognition of changing social and legal attitudes. The California State Supreme Court's decision in *Morrison v. State Board of Education* called for an extensive analysis of the individual's behavior in relation to his or her job responsibilities before employment dismissal was possible. Furthermore, the Court announced that the status of being a homosexual was insufficient grounds for dismissal unless coupled with some related misbehavior. Despite this major advance in employment rights, many courts were able to avoid the *Morrison* criteria for a few years because the parties were still being brought into the dispute through arrests for criminal sexual activity. By 1973, however, *Morrison* was firmly established as one of the strongest statements in favor of an individual's right to retain employment despite a wide variety of personal indiscretions.

In 1973, and until about 1977, the effects of the "sexual revolution" and the legal emphasis on personal freedom, privacy, and minority rights combined with the increasing political effectiveness of the lesbian and gay rights movement to alter the character of homosexual school teacher case law. In this period the typical case involved a male or female teacher who was exposed as a homosexual without criminal behavior, who admitted his or her same-sex orientation, and who challenged the school system's right to abridge employment freedoms solely on the basis of homosexuality.[20] Litigants during this time period appealed to Federal courts, and asserted that their civil rights and constitutional freedoms were being denied by local prejudice. These lesbian and gay male teachers enjoyed the financial and emotional support of special interest groups that advocated homosexual rights and/or the right of school teachers to personal freedoms. Unknown to most of us, for example, is the fact that during their 1974 annual national conference, the National Education Association (NEA) amended their non-discrimination statement to include protection for "sexual preference." Thus, the NEA has been instrumental in funding homosexual school teacher litigation for its union members to this day.[21]

Additionally, by 1973, several states had liberalized their laws concerning sex between consenting adults. Thus the criminal statutes that had previously served as the standard of immoral conduct sufficient for dismissal often were no longer available to local school authorities in homosexual teacher cases. The litigation of this period demonstrated growing support for the homosexual school teacher, although case outcomes were not consistent.

Possibly the best example of this increased support but failed outcome is *Acanfora* (1974). Expert witness testimony by psychiatrists and child development researchers convinced the judge that the role modeling influence of lesbian or gay teachers was minimal because a child's sexual orientation is probably determined by ages five or six. Furthermore, the judge made radical statements about the rights of homosexuals and of school teachers, as though the extension of doctrines like Equal Protection, privacy, and First Amendment freedoms to lesbians and gay men was the obvious outcome given the changes to individual and minority rights over the past decade. In conclusion, however, after finding constitutional infringements upon Acanfora's fundamental rights, the judge resolved the case in favor of the school board on the grounds that Acanfora lied about his political activities as a homosexual on his job application.

Since the case law of this time period is inconsistent, the most striking evidence of social acceptance may be the municipal and school board antidiscrimination ordinances passed in support of homosexuals in general, and homosexual school teachers in particular.[22] I would argue, however, that these policy changes were coat-tailed on the increasingly popular concepts of individual rights and minority freedoms, rather than grounded in mass public education and awareness about the nature and extent of homosexuality. With the lobbying efforts of a few individuals, major political rights were gained, although the evidence suggests that few persons took advantage of their existence. Thus, lesbians and gay men were lulled into a false sense of social acceptance. Things were fairly comfortable, political organization seemed only marginally necessary, and we remained vulnerable to a shift in public sentiment.

Not surprisingly, in the face of these remarkable nationwide advances a conservative backlash arose against homosexual rights during 1977 and 1978. An emergent political coalition, initially led by former Miss America finalist Anita Bryant, was very successful in its efforts to repeal homosexual rights ordinances in Dade County, Florida; Eugene, Oregon; St. Paul, Minnesota; and Wichita, Kansas. Ms. Bryant's initial involvement in the controversy stemmed from four factors.[23] First, the Dade County "gay rights" ordinance was written in such a manner that it was conceivable that private schools, including her church's Christian school, would be barred from discriminating on the basis of sexual preference, while the public school system remained outside its restrictions. Second, Ms. Bryant's minister and her husband strongly urged her to use her notoriety to defeat the ordinance. Third, Ms. Bryant's publicity agent, Richard Shack, had asked her to tape radio endorsements for his wife, Ruth, who was running for county office. Once elected, and to the great embarrassment of Bryant, Shack introduced the widely popular "gay rights" ordinance for adoption. In order to save face, Bryant was mobilized although she admitted to having little knowledge about homosexuality at the time. And fourth, a major source of Bryant's emergent knowledge about homosexuality was a film that graphically linked it to child pornography and violence. These factors, combined with Bryant's strong fundamentalist religious beliefs, provided the conservatives with a highly charismatic public figure who easily aroused support.

It may also be the case, however, that Bryant's repeal campaign tapped the urge by local citizens to vote on the issue of changing social values. During the late 1960s and early 1970s, social change concerning abortion, contraceptives, civil rights, control over education, prayer in the schools, and the war in Vietnam, for example, had all been largely determined by Federal judicial decisions and Legislative and Executive branch action. Voting in opposition to sexual preference protections was one of the few opportunities for the average American to express his or her concern over these breaks with social tradition.

One major concern of this study was how the successful Bryant campaigns were introduced on a state-wide level in California, and later Oklahoma.[24] Apparently, during the Bryant ordinance battle in Florida, California Assembly Speaker Willie Brown, one of the most powerful legislators in the State, traveled to Dade County to express support for gay and lesbian rights. Angered by the impression that Brown was speaking on behalf of all Californians, State Senator John Briggs and his Spanish-speaking wife flew to Miami to assist conservative efforts. Once there, Briggs and several fundamentalist ministers realized the political potential of this highly emotional controversy. Bryant had raised extraordinary sums of money in a very short time, her stance rallied the sympathies of conservative Americans, and her subsequent victory heightened their sense of empowerment. Upon returning to California, Briggs decided to use the issues of homosexual school teachers and the death penalty as the emotional underpinnings of his campaign for governor.

In his Proposition Six, set for public vote in November of 1978, Briggs called for the firing of any school employee who was "advocating, soliciting, imposing, encouraging, or promoting of private or public homosexual activity directed at, or likely to come to the attention of schoolchildren and/or other employees."[25] Polls conducted in August of 1978 suggested that passage of the Initiative was assured.[26] It went down in defeat, however, in part because of opposition expressed by former governor Ronald Reagan. In commenting on the Initiative, Reagan said that it had:

> the potential for real mischief. . . . Innocent lives could be ruined. . . . Whatever else it is, homosexuality is not a contagious disease like measles. Prevailing scientific opinion is that an individual's sexuality is determined at a very early age and that a child's teachers do not really influence this.[27]

In conclusion, Reagan asserted that the Initiative would be too costly to enforce, promoted too much governmental involvement, and set the stage for blackmail of teachers by students and parents.[28] To this day, Briggs blames his defeat on Reagan's reliance on aides, his disinterest in legislative detail, and his deference to Nancy Reagan's apparent support of their gay and lesbian friends in Hollywood.[29]

Briggs maintains that he lost interest in the homosexual teacher issue after the Initiative's defeat, but not before his office fulfilled the request of Oklahoma State Senator Mary Helm for copies of the legislation.[30] Politicized by their fondness for native-daughter and former Miss Oklahoma, Anita Bryant, the Oklahoma legislature unanimously passed the Briggs' proposal in 1978.[31] It seems clear that many members of the Oklahoma judicial and legislative branches wanted to have a law on the books prohibiting school employees from "advocating, soliciting, or promoting homosexual activity" in order to deter homosexual conduct and that they had little or no intention of enforcing the legislation. On the other hand, they expressed little concern over the "chilling effect" of a law that infringed upon Federal and state constitutional protections concerning freedoms of speech and association, and Equal Protection.

Through some extraordinary legal maneuvers, Oklahoma judges were successful in delaying direct challenges to the constitutionality of the law for several years.[32] Finally, in 1984, the United States Court of Appeals, Tenth Circuit, ruled that the law, as written, was unconstitutional. The State appealed to the United States Supreme Court, which in January of 1985 failed to reach a decision because of a 4 to 4 split vote during the illness of Justice Powell.[33] Thus, the lower court ruling was upheld, although there have been subsequent efforts to rewrite the law to withstand constitutional challenges.[34] Since the United States Supreme Court failed to rule on the issue in 1985, and given the increasingly conservative stance of the High Court, it is likely that any future consideration of this issue would be resolved in favor of a state's right to make educational and social policy decisions for its citizens.

FUTURE PROSPECTS

Although the stance of the United States Supreme Court is not appealing to lesbian and gay rights advocates at this time, future prospects for lesbian and gay educators remain promising. Since 1979, there has been a significant shift in public/administrative attitudes towards homosexual teachers, which, if tested, might radically limit the extensive hiring and retention autonomy thus far enjoyed by school administrators.

Additionally, until the early 1970s, the individual teacher bore the cost of litigation against the school board's retained counsel. Now school officials fear the litigation costs in the face of special interest advocates for teachers' unions, minority and homosexual rights, and civil libertarian ideals. Gay and lesbian teacher litigation since 1973 has become a very costly process involving often a decade of legal maneuvering without clear resolution. For example, the *Ross* case in Oregon, commenced in 1979 and was remanded to the lower courts for the third time by the State Supreme Court for an ongoing determination of the meaning of "immorality."[35]

Because of the complexities of the legal and social issues, and because of the seemingly limitless legal and financial resources on both sides, the courts appear to have tried to avoid a direct declaration concerning whether or not gay men and lesbians have a constitutional right to teach school. As long as the judiciary chooses to avoid taking the initiative on this controversial issue, tremendous room is left for negotiation and education. School boards seem more than willing to look the other way with respect to a teacher's sexual orientation unless some indiscretion has occurred, and they certainly seem to be more willing to negotiate than to face the costly expense of litigation.[36]

Having just concluded that a person enjoys tremendous latitude in being "out" in a teaching situation, I would like to offer a disclaimer and some practical advice. My research would suggest that previously impassioned conservative foes of homosexual educators, like former California State Senator John Briggs, fundamentalist minister Jerry Falwell, and many school administrators, have come to believe that trying to fire a lesbian or gay teacher is not worth the hassle unless some overt scandal or community outcry occurs.[37] Unless these persons are newly emboldened by the now firmly Conservative composition of the United States Supreme Court, the danger is less likely to be overt discrimination and job termination. There remains, however, the real possibility of insidious incidents relating to limited advancement, ungranted tenure, mundane duty assignments, and undesirable teaching loads. Assessment of the costs and benefits of being "out" remains an individual task, although it seems clear that gay and lesbian educators have many more options than our invisible presence would lead us to believe.

Somewhat ironically, possibly the major obstacle in gay and lesbian school teacher litigation today is the fact that educators resign their position during a period of "coming out" or administrative conflict, and then wish to be rehired after further reflection. Some recent cases that have been portrayed in the gay press as teacher firings, have in fact been reinstatement attempts after voluntary resignations.[38] If one voluntarily relinquishes an interest in an employment right, the law is quite clear concerning the broad discretionary powers of any employer during the hiring process.

I urge the reader to review my entire analysis of the current state of gay and lesbian teacher litigation as presented in my more extensive writings before taking any personal or collective action, since there are several nuances in the case law that occur depending upon the extent of employment rights established by any given teacher and/or the age of the students involved. For example, as mentioned above, the power of school authorities is greatest during the employment selection process when any idiosyncratic, bureaucratic, or discriminatory reason could convince an education official that a person would not be a welcome addition to their teaching staff. As long as school authorities are able to give rational reasons for their actions when challenged, they usually prevail over an individual claiming prejudice or unfair employment practices.[39] Furthermore, it has been clearly established since the *Acanfora* case in 1973, that one cannot lie on an employment application in order to avoid potential discrimination, and that a school board's concern for young children might be reasonable, but that role modeling influences related to sexual preference were of no consequence after about age six. Thus, the early education teacher, the new applicant, and the non-tenured teacher face the highest risk of job discrimination, which is further complicated by their lack of access to union representation.[40]

In contrast, the case law on tenured teachers demonstrates the power of contractual rights, union clout, and the opportunity to develop a history of professional excellence and community approval.[41] Additionally, despite all of the conflicting court opinions about teacher dismissal, it is very clear that credential revocation on the basis of homosexuality is a thing of the past. First, state boards of education now face a much higher burden of proof because of the *Morrison* nexus requirement between the misconduct and one's job responsibilities. This action acknowledges the severe consequences of completely revoking entitlement to a profession, especially when effective alternative forms of censure are available. Second, since 1975, numerous state legislatures have eliminated most of the situations that previously permitted immediate credential revocation. In fact, even persons found guilty of serious felonies, such as narcotics sales, have the right to petition for credential reinstatement after a period of rehabilitation. School officials seem to have abandoned credential revocation as a procedurally complex maneuver that offers little likelihood of permanent success.

In addition to case law analysis on the basis of hiring, tenured teacher dismissal, and credential revocation, three topics arise that warrant mention — sex with students, the AIDS crisis (Acquired Immune Deficiency Syndrome), and the issue of race.[42] Up until 1986, it seemed conclusive that sexual involvement with students was grounds for immediate termination and likely criminal prosecution, at least as far as the gay or lesbian school teacher was concerned. This process traditionally was carried out swiftly either through teacher resignation or through the previously unrestricted power of school authorities to dismiss a teacher automatically for certain misconduct. Since 1986, however, two Massachusetts cases have arisen that call this outcome into question. In both incidents, the male educators used their social and political connections and the "heterosexual privilege" provided by marriage and children, to shield themselves from involuntary job termination and the harsh potential of the criminal justice system.[43] The lenient outcomes in these cases may speak more to the benefits of being an affluent, educated, married, white male in the very political environment of Massachusetts politics, rather than to an extraordinary change of social perspective towards same-sex molestation of children by their teachers.

Possibly the AIDS controversy offers some more realistic insights into the current status of homosexual educators than do the sex with students cases. The major problem in generalizing about this aspect of the controversy, however, is that litigation takes several years to develop, and the AIDS crisis is a relatively recent phenomena that may not be clearly established in the case law analytical context. After reviewing the existing cases and conducting interviews, I find that the gay educator cases concerning AIDS have focused entirely on the contagiousness of the disease, rather than on sexual preference concerns. Certainly if conservative administrators believed that a homosexual orientation was sufficient grounds for dismissal, they would have raised this argument in conjunction with illness considerations, but this has not been demonstrated in the caselaw.[44] In the most notable case on the subject, for example, *Chalk's* employers, the Orange County Department of Education, expressed regret at terminating Chalk's employment, but did so in order to have judicial clarification of their liability if a parent sued because a teacher known to have the AIDS virus had been permitted to remain in the classroom.[45] Once the court found in *Chalk's* favor, apparently school officials welcomed him back, in part because of his excellent employment record. If one of the most conservative school districts in the nation, led by one of the most vocal opponents of gay and lesbian educators during the late 1970s, former State Secretary of Education Max Rafferty, welcomes a gay teacher with AIDS back to the classroom, certainly the times have indeed changed for lesbians and gay men who teach school.

Information on the issue of race in relation to lesbian and gay teacher employment is less clear, in part because very few cases are available for analysis. My research and interviews would suggest that if a public school or college administrator is interested in attracting minority faculty to their institution in the first place, they are very willing to accept openly gay and lesbian applicants. Conversely, if the administrator has no commitment to affirmative action and civil rights, the applicant faces the same tenuous status as other prospective job candidates as mentioned earlier in this article. On the other hand, given the additional protections afforded racial and ethnic minorities in our legal system at present, it is the case that gay and lesbian minority job applicants have a broader range of legal protections to assert in the face of discrimination than their white counterparts. Since the case of Merle Woo against the University of California at Berkeley is currently unresolved, and since it has received wide coverage in the community press, it deserves special mention. In my opinion, it would appear that much of the problem in this controversy stems from the traditional beliefs about women held by Ms. Woo's Asian colleagues in the University's Asian Studies Department. This extreme cultural bias against women, when combined with Ms. Woo's lack of a doctorate and her very active political involvement in the union (which is a frequent contributing factor in teacher dismissal cases), helped create the complicated and costly conflict. Given the high cost of employment discrimination litigation in time, money, and emotional and physical health, I would urge any person in a similar situation to follow the example set forth in the Woo controversy and elicit the collective support of gay men and lesbians both locally and nationally. Since the precedent set forth in these cases benefits us all, we should be diligent in our efforts to stay informed and involved.

CONCLUSIONS

Although this study has attempted to provide a broad analysis of the controversy over the employment of lesbians and gay men as school teachers, a tremendous amount of research remains to be done. Case law conflict highlights extraordinary moments of dispute, but attention must be given to the everyday incidents, decisions, and negotiations that resolve such a controversy for the average citizen. Does one choose not to enter the teaching profession, or remain in the closet and resign upon discovery? Is it safe to be "out" in the schools, and have our lesbian and gay colleagues experienced acceptance by employers, students, and parents? Can gay and lesbian educators be effective advocates for gay and lesbian youth and still remain in the closet? Is the negative, invisible history that we have been socialized to believe the current reality in the face of increased personal freedom, minority rights, and the sheer number of lesbians and gay men in America today?

I believe that our advances lie in education, not litigation. Several psychological studies have demonstrated that if a heterosexual individual knows a homosexual, then acceptance increases as stereotypical responses decrease.[46] Similarly, my initial research on homosexual educators suggest that if one individual has the courage to reveal his or her sexual orientation to his or her employer in an honest and non-controversial manner, the climate of support and job security extends to the lesbians and gay men who elect to follow that lead. Community deference to the autonomy of school officials remains strong, so the most critical attitudinal responses are those of state legislators and school administrators. It is essential that we lobby our state governments to pass legislation prohibiting discrimination on the basis of sexual preference since the United States Supreme Court and the various inferior courts intend that the matter be resolved on a state level. Additionally, we must work to include lesbian and gay rights issues in school law textbooks so that teachers and administrators are informed of their rights and obligations with respect to this issue. Furthermore, we need to build stronger coalitions with our heterosexual colleagues and other minority educators. All teachers have benefitted greatly from the employment freedoms won in several major homosexual teacher cases, such as *Morrison* and *Neal v. Bryant et al.* [47] Once informed of our accomplishments and contributions, it is my hope that we will educate others and assert our rights. As educators, we have both the opportunity and the obligation to incorporate the contributions of minority individuals into our curriculum. As is often the case, this new information not only enlightens, it empowers.

NOTES

1. State Senator John Briggs, quoted in Ellen Goodman, "Proposition Fever," *The Boston Globe,* 28 September 1978.

2. Karen M. Harbeck, *Personal Freedoms/Public Constraints: An Analysis of the Controversy Over the Employment of Homosexual as School Teachers,* Vols. 1 and 2, Doctoral Dissertation, Stanford University, 1987. Dissertation Abstracts International 48 (7), 1862A. (Order No. DA 8723009).

3. With respect to minority issues and social controversy, reliance on judicial opinions provides a biased perspective on emergent legal rights and changing social opinion. For example, most attorneys commence their legal analysis and court trial briefs on the dismissal of a homosexual educator with the *Sarac* case which was decided in 1967. (*Sarac v. State Board of Education,* 249 Cal. App.2d 58; 57 Cal.Rptr. 69 (1967).) In that case the judge wrote a very vehement opinion stating that homosexuality was "contrary and abhorrent" to society, so the Board of Education in the State of California had a right to revoke Sarac's life teaching credentials because of his conviction for public solicitation of lewd acts (soliciting sex and fondling the genitals of a police officer in a public men's room in Long Beach). The court opinion suggested that Sarac was caught in a flagrant crime, that he was a poor teacher, that no one appeared on his behalf, and that he had engaged in numerous homosexual encounters. Under these extreme circumstances, in fact, one might wonder why Sarac even attempted to challenge his dismissal. Recent correspondence with Sarac's attorney, Norman G. Rudman, portrays a very different scenario of a slightly effeminate Yugoslavian, who walked into a public restroom and was arrested for solicitation. Although Sarac's

wife, his family, and dozens of his colleagues and supervisors at his school testified in his behalf, they were powerless against the judge's personal abhorrence of homosexuals. Decades later, Attorney Rudman expressed frustration about the "miscarriage of justice," the "sanctimonious" decision of the court, and the longevity of its influence in the face of a lack of a mechanism for the presentation of Sarac's side of the story. (Personal correspondence with Sarac's attorney, Norman G. Rudman, 20 February 1986.)

4. An assessment of contemporary educational law and policy textbooks revealed an astounding lack of even the smallest references to homosexual educators. Clearly the legal ramifications for, and the contributions of, lesbians and gay men to the history of employment rights and teachers' rights has been totally ignored. For example, no textbook credits litigation by homosexual teachers in Florida in the 1950s with a major test case that upheld the requirement of school board compliance with established state teacher dismissal procedures. These individuals were illegally purged from their jobs during a state-wide hunt for Communists who supposedly had infiltrated the schools to inculcate homosexuality and Communism in the nation's youth. (See *William Neal v. Farris Bryant, et al., Mary Frances Bradshaw v. State Board of Education;* and *Anne Louise Poston v. State Board of Education,* Fla., 149 So.2d 529 (1962).) Similarly, with the *Morrison* decision in 1969, involving homosexual activity by an educator, the California State Supreme Court articulated a standard concerning the relationship between private action and job-related constraints that remains as the landmark decision in employment restrictions within any profession. (*Marc Morrison v. State Board of Education,* 74 Cal.Rptr. 116; 1 Cal. 3d 214; 461 P.2d 365; 82 Cal.Rptr. 175 (1969).)

5. In the interest of brevity, I have presented an overview of this broader social/legal history, but I refer the reader to the footnotes and original text for more extensive documentation and analysis.

6. Data obtained from *Digest of Educational Statistics, 1989,* National Center for Education Statistics, U.S. Department of Education, pp. 11-12, 67, 70. Because of the publishing schedule, the numbers referenced above pertain to 1988 and projected 1990 data. The reader also should be warned that national census data on teachers varies based upon the data gathering assumptions of each government agency.

7. Estimates of the current number of homosexual men and women in the United States range from 3 to 30 percent. Kinsey's 1948 estimate of 10 percent is still quoted widely, although it predates the emergence of visible, political homosexual subcultures, so 18 percent may reflect a more accurate estimate.

8. Numbers calculated by dividing the total number of teachers (2,724,000) by the total number of public and private elementary and secondary schools in the country (109,623). Data obtained from *Digest of Educational Statistics,* pp. 11-12.

9. For example, a 1975 estimate in San Francisco suggested that over one third of the district's 4,400 teachers were homosexual. ("National Enquirer Equates Mass Murder and Gay Teachers," *Seattle Gay News,* 2 February 1979.)

10. Xenophon, *Lacedaemonians* 2, 13, E.C. Marchant, trans. (London: William Heinemann, 1956). See also Henri Marrou, "Pederasty in Classical Education," in *A History of Education In Antiquity,* George Lamb, trans. (Madison, WI: University of Wisconsin Press, 1948), p. 31.

11. Louis Crompton, "Homosexuals and the Death Penalty in Colonial America," *Journal of Homosexuality* 1 (3), (1976), pp. 282-285.

12. Vern L. Bullough, "Homosexuality and the Medical Model," *Journal of Homosexuality* 1 (1), (1974), pp. 99-110. See also, C.S. Lewis, *Surprised by Joy: The Shape of My Early Life* (New York: Harcourt, Brace and World, 1955), pp. 88-89, 108-110.

13. Such as Abraham Blinderman's volumes on American writers in education, with Jonathan Katz's work on gay and lesbian history. Blinderman, *American Writers on Education,* Vols. 1 and 2 (Boston: Twayne Publishers, 1975, 1976). Katz, *Gay American History: Lesbians and Gay Men in the U.S.A.* (New York: Thomas Y. Crowell, 1976).

14. Madelon Bedell, *The Alcotts: Biography of a Family* (New York: Clarkson N. Potter, Inc., 1980), pp. 17-18, 175, 180, 189, 208, 227-230.

15. See William Blackstone, *Commentaries on the Laws of England* (London: William Reed, 1811), pp. 215.

16. John D'Emilio, *Sexual Politics, Sexual Communities: The Making of a Homosexual Minority in the United States, 1940-1970* (Chicago: University of Chicago Press, 1983).

17. D'Emilio, *Sexual Politics,* p. 112. See also, Walter Barnett, *Sexual Freedom and The Constitutionality of Repressive Sex Laws* (Albuquerque, NM: University of New Mexico Press, 1973).

18. *George Fountain v. State Board of Education,* 157 C.A.2d 463; 320 P.2d 899 (1958). See also *Lerner v. Los Angeles City Board of Education,* 59 C.2d 382; 29 Cal.Rptr. 657; 380 P.2d 97 (1963).

19. *Neal, Bradshaw, and Poston* (1962).

20. In *Acanfora v. Board of Education of Montgomery County,* 359 F.Supp. 834 (1973), 491 F.2d 498 (1974), *Cert. denied,* 419 U.S. 839 (1974); *Burton v. Cascade School District,* 353 F.Supp. 254 (1973), 512 F.2d 850 (1975), *Cert. denied,* 423 U.S. 859 (1975); *Gaylord v. Tacoma School District No. 10,* 85 Wn.2d 348, 88 Wash.2d 286, 559 P.2d 1340 (1977), *Cert. denied* (1977); *Aumiller v. University of Delaware* 434 F.Supp. 1273 (1977); and *Gish v. Board of Education,* 145 N.J. Super. 96, 366 A.2d 1337 (1976), *Cert. denied* (1977), the judiciary were presented with exemplary citizens and educators who also were comfortable with and political about their sexual orientation.

See Chapter Five of Harbeck, *Personal Freedoms,* for a more extensive discussion of gender distinctions in the case law.

21. Interview with National Education Association officials, Michael Simpson, Assistant to the General Counsel (5 March 1986), and Al Erickson, Manager of Governance and Policy Support (10 March 1986). See also 1974-75 Book of Resolutions adopted in Chicago (1974), p. 252.

22. Ordinances were passed in such diverse communities as Washington, DC, Palo Alto, CA, Wichita, KS, St. Paul, MN, Eugene, OR, and Dade County, FL.

23. See Harbeck, *Personal Freedoms,* Chapter Nine.

24. These questions were answered after extensive research through newspapers and articles, and a three-hour interview with former California State Senator John Briggs (January 1988).

25. See Harbeck, *Personal Freedoms,* Appendix C, for a complete text of the Initiative.

26. A Field poll showed the Initiative passing by a 61 to 31 percent margin. ("Poll Shows Californians Support Controversial Initiatives," *Washington Post,* 20 September 1978).

27. "After Low-Key Campaigns, Comeback Is Seen For Gay Rights," *Washington Post,* 27 October 1978. See also, Ronnie Dugger, *On Reagan, The Man and His Presidency* (New York: McGraw, 1983), pp. 264, 559.

28. See Harbeck, *Personal Freedoms,* Chapter Ten.

29. Briggs aides met with Ronald Reagan after the anti-Initiative speech was given in the hopes of changing his mind. Reagan seemed willing to do so after hearing arguments in favor of the Proposition, but expressed concern that he would need to check the matter out with Nancy Reagan first. A retraction was never issued. (Personal Interview with Briggs, January 1988.)

30. Both State Senator Helm and the House sponsor, Representative Monk, were members of the John Birch Society and active opponents of the Equal Rights Amendment. Helm may have been using the Bill to boost her failing bid for re-election.

31. Oklahoma Stat. tit. 70, section 6-103.15 (A) (2).

Additional research suggests that the Ku Klux Klan was very active in Oklahoma high schools during this time period. Grand Wizard David Duke publicly discussed recruitment efforts and school endorsed club meetings that focused on a hatred of Blacks, Catholics, homosexuals, and women. ("Klan Leader Affirms Oklahoma City High School Organizational Activity," Source Unknown; "KKK Head In UK On Recruiting Trip," *Gaysweek,* May 1977; "Klan Chapters Terrorize Gays In Oklahoma," *Gay Community News,* 11 February 1978; "Teens Turn To Klan To Combat Gays," *Washington Star,* 26 January 1978; and "High School Ku Klux Klan Terrorizes Gays In Oklahoma City," *Gaysweek,* 6 February 1978.)

Klan members also served as bodyguards for Anita Bryant during her numerous public appearances against the Dade County Homosexual Rights Ordinance. ("KKK 'Protects' Anita At Rally," Source Unknown, 23 July 1977.)

32. For example, in initial legal proceedings the judge refused to permit anonymous plaintiffs, although this procedure has been affirmed by the Courts in situations where identified individuals might face potential harm, such as loss of employment or physical threats.

33. *National Gay Task Force v. Board of Education of the City of Oklahoma, State of Oklahoma,* 729 Fed.2d 1270 (1984), 33 FEP 1009 (1982).

34. In addition to Oklahoma and California, the states of North Carolina, Ne-

vada, Texas, and Arkansas considered similar legislation. ("Bill Against Gay Teachers Withdrawn," *Gay Community News,* 20 July 1985; George Michaelson, "Teachers Under Fire In Nevada," *Gay Community News,* 5 May 1979; and, "Gay Rights Backlash Repeals Local Ordinances," *Gay Community News,* May 1978.)

35. *Frank Ross v. Springfield School District No. 19,* 56 Ore.App. 197, 641 P.2d 600 (1982), 71 Ore.App. 111, 691 P.2d 509 (1984), 294 Ore. 357, 657 P.2d 188 (1982). Most recent decision of the Oregon State Supreme Court, 11 February 1986.

36. I refer the reader to the full text of this study in order to substantiate this conclusion.

37. Briggs interview, January 1988.

38. Probably the best example of this is the recent West Virginia case, *Conway v. Hampshire County Board of Education,* 352 S.E.2d 739 (1986). *Rehearing denied,* 17 February 1987.

39. See *Acanfora, Rowland, Burton, Aumiller, and McConnell v. Anderson,* 451 F.2d 193 (1971). *Cert. denied,* 405 U.S. 1046 (1972).

40. In the *Acanfora, Rowland, and Burton* cases, for example, the court concluded that these non-tenured teachers' rights had been violated, yet none of them was permitted to regain his/her employment.

41. See *Jarvella v. Willoughby-Eastlake City School District Board of Education,* 12 O.Misc. 288, 41 O.O.2d 423 (1967); *Lish v. Anchorage School District,* Superior Court, Alaska (1978); *Amundsen v. State Board of Education,* Civ. No. 37942, Cal. Ct. App. (1971); the two Iowa cases, and Neal, Bradshaw, and Poston (1963).

42. See Chapter Five of Harbeck, *Personal Freedoms,* for an extensive discussion of gender distinctions in the case law.

43. Francis J. Pilecki, former President of Westfield State College, Westfield, Massachusetts (1986-87), and the Buckingham, Browne and Nichols Academy scandal (1987).

44. In *Rice v. Bloomer,* Prince William County, Virginia (1986-88), attorneys for the school board knew of Rice's sexual orientation and tried only once to raise this issue at trial. Rice's attorney objected to the question, and the judge ruled that an answer was not relevant to the case. In a subsequent settlement arrangement, Rice agreed to resign from his teaching position in return for "generous" support payments until his death In April of 1988. It should be noted that the same school district welcomed a six-year old HIV positive child into mainstream classes in December of 1987, without debate. (Personal correspondence, Rice's attorney, Kenneth E. Labowitz, 31 October 1988.)

45. See *Chalk v. U.S. District Court,* 46 FEP 279 (9th Cir., 1988). See also Briggs Interview, January 1988. Vincent Chalk died in October of 1990.

46. Katy Butler, "Perils For Gays Fighting Briggs Initiative," *San Francisco Chronicle,* 26 August 1978. See also, R. Bowman, "Public Attitudes Toward Homosexuality In New Zealand," *International Review of Modern Sociology* 9, (1979), pp. 229-238; B. Glasser and C. Owen, "Variations In Attitudes Toward

Homosexuality," *Cornell Journal of Social Relations* 11 (2), (1976), pp. 161-176; G. Hansen, "Measuring Prejudice Against Homosexuality (Homosexism) Among College Students," *Journal of Social Psychology* 117, (1982), pp. 233-236; Jim Millham, Christopher San Miguel, and Richard Kellog, "A Factor-Analytic Conceptualization Of Attitudes Toward Male And Female Homosexuals," *Journal of Homosexuality* 2 (1), (1976), pp. 3-10; and, C. Weis and R. Dain, "Ego Development and Sex Attitudes In Heterosexual and Homosexual Men and Women," *Archives of Sexual Behavior* 8 (4), (1979), pp. 341-356.

47. See Endnote 4 above.

Living in Two Worlds:
The Identity Management Strategies
Used by Lesbian Physical Educators

Sherry E. Woods, EdD

University of Massachusetts, Amherst

Karen M. Harbeck, PhD, JD

Clark University and University of Massachusetts, Boston

SUMMARY. Twelve lesbian physical educators participated in an in-depth phenomenological study of their work experiences in relation to their identities as lesbians and teachers. All study participants held two assumptions: that they would lose their jobs if their lesbianism were revealed, and that female physical education teachers are negatively stereotyped as being lesbian. Participants most often engaged in identity management strategies designed to conceal their lesbianism, such as passing as heterosexual, self-distancing from others at school, and self-distancing from issues pertaining to homosexuality. The less common risk-taking behaviors included obliquely overlapping their personal lives with their professional, actively confronting homophobia and supporting gay and lesbian students, and overtly overlapping the details of their personal and professional lives. The authors conclude this paper with recommendations for challenging homophobia and heterosexism in physical education.

Sherry E. Woods recently completed her doctorate at the University of Massachusetts, Amherst. Correspondence should be addressed to her at: 1711 Rutland Drive #1323, Austin, TX 78758.

Karen M. Harbeck is the Editor of *Coming Out of The Classroom Closet: Gay and Lesbian Students, Teachers, and Curricula*. She is currently a Fellow at the University of Massachusetts' New England Resource Center for Higher Education and a Lecturer at Clark University, where she teaches a course on gay and lesbian issues in education. Her correspondence should be addressed to the author at: P. O. Box 1809, Brookline, MA 02146.

141

In February of 1991, "Ms. Greene," a physical education teacher at a suburban, Boston, Massachusetts, junior high school, had to request a sudden leave of absence. Although many people knew that she was going out of state to attend to an ailing parent, her rapid departure left the situation open for interpretation. Almost immediately, a rumor was started stating that "Ms. Greene" had been suspended by the Principal pending an investigation into accusations that she had molested two female students during a mandatory scoliosis check. By the end of her two-week absence the rumor had grown to include administrative and criminal investigations into the rape of two students by the physical education teacher in the girls' locker room. Apparently, the administration did nothing to correct this student and parental perspective. Upon her return "Ms. Greene" obliquely informed several classes that "whatever rumors they had heard were not true."

Unfortunately, incidents such as this one are not uncommon for women physical education teachers who are perceived to be lesbians. This paper is a brief summary of the senior author's doctoral research on how lesbian physical educators cope with some unique occupational stresses relating to society's perspectives on homosexuality and women in sports.

Throughout American history, some members of society have viewed homosexual acts as a sin, a crime, and/or a mental disorder. Since the 1960s, however, our nation has undergone a liberalization of attitudes about sex between consenting adults and a greater politicization of minority individuals, including homosexual women and men. While lesbians and gay men enjoy much greater freedom and societal acceptance, it is still the case that certain circumstances trigger a high level of hostility and prejudice. In his study of the American legal system and homosexuality, Goldyn (1979) documents that in situations where children are involved, society and the law seem much more righteous about abridging the freedoms of lesbians and gay men for the supposed "best interest of the child." Powerful prejudicial themes emerge concerning molestation and recruitment—that homosexuals are intensely sexually attracted to young children and continually attempt to recruit new members into their deviant lifestyle. Ironically, these prejudices survive in the face of scientific research that clearly renders them inaccurate (Kinsey, Pomeroy, & Martin, 1948; Barnett, 1973; Groth & Birnbaum, 1978).

While litigation concerning child custody or foster care arrangements demonstrate individual instances of societal prejudices against lesbians and gay men, the nation's educational complex serves as a large scale exemplar of this bias. Since the schools historically have been charged with the inculcation of society's morals and values on a population considered to be highly impressionable, lesbian and gay male educators have often faced tremendous hostility when their sexual orientation has been revealed. Furthermore, school administrators traditionally have enjoyed tremendous autonomy in controlling educational institutions and their employees, in part because of a belief that local decision-making will best reflect local values and interests. Thus, despite a trend towards nationalization and standardization of curriculum and control, local determinations of what constitutes moral conduct are still viable in schools, particularly in situations involving very young children.

It is not surprising, then, to find that many gay and lesbian educators believe that they would be fired if their homosexual orientation were to be disclosed. Especially vulnerable are gay and lesbian teachers whose subject areas are not consistent with traditional gender roles, such as a male librarian or preschool teacher, or a female shop teacher. The lesbian physical educator is, however, the most vulnerable target of all. Not only does she teach in the firmly entrenched male domain of sport, but her professional responsibilities require her to supervise locker rooms where girls are changing clothes and to touch students in the course of instructing the techniques of a particular physical skill. After school, she often spends many hours coaching an all female team where teamwork and togetherness are stressed. For those who believe homosexuals are child molesters that recruit young children to their ranks, just the presence of a lesbian physical educator doing her job is cause for concern and homophobic accusations.

While Harbeck argues that lesbians and gay educators have many more rights at the present time than they did historically (Harbeck, 1987, 1989), it would appear, according to the research presented in this paper, that homosexual educators still actively fear reprisals if their sexual orientation is discovered. Many of them choose to remain silent and to keep their sexual orientation a secret, a phenomenon typically referred to as "being in the closet" (Kingdon, 1979), rather than risk disclosure and possible job termination. Many actively seek to create the impression that they are heterosexual by using opposite sex pronouns and appearing at school functions with dates of the opposite sex. If Harbeck's analysis is correct and educators can enjoy a great deal of personal freedom within the teaching profession, it is important to understand the perspective of those teachers that are intensely vulnerable to local prejudices and hostilities. While their perceived and actual hostile environment provides the backdrop for understanding the homosexual educators' silence, it also sets the stage for an examination of why this silence must be broken.

The senior author's doctoral research was a phenomenological study whose purpose was to have lesbian physical educators describe and make meaning of their work experiences. This paper focuses on one aspect of that research: to describe the identity management strategies used by the participants to conceal or reveal their lesbianism.

Ironically, a female physical education teacher is frequently assumed to be lesbian whether or not this is, in fact, her sexual orientation (Guthrie, 1982). Within the culture of American sport and physical education there appears to be a belief in a relationship between traditional gender roles and sexuality (Lenskyj, 1986), meaning that to be athletic is equated with masculinity. Thus, masculine women are perceived to be lesbian, rather than feminine and heterosexual. These allegations of lesbianism are used to intimidate and harass women in physical education and sport (Fields, 1983). As Cobhan asserts, the "de facto evidence" that sport is the province of lesbians "will be used as ammunition by those who deny a woman's right to participate in athletics" (1982, p. 179).

Threats and allegations of lesbianism are manifestations of homophobia, which is defined as the irrational fear and/or intolerance of homosexuality (Hudson & Ricketts, 1980). Homophobia is a relatively new concept (Weinberg, 1972). Acknowledging its existence marks a shift from defining homosexual behavior as deviant to defining prejudicial attitudes toward homosexuals as deviant. Homophobia can be conceptualized on two levels: external and internal. External homophobia refers to any belief system that maintains and encourages negative myths and stereotypes about homosexuals. Internal homophobia refers to a person's acceptance and internalization of negative attitudes and irrational fears about homosexuality (Morin & Garfinkle, 1978).

Lesbians in sport and physical education often experience both forms of homophobia. Subjected to derogatory innuendos from others, these women internalize many of these negative stereotypes and adjust their behavior accordingly. To avoid being stereotyped as homosexual, many female physical education teachers—heterosexual and lesbian alike—assume what Felshin (1974) called "apologetic" behaviors. To assure the world of their "womanhood," for example, many physically active women may act (and are often publicly described) in ways that accent stereotyped notions of "femininity."

Similarly, in actual athletic competition, women may play less assertively and be less willing to demonstrate their full athletic potential for fear of appearing too "masculine" (Lenskyj, 1986). Apologetic behaviors, both on and off the playing fields, are calculated to counteract any questions regarding one's sexual orientation in the belief that these behaviors will protect one's reputation, relationships, and employment status. This feminine role playing, combined with silence, perpetuates the negative stereotypes associated with lesbianism in sport and physical education.

THEORETICAL PERSPECTIVES

Much of the research on the experience of lesbians and gay men in this society has used deviancy theory as a conceptual framework (Goffman, 1963; Becker, 1963). Under this analysis, one is able to determine what is socially and culturally "normal" based upon the expressed beliefs of the majority population. Persons outside this "norm" are considered to be deviant. While this terminology may have been originally intended to be value free, it easily lends itself to pejorative interpretations. Furthermore, since deviancy theory has been used to study racial, ethnic, sexual preference, and lower-economic minority groups that are also perceived to have greater problems with crime, poverty, illiteracy, and poor health, those assigned the deviant label are blamed for causing social and economic problems for the larger society as a whole.

Over the past few decades social scientists and minority activists have challenged the underpinnings of deviancy theory, and have developed "oppression theory" to provide alternative insights into social behavior. Oppression theory (Jackson & Hardiman, 1988; Freire, 1972; Goldenberg, 1978; Baker-Miller, 1976; Memmi, 1965) focuses on the majority group's ideological domination and institutional control, and the promulgation of the oppressor group's ideology, values, and culture on the oppressed group. This results in the exploitation of one social group by another for the dominant group's own benefit. Within an oppressive society, persons in social group "A" hold a set of negative beliefs about people in social group "B" and act toward people in social group "B" based on those beliefs. Harro argues that these beliefs and actions are:

> supported, sanctioned, enforced, and empowered by cultural ideologies and institutions and result in a privileged existence for social group "A" and a limited existence for social group "B" and the dehumanization of both. (1983, p. 1)

This analysis of oppression has been used as a conceptual framework for understanding the unequal relationships between many different social groups: white and black, rich and poor, male and female, and heterosexual and homosexual. Because of the refocused perspective inherent in oppression theory, several insights emerge with respect to the minority group or individual's experience. First, that group or individual is permitted to characterize their life experience rather than merely juxtapose their behavior against the majority's definition of what is normal. Second, the focus of the problem and potential solutions shifts from the minority population on to the majority's abuse of power. Finally, each minority group's experience can be more precisely analyzed within its own context rather than further stigmatized by the majority's distortions. For example, lesbians and gay men have been labeled by the majority as rapists who prey on young children, Communists with strong desires to sabotage the American political system, and non-Christian, anti-God heretics. Given this plethora of additional unpleasant characteristics, it is little wonder that one might seek to hide one's sexual orientation from one's self, let alone from employers and family members. By examining the belief system within the lesbian and gay experience, one can begin to alter one's self-image and that held by society at large.

RELEVANT RESEARCH

While there is finally some research available about homosexual educators (Fischer, 1982; Harbeck, 1987, 1989; Griffin, 1989, Olson, 1987; Nickeson, 1980; Sciullo, 1984; Smith, 1985), there is no research focusing specifically on lesbian physical education teachers. Similarly, only three studies were found that directly or indirectly addressed the issue of lesbianism in physical education and sport. Guthrie (1982) examined homophobic attitudes towards females in sport; Beck (1976) studied the lifestyles of "never married female physical educators" in higher education; and Locke and Jensen (1970) explored the heterosexuality of women in physical education. As difficult as it is to believe, these latter two studies conspicuously managed to avoid a direct discussion of lesbianism. While a few writers have addressed the issue of sexual orientation in sport and physical education (Beck, 1980; Bennett, Whitaker, Smith, & Sablove, 1986; Boutilier & SanGiovanni, 1983; Cobhan, 1982; Gondola & Fitzpatrick, 1985; Griffin, 1983, 1987; Hart, 1974; Lenskyj, 1986), for the most part, the topic of lesbians in physical education has remained an unexamined area of research.

METHODOLOGY

In order to obtain information about these lesbian physical educators and to understand the meaning they make of their experiences, a phenomenological interviewing technique was used. Taken from the work of Schuman (1982), the specific interviewing format employed was formally developed by Seidman, Sullivan, and Schatzkamer (1983) and consists of three, in-depth open-ended interviews. The goal in these interviews was to have the participants reconstruct their experience and reflect upon its meaning. An underlying assumption of this approach is that the meaning people make of their experience is "crucial to the way they carry out their work" (Seidman et al., 1983, p. 638).

One focus question guided each 90-minute interview. In the first interview the participants were asked to provide personal and professional background for describing their experiences as lesbian physical educators. They were asked in the second interview to recreate the concrete details of their day-to-day work experiences, and the objective of the final interview was to have them reflect on the meaning they make of their experiences as lesbian physical educators.

PARTICIPANTS

The participants in this study were 12 elementary and secondary public school physical education teachers who identified themselves as lesbians. Access to the 12 participants was gained through researcher contacts and from referrals by participants. Their ages ranged from 25 to 50 years old: five were in their 20s, four in their 30s, two in their 40s, and one in her 50s. Eleven were White, and one was Black. The majority of the participants identified themselves as coming from middle class backgrounds based upon their parents' occupational status, while two were from upper middle class, one from lower middle class and one from working class backgrounds. Four persons identified themselves as Catholic, and the rest as Protestant.

Seven of the teachers interviewed were employed in suburban schools, while three taught in rural and two were in urban settings. Five teachers taught at the high school level, and three taught at junior high or middle schools. One teacher taught physical education to grades K-8 and another taught grades K-12. One teacher taught adapted physical education for a large school system. In addition to her regular teaching duties, one participant served as the athletic trainer for a high school. Five of the participants were coaching a girls' athletic team, and all but two had coached at some point during their tenure as teachers.

FINDINGS

The participants held two underlying assumptions about their experience: (a) that as lesbian teachers, they would lose their job if they were open about their sexual orientation, and (b) female physical education teachers are often negatively stereotyped as lesbians. These assumptions were shared by all the participants and were reflected in everything they said and did, including the identity management techniques they used to conceal or reveal their sexual orientation.

Of the 12 participants, 11 believed they would be fired if their sexual orientation was publicly disclosed. Although the twelfth participant stated that she would probably not lose her job, she did admit to engaging in "passing" behaviors so that her colleagues would assume that she was heterosexual. The following statement reflects the sentiment held by the majority of participants:

> I guess I don't put the two words together, lesbian and p.e. teacher. Because it means not having a job if I [do], if I was out. My lesbian life is separate. I've kept it, and I'm trying to keep it very separate from my teaching. (Caren)

A love of teaching coupled with the fear of professional repercussions often outweighed a participant's need to be open about her lesbian identity. The bottom line for many was that being a teacher was more important than being out as a lesbian.

The second underlying assumption expressed by the participants was that female physical education teachers are frequently negatively stereotyped as lesbians by students, teachers, administrators, and parents. Much of the stigma centered around the labeling of female physical educators as "locker room peepers":

> We used to require showers, I remember we did that in the '60s. "You will take gym. You will sweat, and you will take a shower." One of my colleagues overheard [this one young lady say to a friend of hers], "They make us take showers so they can look at us. They're all queer." Geez, now who told her that? Somebody must have told her that because it didn't just pop into the kid's head, did it? Most of our ideas come from our parents or from our peers but

our peers got those questions and those wise remarks from some place. (Jackie)

The participants believed that today's students are very aware of the stereotype that physical education instructors are lesbians, and that they are more willing to confront teachers about it.

"All gym teachers are queer." How do you know? "My mother told me." Her mother told her. It's like that's common knowledge: P.E. teachers are queer. "Miss Carlson, are you over 30?" Nope, I'm 29. "Oh, you're all right, you're still safe." If you're over 30 and you're a p.e. teacher and you're single, you're a lesbian. (Susan)

From the perspective of the participants, being fired was a daily threat because of the prevailing stereotype that female physical educators are lesbian. These two assumptions shaped the foundation from which they viewed their day-to-day worlds as lesbian physical educators.

IDENTITY MANAGEMENT TECHNIQUES

If placed on a continuum with one end labeled total concealment of their lesbian identity and the other total disclosure, the majority of participants fell on the half representing greater concealment. None of the twelve participants interviewed was totally out as a lesbian teacher; yet all had disclosed their sexual orientation at some point in their teaching career to at least one other teacher, colleague, ex-student, or current student from their school. The two categories of lesbian identity management techniques identified from the data were: (a) strategies to conceal one's lesbian identity, and (b) risk-taking behaviors that could disclose one's lesbian identity. In terms of the choices made by the participants in managing their lesbian identity, no simple pattern emerged. For instance, a participant on one occasion may have chosen to confront a homophobic remark made by a teacher, but on another occasion under similar circumstances, she may have totally ignored it. The following is a brief discussion of the concealment and risk-taking behaviors engaged in by the participants.

Strategies to Conceal One's Lesbian Identity

All the participants employed strategies to hide their sexual orientation in their relationships with both heterosexual and homosexual members of the school community. The strategies employed to conceal their lesbian identity can be broken down into three categories: (a) passing as heterosexual, (b) self-distancing from students, teachers, and administrators, and (c) self-distancing from issues of homosexuality.

A. Passing as Heterosexual

In order to conceal their lesbian identity, the participants in this study frequently adopted strategies that actively mislead their colleagues and students into believing that they were heterosexual. This process of "passing as heterosexual" usually took the form of changing pronouns and names of lovers and friends from female to male:

> I'll tell the kids stuff about Carrie but just change the name. They'll ask how long I've been going out with my boyfriend, and I just say, "Oh, for a year." (Pam)

Several of the participants, however, were prepared to go to even greater extremes to falsify information about themselves and their activities. Toni, for example, made sure that she knew the names of a couple of local straight bars and some details about these businesses, so that she would have a heterosexual scenario in mind if colleagues asked more extensive questions about her weekend activities:

> There was always a fear that somebody would really pursue what I did [on the weekends]. "I went out to a bar." God forbid anybody would ever question what bar I went to. I'd have a couple of names [of straight bars] I'd pull out of my pocket. (Toni)

A few of the participants disclosed information about a prior relationship with a man in order to imply that they had been in love or involved with some special man at an earlier time in their life, and that this loss had not been recovered from or replaced. This strategy may have been more effectively employed by the older participants in this study, who seemed to face less pressure from colleagues to be dating. Participants who felt uncomfortable about appearing at school functions without a date often made arrangements with a gay male friend to serve as their "significant other," and they would return the favor for him at his place of employment. Appearing at social events with the same man raised questions about an impending marriage, while appearing with different men often involved explaining why the previous relationship had failed.

In the face of their firm belief that they would lose their job if their lesbian identity were disclosed, this process of passing as heterosexual was viewed by the participants as being an unpleasant reality of the circumstances. Many of them expressed upset at a system that required deception and lies, and at their daily stress levels as they worried about being discovered through accident or inconsistency. In light of this latter concern, the changing of pronouns and names seemed the least complicated method of passing because it permitted discussions about current personal occurrences and activities without more elaborate falsifications if one did not disclose too many specific details. Conversely, appearing at a school function with a date raised the possibility of being found out because of conflicting personal details revealed in casual conversation.

In order to justify passing as heterosexual, a surprising number of participants referred to the process as a game:

> There's nothing that I keep hidden from my kids except my real personal life. Last weekend I told them I was on a date. I was down at John's who is my gay friend, but I told them I was on a date with John. You've got to play a little game. I have no intentions of my kids knowing that I'm gay. (Alice)

> * * *

> The kids would say, "Oh, you're *Miss* Johnson. You're not married." "No, no, I'm not. I haven't found the right one yet. Prince Andrew is busy." I'd make up all these things, and they'd laugh. They think I'm having a romance right now with a science teacher, this guy, [Steve]. We hang around together in school. So some of the freshman kids started a rumor last year that we were engaged. These kids just thought it was the most wonderful thing, and we let it go. It was kind of fun for a while. And they wanted to be invited to the wedding. So I guess you could say that every once in a while I have all these little games that either I play or a group of kids play, and I just don't push the rumors down that hard. (Nancy)

For some participants, the passing game was second nature:

> I have to do it. It's just a natural response. I don't even think about it. You have to be quick. I just do it. (Jackie)

Not every participant engaged in passing behaviors, but for those who did, the intent was to counteract the assumption that female physical education teachers are lesbian. By misleading others to believe they were heterosexual, the participants hoped to keep suspicions about their sexual orientation to a minimum.

B. Self-Distancing from Others

The process of self-distancing was consciously employed by the participants in order to avoid interactions with colleagues, superiors, and students that would call for an exchange of personal information or feelings. Unlike the process of passing described above, in this strategy the participants sought to rigidly avoid communicating with others. This strategy, then, provided the participants with a first level of defense so that more elaborate and more dishonest passing behavior could be avoided.

Self-distancing from others was a relatively constant and diverse activity. Regardless of the personalities, participants sought to maintain an image of themselves as stern, businesslike, efficient, task-oriented, and unamused. By keeping interactions short and to the point, and by remaining aloof from others, they sought to avoid longer, more intimate conversations about personal details and feelings that might ultimately reveal their sexual orientation.

> You kind of walk a fine line of how much you want to reveal to these people. I have a tendency not to get too over friendly or warm to my students. I always kind of keep this little front up and sometimes I think the front is sternness. Not that I am a stern teacher, but I hold that front a little bit to kind of keep everybody at arm's length. So that maybe they don't want to pursue too much my personal life. (Toni)

When choosing to share personal information, many of the participants carefully selected their words, making sure not to reveal too much information at once.

> You really have to guard your words. . . . I don't know as I would often volunteer it. I don't know whether I dole out pieces at a time and not all at one time so they don't put them all together. I don't know whether I'm being extraordinarily guarded, or I have this real fine line about professionalism, and I have a real fine line about personal life. I think [volunteering information is] giving away too much of myself. I'm a little afraid to give that much away of myself. (Sara)

Because of engaging in self-distancing behavior, many of the participants felt misunderstood, isolated, and dishonest. They were very aware that often they were harming relationships that were otherwise important to them both personally and professionally.

> This is the first year that I am in conflict with becoming a pretty good friend of a [teacher] who is straight and does not know anything about me. The worst part is being so secretive to the point where I am with this new person, Elaine. It is a friendship right now that is based on lying, because I do lie. She'll ask me, "Who [are] you seeing?" And I say, "I'm not seeing anyone." That's hell for me. (Susan)

Again, despite the cost to them in their interpersonal relationships, self-esteem and honesty, the participants felt that it was better to avoid any and all situations that might lead to disclosure or to the more complex process of having to lie.

While the stress of having to manage information and intimacy in relationships is significant for any gay and lesbian educator, as physical education instructors these women faced numerous added complications in their school interactions. In the locker room, for example, some participants consciously avoided eye contact with students who were changing clothes, while others avoided the locker room altogether. The most common strategy employed was to avoid physical contact with female students. Even when students initiated physical contact, participants consciously chose not to reciprocate for fear of repercussions.

> [The kids] don't feel bad about coming up to me, like some of my hockey players slap me on the back or put their arm around me. But I won't do it to them. That probably will never change. You don't know who's watching or who might go home and say something to their mother. I just wouldn't want any controversy to start when there's nothing to be talked about. But I do worry about it, and I think about it consciously. (Nancy)

C. Self-Distancing from Issues of Homosexuality

Most of the participants believed that if they intervened in school situations concerning homosexuality, such as name-calling, AIDS education, and assisting students with questions about sexuality, that they would be revealed as lesbians. Thus, when confronted either directly or indirectly with the issue of homosexuality, the participants employed a variety of strategies to remove themselves from the situation altogether. When confronted with homophobic comments made by students, teachers, or administrators, for example, they would pretend that they had not heard it:

> The boys are into calling each other "faggots" or "He's queer." I
> pretend I don't hear those. I try not to make a big deal about it. Kids
> are into name calling, no matter what they use, they're into name
> calling. If it's not that, it's something else. (Mona)

Even when homophobic comments were directed at them, many participants chose to ignore the incident:

> I was taking my roll this year the first day of class. I'm checking
> them off, and I hear in the back, "Oh, she's the lesbian." Now, one
> girl is saying this to another girl. There's no question [but] that they
> were talking about me. And I'm thinking to myself, whoa. What is
> this? Already the first day of class, brand new year, and this has
> happened. The only thing I could think of was somewhere along the
> line, [a] girl the year before tipped them off. Maybe that's my para-
> noia about them really and truly knowing it or whether or not they
> just thought it, and the rumor had just passed around. I didn't ac-
> knowledge it. I suspect that they didn't think I heard it, but I didn't
> acknowledge it. (Sara)

When the topic of homosexuality or jokes about gays came up in the
teachers' room, some participants dealt with this by remaining silent,
while others tried to make an inconspicuous exit.

> My own reaction to that is to pretend that I'm busy, and I don't hear
> what's going on. I'll wait a reasonable amount of time, and then I'll
> leave. So it isn't too obvious. It's an escape. I know that. (Mona)

The participants in this study were deeply upset about their own failure
to intervene in anti-gay and lesbian situations. Had these incidents occurred concerning another minority group, however, they felt empowered
and, in fact, obligated to take action against the prejudice and discrimination being expressed.

When dealing with a gay or suspected gay student, many participants
took a cautious approach. Some avoided being alone with students they
thought were gay, and they always left the door open for safety:

> You know how you peg kids, this is awful, but you peg them. Like,
> "Oh, that kid's going to be gay. I don't want to be near her." So I
> never went near [this one] kid. Then she got hurt, she pinched a
> nerve in her neck. She brought in a doctor's note, and the doctor
> wanted her to get massages every day. I was like, oh, no. So I
> always had the doors wide open. I always made sure there were

about five kids in the trainer's room. I was real paranoid. I had to massage [her] neck and shoulders. It was for about three weeks, and I was paranoid every single day. (Pam)

Other participants made a choice not to counsel gay students or those they thought might be gay.

There [are some students] that I would love to be able to talk with, but that's one place where I'm afraid. I would not sit down and talk to anyone and give them any counseling about being gay. That's something that's really important that the students have someone to talk to, but unfortunately, I don't feel like I could do that now. (Jody)

Clearly, the participants felt that their avoidance of potentially gay and lesbian students was a betrayal of these young people who were searching for help in defining who they were as human beings. By hiding their own sexual orientation, the participants felt that they were failing to be positive role models and failing to provide accurate information about homosexuality. Furthermore, they realized that they were covertly communicating the message that being gay or lesbian was bad because of the need for denial. While the participants all felt quite positive about their lesbian lifestyle outside the school environment, they uniformly believed that bringing that lifestyle into their work situation would be hazardous to their careers.

Overall, then, the strategies the participants employed to conceal their lifestyle reflected the separation between their personal identities as lesbians and their professional identities as teachers. Yet at times, they chose not to separate these two identities and engaged in behaviors within the school environment that disclosed or risked disclosure of their sexual orientation. These risk-taking behaviors are examined next.

RISK-TAKING BEHAVIORS

The participant group took risks much less frequently than they used strategies to conceal their sexual orientation. The behaviors engaged in that disclosed or risked disclosure of their lesbian identity fell into three categories: (a) obliquely overlapping personal with professional, (b) actively confronting homophobia and supporting gay and lesbian students, and (c) overtly overlapping their personal and professional lives. Most of the risks taken were premeditated.

A. Obliquely Overlapping Personal with Professional

This type of risk was characterized by a participant sharing personal information about herself with students or colleagues in a vague, but honest manner. For instance, a participant might acknowledge that she owns a house with a "roommate," or bring her partner to school events and describe her as a "friend." A participant also might invite students to her home but not clarify the living arrangements. The consequences of such risks were not clear to the participant. For example, some participants socialized with their colleagues extensively, but they were not sure if their lesbianism had been ascertained.

> We did have a group of teachers at the [school], women that used to get together. I enjoyed going out with this group, but I felt uncomfortable for several reasons. One being my sexual preference being gay. I was always hoping that nobody ever really talked to me and said, "Well, are you seeing anybody, are you dating anybody?" There wasn't time to delve too deeply into my background. I was always thankful for that, but I could never figure out whether it was really because maybe deep down inside they knew. (Toni)

Another vague way of potentially declaring one's lesbiansim was to associate with another gay teacher in the school.

For most participants, this kind of limited personal disclosure was viewed as being relatively low risk because it was vague and because nothing about their lesbianism was overtly or irrevocably confirmed. Integrating their personal and professional lives, even in these small ways, lessened their conflict about living in two worlds. It also heightened their self-esteem because it permitted them to express some aspects of who they truly were and it avoided the deceit and dishonesty that they often experienced during their concealment efforts.

B. Actively Confronting and Supporting

Many participants took risks that heightened the chance of disclosure of their lesbian identity. Susan, for example, took the opportunity to challenge her students on their use of the word "gay."

> Other than, "This sucks" or "That sucks," the other most frequently used word is, "This is gay." Everything's "gay" in junior high school. Most often when anyone uses the word gay, I talk to them, and I ask them, "What does gay mean?" It's really interesting to listen to their definitions. As a matter of fact, under my blotter

on my desk, I have a piece of paper saying definitions of gay. And when somebody gives me a new definition, I write them down. They range from it's just geekish, it's something from being nerdy to two guys that love each other. But it can be anything in between. A lot of lesbian p.e. teachers would sort of shy away from that stuff, at least ones that I know. If somebody says gay, you sort of just turn your head and make believe you didn't even hear the word. I love finding out what they're thinking. (Susan)

Susan's behavior was atypical, both because of its directness and because the risk-taking occurred in a group setting. Conversely, other participants were more comfortable in one-to-one situations. Instead of avoiding students who were questioning their own sexual orientation, for example, some participants chose to talk with them. It should be noted, however, that the participants were much more likely to have an honest discussion about homosexuality, and even their own sexual preference, if the young person involved was a former, rather than a current student.

I had [a] kid that was on my team a couple years ago that came to me. She said she had something really important to talk to me about, and she didn't know if she could tell me. And I said, "Well, what is it?" And she wouldn't tell me, and so I said, "Well, is it about being gay?" She said, "Yeah, how did you know?" And I just talked to her a lot about it. We weren't talking about her. We were talking about gay in general. So I just told her how I felt about people and being different [and that] it doesn't make a difference to me. (Caren)

* * *

There was [a] kid my second year as head coach who was a senior. [Jamie] had a lot of problems at home. And I just spent hour on hour, sitting and talking to Jamie and helping her through a lot of situations just [by] talking to her.

Jamie got back in contact with me after her senior year, and she spilled her guts to me. She told me she was in love with me, and she had been. She had evidently spent many emotional evenings and days and weeks and months on end not knowing how to deal with this. Keeping it inside, not knowing who to talk to, so eventually she came back to me. And boy, I'll tell you, I choked on my coffee that day.

I just didn't know what to do. I told her I was flattered. And I told her that in fact I was gay. She asked me. She knew that she had these feelings and attractions toward different women. And she was struggling with what she was feeling. I knew that there was no way I could sit there, looking across the table at this kid and say, no, that I wasn't gay. I couldn't do it. And I didn't want to. I knew that Jamie was having a lot of emotional problems herself, so I knew that I had to be very upfront and honest with her. (Toni)

While the teachers involved in this study were likely to overlook hostile remarks about homosexuality made generally or aimed at them, they did take action when people they felt emotionally close to were being victimized by unkind student behavior.

One day, I was sitting outside the local pizza place in the car, and Jeannie [my partner] had gone into the restaurant. These students called out, "Hey Lezzie." I got out of the car and I walked across the street. I said, "Becky, come here." She looked, and then she turned around. So I threatened her, you know, that she was fooling with the wrong person right now. And if I heard that from her again, she would be dealt with severely. Every time after that I saw her in school, I just gave her this real bad look. I didn't say anything to her. I just stared her right in the eye. I didn't take my eyes right off of her, even if she looked. I made her eyes turn away. And I haven't heard anything from her since. (Jody)

Participants in this study felt that as teachers they were obligated to confront harassment, educate students about minority differences and social/individual tolerance, and provide students with information and support to help their emotional, social, and intellectual development. Thus, they felt they had a duty to intervene and to educate when the issue of homosexuality surfaced. Despite a strong commitment to this obligation, most of the participants acknowledged that their own fear of losing their jobs made them less likely to act. Thus, they felt self-critical of their perceived failure to be the resource that they believed was needed by many students within their schools, both homosexual and heterosexual.

C. Overtly Overlapping Personal with Professional

Every participant had revealed or acknowledged her sexual orientation to at least one other member of the school community during their tenure as teachers. Coming out to a teacher, colleague, student, or ex-student took many forms, ranging from overt declarations to non-denial of accusations. Sometimes it was the other person who let the lesbian physical education teacher know that he or she knew of her sexual orientation, in order to protect her or put her at ease. For example, one participant was informed by a student that if she was going out that weekend, maybe she should avoid a certain local (lesbian) bar because some underage students intended to use their false identification to gain entry.

> I just said, "Thank you, Nina." I spoke to Nina after that one day, and she finally said to me, "I know," [referring to me being gay]. And I said, "Well, just keep it to yourself, lady, because this job is kind of nice." She said, "I know. Don't worry." (Alice)

Other participants shared their lesbian identity in similar circumstances where the other person had already guessed, or when their own emotional upset was too extreme to manage, such as during a painful relationship ending.

> [When] my relationship with Terri was dissolving, for the first time in my life, I couldn't get a grip on things. I lost probably 20 lbs. So there were some noticeable things that were going on. Teaching, I loved. I was still high energy. As a matter of fact, I hated for the day of teaching to end, because I really put all my energy into it.
>
> At one point I was very close to a guy, the art teacher in this school system. I remember him coming out one day and saying, "Susan, I'm sick because I really think my wife is cheating on me. I think my wife is going to leave me." And I remember turning and looking at him and saying, "Larry, I understand that. My wife just left me." And I remember saying it like that, and I remember him looking at me and him saying, "Are you gay?" And I said, "Yeah. And I'm going through hell." And since then we have developed a great friendship. (Susan)

For some, coming out was considered a better alternative to lying. Others came out to a colleague because they were caught off guard. Pam, for example, confirmed her boss's inquiry about her lesbianism when he casually mentioned that he was from the same town as her roommate, and that he knew that her roommate was a lesbian.

> He caught me off guard. I didn't know what to do. I was going to deny it, but no, why should I? I've never lied to him before, why should I now? So I didn't. I figured he wouldn't say anything because he had hired me and that would make him look like a fool, according to his standards.

One might assume that the more risks a participant took, the fewer concealment strategies she employed. This was not the case. Nor was it the case that the longer a participant had been a lesbian or the more accepting she was of that identity, the less active she was in hiding her sexual orientation. A consistent pattern with respect to how and when participants concealed or revealed their sexual orientation did not evolve. Rather, each decision was made on a case-by-case, day-to-day, person-to-person basis, contingent upon numerous factors. The differences in behavior could be attributed to something simple, like whether or not she was having a good day, to something more complex, such as how deeply the negative stereotypes associated with lesbian physical education teachers affected her acceptance of her own lesbian identity.

CONCLUSIONS

The participants in this study described school environments that were deeply enveloped in homophobia and heterosexism. Heterosexuality was acknowledged and celebrated as the norm, while homosexuality was discredited and silenced. The participants experienced homophobia on both external and internal levels. Externally, they were subjected to blatant and subtle forms of homophobic harassment, ranging from direct threats of dismissal to casual displays of heterosexual privilege. Internally, they bifurcated their existence, so that their identity as lesbians did not impact on their identity as school teachers. They survived by constantly denying and hiding their lesbianism in order to work within their chosen profession. They accepted living in these two worlds as a necessary way of life for a lesbian physical education teacher, yet their stories revealed a high cost in emotional energy and self-esteem as a consequence of this bifurcated existence.

Regardless of the degree to which the participants accepted their lesbian identities, each paid a personal and professional toll for concealing it in school. For some, the personal toll was self-hatred and non-acceptance of her lesbianism; for others, the frustration, fear, and isolation associated with hiding a lesbian identity. Professionally, the participants felt unable to be fully functioning and honest members of the school community. They distanced themselves from students, as well as colleagues, and they avoided any overlap in their personal and professional lives. While aware of the limitations of their less-than-honest participation in their schools, they also suffered remorse that they were failing to be positive lesbian role models for both homosexual and heterosexual students. Perhaps the heaviest toll was the energy required day in and day out to maintain their cover.

For some, this became second nature—a tragedy in itself—but for others it was a daily struggle.

To outsiders, the risks these participants did take may appear minimal. Given the homophobic climate of their work worlds, however, their risk-taking behavior should not be minimized. Participating in this study, for example, involved considerable risk and self-exploration, as did coming out to students and colleagues. In acknowledging their sexual orientation to one or more members of the school community, these teachers took very significant, irreversible stands that required their colleagues to deal directly with issues of homophobia. Research about homophobia indicates that peoples' attitudes about homosexuals are positively affected by personally knowing a gay or lesbian person (Herek, 1984). By acknowledging their lesbian identity to others in the school community, the participants interrupted the oppressive pattern of invisibility and prejudice.

In interactions with students and ex-students who were questioning their own sexual orientation, many participants either came out directly and/or supported the student's choice to be gay or lesbian. A recent study indicates that as much as 30% of teen suicide may be related to sexual orientation confusion (Adams, 1989). This figure underscores the need for positive lesbian and gay role models in the schools. Although their visibility was limited, many participants in this study assumed this role despite their belief that to do so risked their careers. Unfortunately, the message these participants felt forced to communicate, veiled in secrecy and caution, was: "It is okay to be gay or lesbian, but don't be open about it and be selective in whom you tell."

Just as the participants in this study struggled to break the silence surrounding the lesbian presence within physical education, it is our hope that this research will be used as a catalyst for dialogue and change. While we are aware that change concerning attitudes about lesbians and gay men needs to occur on individual, local, state, national, and global levels, we will limit the balance of our discussion to areas within physical education that offer some hope of change.

Available research and shared experiences reveal that homophobia and heterosexism effect not only lesbian physical educators but all physical educators, heterosexuals as well as homosexuals, men as well as women. As such, these are issues that could be effectively addressed by the entire physical education profession. Collective reflection would permit us to examine the silence, fear, and isolation that continues to harm our personal and professional lives. Informal networks of gay and lesbian physical educators can be used as sources of support, but formal networks are necessary to publicly acknowledge and embrace the lesbian and gay presence within physical education. The goal is to move away from private discussions veiled in secrecy and coded language toward more visible and open exchanges distinguished by honesty and directness. Risks must be taken, and we must openly acknowledge our sexual orientation. Our closet doors must be opened, perhaps cautiously at first, but eventually they must be taken off the hinges. One major step in achieving this goal would be the protection offered by a large group of professionals who are willing to use their collective influence for the benefit and protection of minority members.

Another value of collective reflection is the possibility of a broadbased commitment to eradicating homophobia and heterosexism. Professional workshops and teacher training could be expanded to help our colleagues deal with the overt and subtle forms of prejudice that go on in the schools. We could be encouraged to take action and trained to intervene when words like "faggot," "queer," and "lezzie" are used in our classes. Given the high rate of teen suicide over sexual preference issues and the harm of damaged self-esteem, these terms can no longer be excused as innocuous name-calling. If unchallenged, these pejorative words validate and support a school climate that perpetuates a fear and hatred of homosexuality.

Similarly, our profession needs to examine the role of gender socialization in perpetuating homophobia and heterosexism. The labelling of athletically skilled girls as "tomboys" and athletically unskilled boys as "sissies," for example, are manifestations of this prejudice. Behind these labels are negative innuendos about one's sexual orientation. As long as those individuals who do not qualify as "real men" are differentiated from those who do, sport is maintained as a masculine rite. In this masculine realm, females and unathletic males are treated as intruders or "marginal participants in an alien environment" (Griffin, 1989, p. 18). Given the importance of physical fitness and activity in maintaining the quality of one's life, we perpetuate a tremendous disservice to countless men and women by failing to reflect on our biases and outdated perspectives.

And finally, as a strong and politically influential professional body, we have the opportunity to successfully lobby for anti-discrimination clauses on local, state, and national levels. A united front of heterosexual and homosexual teachers would be a powerful political force and would provide positive role modeling of acceptance for and appreciation of diversity. Without such an alliance, homophobia and heterosexism will continue to divide and isolate heterosexual and homosexual physical educators.

As researchers in the field of physical education, we have the ability to study the effects of homophobia and heterosexism within our profession. We must ground our research in the contextual realities of people's experiences, using a theoretical perspective that acknowledges gender construction in maintaining homophobia and heterosexism (Griffin, 1987). The perspectives of both homosexual and heterosexual, male and female physical educators who work at the elementary, secondary, college, and university levels should be solicited. A variety of methodologies should be employed, but researchers should give special consideration to the type of empowerment research recently undertaken by Griffin as a way to document experience and effect social change. Obviously, the support of colleagues, organizations, and institutions would be very important in funding this type of research and in providing a wider mechanism for the consideration of the findings.

As professionals, we have an opportunity to positively impact society by increasing our recent efforts to make education about homophobia and heterosexism within physical education a priority. Homophobia workshops have been offered at recent national conventions of the American Alliance for Health, Physical Education, Recreation and Dance (AAHPERD), but more are needed at the district and local levels to facilitate the learning process. Subgroups within AAHPERD, like the National Association for Girls and Women in Sport (NAGWS) and the National Association for Sport and Physical Education (NASPE), have begun to address the issue of homophobia within physical education and sport, but more open dialogue is necessary to bring this topic fully out of the closet.

The potential outcome of such research and workshops will depend upon its reception by the entire physical education community. The "L-word" is very powerful, and it historically has been avoided, rejected, and feared by homosexuals and heterosexuals alike within physical education. This study, and others like it, may fall victim to the same kind of reaction, or they may begin a process of personal and professional reflection and exchange that is long overdue. Homophobia and heterosexism affect all physical educators, not just lesbian physical educators. "Lesbian" is a very powerful word, and until we individually and organizationally take the opportunity to use it and to examine the realities of the lesbian experience, the power of the label "lesbian" lies with others who are insensitive to issues of oppression and personal freedom.

REFERENCES

Adams, J. M. (1989, January 3). For many gay teenagers, torment leads to suicide tries. *Boston Globe*, 1, 8.

Baker-Miller, J. (1976). *Toward a new psychology of women*. Boston: Beacon Press.

Barnett, W. (1973). *Sexual freedom and the constitutionality of repressive sex laws*. Albuquerque: University of New Mexico Press.

Beck, B. (1976). Lifestyles of never married women physical educators in institutions of higher education in the U.S. *Dissertation Abstracts International, 37*, 2715A. (University Microfilms No. DA 76-24, 936).

Beck, B. (1980). No more masks! A feminist perspective on issues and directions in professional preparation. *Proceedings of the National Association for Physical Education in Higher Education (NAPEHE) Annual Conference, 2*, 126-135.

Becker, H. S. (1963). *Outsiders: Study in the sociology of deviance*. London: Free Press of Glencoe.

Bennett, R. S., Whitaker, G., Smith, N., & Sablove, A. (1987). Changing the rules of the game: Reflections toward a feminist analysis of sport. *Women's Studies International Forum, 10* (4), 369-79.

Boutilier, M. A., & SanGiovanni, L. (1983). *The sporting woman*. Champaign, IL: Human Kinetics.

Cobhan, L. (1982). Lesbians in physical education and sport. In M. Cruikshank (Ed.), *Lesbian studies: Present and future* (pp. 179-186). Old Westbury, NY: Feminist Press.

Felshin, J. (1974). The dialectic of women and sport. In E. Gerber, J. Felshin, P. Berlin, & W. Wyrick (Eds.), *The American woman in sport* (pp. 179-210). Reading, MA: Addison-Wesley.

Fields, C. (1983, October 26). Allegations of lesbianism being used to intimidate, female academics say. *Chronicle of Higher Education*, pp. 1, 22.

Fischer, T. R. (1982). A study of educators' attitudes toward homosexuality (Doctoral dissertation, University of Virginia). *Dissertation Abstracts International, 43*, 3294A.

Freire, P. (1972). *Pedagogy of the oppressed*. New York: Herder and Herder.

Goffman, E. (1963). *Stigma: Notes on the management of spoiled identity*. Englewood Cliffs, NJ: Prentice Hall.

Goldenberg, I. (1978). *Oppression and social intervention*. Chicago: Nelson-Hall.

Goldyn, L. M. (1979). *Legal ideology and the regulation of homosexual behavior* (Doctoral Dissertation, Stanford University). *Dissertation Abstracts International*.

Gondola, J. C., & Fitzpatrick, T. (1985). Homophobia in girls' sports: "Names" that can hurt us . . . all of us. *Equal Play, 5* (2), 18-19.

Griffin, P. S. (1983, November). *How can a female sports performer avoid, diminish, or disarm threats to her own sense of femininity?* Paper presented at the New Agenda for Women in Sport Conference, Washington, DC.

Griffin, P. S. (1987). Gender as a socializing agent in physical education. In T. Templin & P. Schempp (Eds.), *Socialization in physical education: Learning to teach*. Champaign, IL: Human Kinetics.

Griffin, P. S. (1989, March). *Using participatory research to empower gay and lesbian educators.* Paper presented at the annual meeting of the American Education Research Association, San Francisco, CA.

Groth, A. N., & Birnbaum, H. J. (1978). Adult sexual orientation and attraction to underage persons. *Archives of Sexual Behavior, 7* (3), 175-181.

Guthrie, S. P. (1982). *Homophobia: Its impact on women in sport and physical education.* Unpublished master's thesis, California State University, Long Beach.

Harbeck, K. M. (1987). *Personal freedoms/public constraints: An analysis of the controversy over the employment of homosexuals as school teachers,* Vol. I and II (Doctoral dissertation, Stanford University). *Dissertation Abstracts International 48* (7), 1862A. (University Microfilms No. DA 8723009).

Harbeck, K. M. (1989, March). *The homosexual educator: Past history/future prospects.* Paper presented at the annual meeting of the American Education Research Association, San Francisco, CA.

Harro, R. L. (1983). *Heterosexism 101: Content for an educational experience.* Unpublished manuscript, University of Massachusetts, Amherst.

Hart, M. M. (1974). Stigma or prestige: The all-American choice. In G. McGlynn (Ed.), *Issues in physical education and sports* (pp. 214-220). Palo Alto, CA: National Press Books.

Herek, G. M. (1984). "Beyond homophobia": A social psychological perspective on attitudes toward lesbians and gay men. *Journal of Homosexuality, 10* (1/2), 1-21.

Hudson, W. W., & Ricketts, W. A. (1980). A strategy for the measurement of homophobia. *Journal of Homosexuality, 5*(4), 357-372.

Jackson, B., & Hardiman, R. (1988). *Oppression: Conceptual and developmental analysis.* Manuscript submitted for publication.

Kingdon, M. A. (1979). Lesbians. *The Counseling Psychologist, 8*(1), 44-45.

Kinsey, A. C., Pomeroy, M., and Martin, C. E. (1948). *Sexual behavior in the human male.* Philadelphia: Saunders.

Lenskyj, H. (1986). *Out of bounds: Women, sport & sexuality.* Toronto, Ontario: The Women's Press.

Locke, L. F., & Jensen, M. (1970). The heterosexuality of women in physical education. *The Foil,* Fall, 30-34.

Memmi, A. (1965). *The colonizer and the colonized.* Boston: Beacon Press.

Morin, S., & Garfinkle, E. (1978). Male homophobia. *Journal of Social Issues, 34* (1), 29-47.

Nickeson, S. S. (1980). *A comparison of gay and heterosexual teachers on professional and personal dimensions. Dissertation Abstracts International, 41,* 3956A. (University Microfilms No. DA 8105601).

Olson, M. (1987). A study of gay and lesbian teachers. *Journal of Homosexuality, 13*(4), 73-81.

Schuman, D. (1982). *Policy analysis, education, and everyday life.* Lexington, MA: D. C. Heath.

Sciullo, A. A. (1984). *Tolls at closet doors: A gay history for teachers. Dissertation Abstracts International, 45,* 497A. (University Microfilms No. DA 8412076).

Seidman, E., Sullivan, P., & Schatzkamer, M. (1983). *The work of community college faculty: A study through in-depth interviews* (Grant No. NIE-G-81-0056). Washington, DC: National Institute of Education.

Smith, D. (1985). *An ethnographic interview study of homosexual teachers' perspectives. Dissertation Abstracts International, 46,* 66A. (University Microfilms No. DA 8506864).

Weinberg, G. (1972). *Society and the healthy homosexual.* New York: St. Martins Press.

From Hiding Out to Coming Out: Empowering Lesbian and Gay Educators

Pat Griffin, EdD

University of Massachusetts, Amherst

SUMMARY. The purposes of this participatory research project were to describe the experiences of thirteen lesbian and gay educators and to empower the participants through collective reflection and action. Each participant was interviewed and given a copy of her or his audio-tape and transcript. Using these materials, each participant developed a profile of themselves to share with the other participants. During a series of group meetings that spanned fifteen months, participants discussed their experiences, searched for common themes, and planned two collective actions. This chapter describes the professional experiences of these lesbian and gay educators and the process of empowerment that changed their lives.

Lesbian and gay educators constitute a large, but often invisible minority group in the schools. Most choose to remain closeted rather than risk being subjected to prejudice, discrimination, and accusations that they are child molesters or recruiters to an immoral lifestyle. As a result of this invisibility and the stigma attached to research on homosexuality in education, little is known about gay and lesbian educators.

Though the popular press, lesbian and gay publications, and some edu-

---

Pat Griffin is Associate Professor of Education. Her research and teaching interests include sexism, racism, and heterosexism in education; homophobia in education and sport; and qualitative research methods. The author would like to acknowledge her co-researchers, Georganne Greene and the 13 other lesbian and gay educators who participated in the project. Correspondence to the author should be addressed to: 464 Hills South, University of Massachusetts, Amherst, MA 01003.

167

cation and law journals include articles about gay and lesbian teachers, there is little formal research available. Fischer (1983) surveyed the attitudes of a group of educators toward homosexuality; Harbeck (1988) completed an extensive historical review of litigation involving homosexual teachers; and Nickeson (1981) compared the responses of 30 gay and lesbian teachers with those of 30 heterosexual teachers on a teacher characteristic scale and a sex role inventory.

Fewer than ten studies focus specifically on the professional experiences of gay or lesbian educators (Fogarty, 1981; Griffin, in press; Moses, 1978; Olson, 1986, 1987; Sciullo, 1984; Smith, 1985; Woods, 1990). Fogarty, Smith, and Woods used open-ended interviews with small numbers of respondents (twelve and under). Olson, using a mail questionnaire, received 97 responses and followed-up with a telephone interview of 21 selected respondents. Moses also distributed a questionnaire to 300 professionally employed lesbians; eighty-two were returned. Sciullo's study is an autobiographical account of the researcher's experience as a gay teacher who was fired. Though Fogarty and Moses included lesbian teachers among the participants in their investigations, only the Smith, Sciullo, Olson, and Woods studies focused exclusively on the experiences of lesbian and gay teachers.

The consistency of responses in these studies is striking: Gay and lesbian educators believe that a strict separation between their personal and professional lives is required and that to be publicly "out" at school would cost them their jobs. Thus, they describe themselves as constantly vigilant about protecting their secret identities, and the energy required to maintain this false public facade takes a tremendous psychological toll. This fear affects relationships with colleagues, students, and parents, creating a sense of isolation for the educator. Finally, these teachers experience frustration about changing the public's negative image of lesbian and gay people to match their own sense of themselves as worthy people and good teachers.

PURPOSE OF THE PROJECT

The purpose of this study was twofold: to describe the experiences of a selected group of gay and lesbian educators, and to empower these educators through collective reflection and action.

Given our empowerment goals, participatory research was chosen as an appropriate inquiry style. Participatory research, as a form of critical inquiry (Carr & Kemmis, 1986; Freire, 1970; Hall, 1975; Lather, 1986; Mies, 1983; Popkewitz, 1984), is grounded in the following assumptions:

(a) it is essential to acknowledge and address power imbalances among different social groups, (b) research is political, (c) research should move beyond description to facilitate social change, (d) research should enlighten and empower the participants to develop a critical understanding of their situation and should provide the means for them to take collective action to gain greater control over their lives, and (e) this action should begin with dialogue and reflection among participants about their personal experiences. The purposes of a participatory research project are to create a process in which members of a disempowered social group (in this case gay and lesbian educators) can work together collectively to articulate and validate their common experience and then act to change power inequities resulting from their social group membership.

PARTICIPANTS IN THE STUDY

In addition to two lesbian co-researchers who teach at the university level and are publicly "out" on their campus, thirteen self-identified gay and lesbian educators (six men and seven women) participated in the study. All levels of teaching were represented (pre-school, elementary, middle, and high school). Participants included teachers of a variety of subject matter areas, a librarian, a guidance counselor, and a principal. One participant was black and 14 were white. Participants ranged in age from 36 to 45, and their experience in education ranged from 6 to 23 years. The number of years that participants had known they were gay or lesbian ranged from 5 to 21 years. Participants represented nine different school districts. Some of these districts were small and rural, others were mid-sized cosmopolitan college town systems, and still others were large urban systems.

Nine of these educators were identified through their participation in a weekend program for gay and lesbian educators in which the researchers also participated. The remaining participants were identified through contact with the first nine. None of these teachers was publicly out at school, nor were any of them totally closeted when the project began.

Because of the group's small number and by virtue of their willingness to participate in this study, these educators are not necessarily representative of all gay and lesbian teachers. Moreover, all of the educators in this group began the project with the belief that societal homophobia is the problem, not their homosexuality. Not all lesbian and gay educators share this perspective.

DESIGN OF THE STUDY

The study spanned 15 months from November, 1987, to February, 1989. This time span predated the passage of the Massachusetts Gay Rights Law which protects the employment rights of lesbian and gay teachers. After an initial group meeting in November to introduce participants, describe the project, and sign consent forms, each participant scheduled time for a 90-minute individual interview with one of the researchers (who also interviewed each other). These open-ended interviews focused on the question, "What is it like to be a gay/lesbian educator?" All interviews were audio-taped and then transcribed verbatim. Interviewing and transcribing continued through December and the first part of January.

During the last two weeks in January each participant was hand-delivered a copy of her or his interview audio-tape and transcript to review. At a second group meeting in February, participants received guidelines for editing the transcripts to create a six to eight page profile of themselves. These profiles would be shared with the rest of the group. During February each participant, including researchers, worked individually to construct her or his profile.

A two-day group meeting in March focused on sharing all profiles with each other and identifying common themes. Three meetings in April, May, and June focused on continuing to share experiences, and identifying and planning two group action projects. Researchers took fieldnotes following all group meetings and individual interactions with participants. From June to November one of the co-researchers, using inductive analysis (Patton, 1980), worked with the interview data to refine, elaborate, and confirm the themes identified by the group. In November and December the second researcher reviewed the analysis process to confirm the grounding of the analysis in the interview data. In January a group meeting was held to describe the elaborated analysis of the interview data to the participants and to incorporate their reactions into this analysis.

Finally, in February, the researchers conducted two group interviews (Morgan, 1988) with participants (six in one interview and seven in the other). These interviews were audio-taped and transcribed. The focus of these open-ended interviews was, "Compared to my first interview, what is different and the same for me as a gay/lesbian educator over the past year?" These interviews were analyzed with the same previously discussed procedures.

This report will focus on detailing the experiences of the participants as described during the initial individual interviews and describing the empowerment process as experienced by the participants throughout the study. Though both researchers participated in all phases of the study with the other participants, the information presented in this report focuses on the experiences of the 13 pre-school through high school educators.

STORIES FROM THE CLOAKROOM

During the individual interviews, participants described their experiences as lesbian and gay educators. Analysis of the interviews yielded several themes that provide insight into the professional lives of the 13 participants in this study.

Fear of Accusation
vs. Wish for Self-Integrity

Because none of the gay and lesbian educators in this group was either publicly out or totally closeted in school, decisions about how to manage their gay or lesbian identities were made on a person-by-person and day-by-day basis. As personal and professional lives and relationships changed over the course of a school year and a career, participants needed to constantly reevaluate how to manage their identities. These decisions were made in the context of an underlying tension between their fear of public accusation and their wish for the integrity that they believed could come only from the integration of their lesbian/gay and educator identities.

Participants believed that a public accusation would inevitably result in one of two equally negative consequences: loss of job or loss of credibility among students, colleagues, and parents (see Figure 1). Moreover, participants feared public accusation as a result of three specific instances. One instance was to be accused of child molestation or making sexual advances to students. As a result, all participants were conscious of how physical contact with same-sex students might be misinterpreted. The second instance was to be accused of recruiting students to a lesbian or gay lifestyle. This fear made participants cautious about talking with lesbian or gay students who sought them out as sympathetic adults. The third instance was to be accused of being lesbian or gay as a result of being seen at a gay-identified place or event, such as a gay pride march, a gay-identified resort, a lesbian bar, or a women's music concert. In all instances, participants feared that public accusation would mean that they had lost control over the management of their lesbian or gay identities and that they would be isolated and vulnerable because of a lack of legal protection.

The dishonesty and secrecy that they believed was necessary to protect

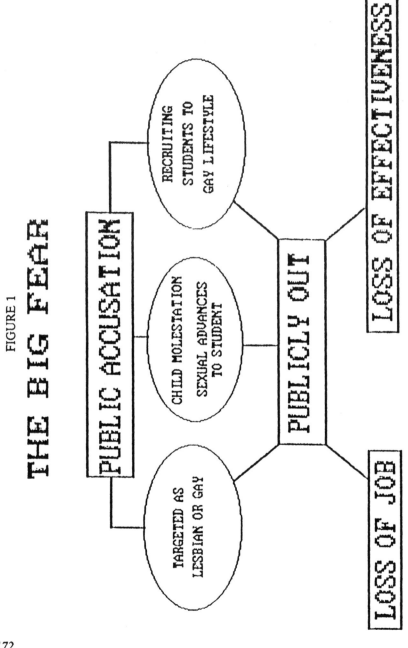

FIGURE 1

THE BIG FEAR

PUBLIC ACCUSATION

- TARGETED AS LESBIAN OR GAY
- CHILD MOLESTATION SEXUAL ADVANCES TO STUDENT
- RECRUITING STUDENTS TO GAY LIFESTYLE

PUBLICLY OUT

LOSS OF JOB

LOSS OF EFFECTIVENESS

their gay and lesbian identities was uncomfortable for them. Working silently in the shadow of gay and lesbian stereotypes held by students and colleagues made some participants feel ashamed of their fear of speaking out. This self-betrayal for the sake of safety felt like selling-out their integrity. All participants wished to integrate their gay or lesbian identities with their professional identities to end the constant sense of division. There was, however, a wide range of belief about how realistic this wish for integration was. Some participants envisioned a day when they would be publicly out in school. Others believed they would never be able to be open about who they were with more than a few trusted colleagues or former students.

This tension between fear of public accusation and the wish for self-integrity and integration of their lesbian/gay and educator identities was an underlying factor in every situation in which participants had to make choices about how much of their identities to reveal. The conflict between concealing and revealing their lesbian or gay identities was as much a part of every school day as were lesson plans and faculty meetings.

Generalized Protection Strategies

The participants described several strategies they used to prevent colleagues and students from knowing that they were gay or lesbian and to minimize the damage if this information was revealed publicly. These protection strategies can be clustered into four groups: (a) reputation, (b) preparation, (c) regulation, and (d) separation.

Reputation. Participants hoped to limit the negative effects of being publicly accused of being lesbian or gay, should that ever happen, by establishing several kinds of protective reputations. All participants sought to establish themselves as "super teachers": totally competent, above reproach, and conscientious about their professional responsibilities.

Some participants attempted to establish reputations as well-liked and accommodating colleagues, while others tried to establish a reputation as someone "not to mess with." These participants believed that being known as someone who fights back and who would not "go quietly into the night," discouraged the school administration, teachers, or students from ever challenging their fitness to teach because of their lesbian or gay identity.

One participant believed that, because he had established a reputation in school as an activist on a number of social issues over the years (racism, anti-war movement, sexism), when he spoke out about AIDS education or homophobia, his concern was perceived by colleagues as just another of his "liberal causes," and thus reduced his risk. Finally, seniority and tenure were perceived by the participants as other ways to develop a reputation in school that might protect them in the event that they were publicly accused of being lesbian or gay.

Preparation. Another group of strategies involved careful advanced planning on how to respond to direct confrontation or generalized homophobic remarks made by students or colleagues. Some participants actually rehearsed their responses to accusations about being lesbian or gay so that they would be prepared for this dreaded event. Other participants talked about deliberately developing the ability to maintain a cool and unruffled external appearance even when they were terrified.

Participants who chose either to disclose their lesbian or gay identities to someone in school or to initiate a discussion about homophobia among students or colleagues did so after careful planning and preparation. They considered all the possible consequences, checked out all procedural details, and arranged "escape routes" if their plans went awry.

Regulation. Participants also protected themselves by regulating how much information about themselves they allowed to become known in school. This required constant vigilance. Decisions about clothing, informal interactions with students, personal sharing with colleagues, and speaking out about homophobic name-calling or jokes were all carefully regulated in an attempt to maintain control over who might know or suspect a participant's lesbian or gay identity. Participants described this regulation as "wearing a mask," and "keeping my guard up." In addition to careful decision-making about what information to share with whom, participants also constantly monitored others' reactions to detect any sign of hostility or disapproval.

Separation. All participants were aware of maintaining a strict separation between their personal (lesbian/gay) identity and their professional (educator) identity. Participants described this separation as "living in two worlds," "being schizophrenic," and "putting up walls." Two participants actually went by separate names in their personal and professional lives: "In school I think of myself as Mrs. Marcel, out of school I'm Rhea." Another participant consciously sought to create a separation between himself and his students by establishing a reputation as a hardnosed disciplinarian.

In addition to creating a psychological and social distance between their personal and professional lives, some teachers intentionally chose to live out of the school district in which they worked. This physical distancing minimized the chance that information about their personal lives would become known to the school community.

Some participants worked so hard at creating a separation between their lesbian or gay identities and their educator identities that they found it initially difficult to talk about their experiences.

> Until this interview, I never thought of myself as a gay educator, just a teacher who happens to be gay.

* * *

> It's hard to think of being gay and being a teacher together. I work to separate them so.

To summarize, participants used these four general protection strategies daily to maintain control over disclosure of their gay or lesbian identities. The function of these was to create a sense of safety in a work environment where they believed that public disclosure of their identities would result in either loss of job or loss of credibility.

Safety-Making or Risk-Taking

Safety-making and risk-taking represent the choice between maintaining secrecy or risk revealing their lesbian or gay identities. For all participants, protecting themselves and maintaining secrecy was their reflexive response. In considering risk-taking, participants balanced potential benefits and importance to themselves and others against the potential negative consequences of taking a risk in each particular situation. Other factors considered were their own sense of confidence and well-being on a particular day, their relationship with the people in the situation, the location where an incident occurred, and the public or private setting of the situation. In general, participants were more inclined to take risks (a) in their own classrooms or offices where they felt more in control, (b) with trusted colleagues, especially those who expressed intolerance for other kinds of prejudice, (c) in private settings, or (d) with students struggling with their own sexual orientation who sought participants out in private. All decisions to take a risk were accompanied by fear. Safety-making decisions were often accompanied by a sense of self-betrayal. Safety-making and risk-taking decisions can be further divided into direct and indirect acts.

Direct Disclosure or Concealment

In managing their gay or lesbian identities in school, participants described strategies that clustered into four categories: (a) passing, (b) covering, (c) being implicitly out, and (d) being explicitly out. Participants thought of these categories of identity management as a continuum: Passing was the safest strategy and being explicitly out involved the most risk (see Figure 2).

Passing. Passing strategies were used to lead others to believe that the participant was heterosexual. Passing strategies were active or passive. Active passing strategies included making up stories about a romantic partner of the other sex, changing the name or pronoun references to a partner when talking about weekend activities, or attending school functions with a date of the other sex. One passive passing strategy used was to allow others to assume the participant was heterosexual because he or she was formerly married or had children. Even for participants who had never been married or did not have children, the heterosexual assumption was so prevalent among colleagues and students that it was relatively easy to pass without actively promoting a heterosexual image. The problem with passing, however, was that participants who used this strategy felt dishonest and, in some cases cowardly, because they were not doing more to challenge lesbian and gay stereotypes and were not being true to themselves.

Covering. When covering, the participants were not trying to lead others to believe that they were heterosexual. Instead, they were trying to prevent others from seeing them as gay or lesbian. Though the difference between passing and covering might appear to be negligible, participants perceived covering to be different from passing because they were no longer lying or intentionally deceiving colleagues and students. Rather, they were omitting information or censoring what they shared, not to pretend to be heterosexual, but to keep others from knowing that they were lesbian or gay. This distinction was important to the participants because it felt more honest and allowed a greater sense of integrity. As one lesbian participant stated, "I never make up stories about men. I just don't tell everything. There are omissions."

Covering strategies included omitting gendered pronouns when talking about a lover: "I avoid personal pronouns. I use 'my friend,' 'my special friend,' or 'my relationship.' I avoid 'he or she.'" Covering also included attending all obligatory school social events solo, avoiding all other events, avoiding local gay-identified social events and places, and carefully monitoring not only such in-school behavior as clothes selection and mannerisms, but also out-of-school public behavior when with a partner.

Being Implicitly Out. This group of strategies involved honest sharing about one's personal life and intimate relationships without actually labeling one's self as gay or lesbian. Participants who were implicitly out to others did not lie or cover. Instead, they talked openly about themselves

FIGURE 2

LESBIAN AND GAY EDUCATORS
IDENTITY MANAGEMENT STRATEGIES

	TOTALLY CLOSETED	PASSING	COVERING	IMPLICITLY OUT	EXPLICITLY OUT	PUBLICLY OUT
OUT TO NO ONE AT SCHOOL		Lying	Censoring	Telling Truth w/o Gay/Lesbian Labels	Affirming Lesbian/Gay Identity	OUT TO SCHOOL COMMUNITY
		I assume you don't know	I assume you don't know	I assume you know, but I'm not sure.	I know you know. You know I know you know.	
		See me as Heterosexual	Don't see me Lesbian/Gay	You can see me as Lesbian/Gay if you want to	See me as Lesbian/Gay	

SEPARATION — FEAR — SELF-INTEGRITY — INTEGRATION

PERSONAL/PROFESSIONAL SELF

177

and their relationships and let others make whatever sense of this information they chose to.

> I never lie about my identity, but I'm never explicit either. There are no pretenses now. It's just the unspoken word.

*   *   *

> I'm pretty much myself. I just don't put a gay label on it.

The key distinction between being implicitly out and being explicitly out was that when participants were implicitly out, labels were never used and their gay or lesbian identity was never confirmed. Participants who were implicitly out to people at school assumed that their identity was known, but they were never sure.

> I'm acknowledging what I think everyone knows anyway. I'm not sure what everyone knows. It's sort of understood.

Being implicitly out included inviting selected colleagues to dinner in the home shared with a partner, talking about a partner by name in school, using the appropriate gendered pronoun when talking about a partner, and telling colleagues about plans to spent a vacation with a same-sex friend at a well-known gay-identified resort. Some participants were more aggressively implicit about their identity. By wearing lesbian/gay-identified symbols (one earring, lavender clothes, a labrys necklace, or a pink triangle pin), these participants believed they were making a statement about their identity without directly labeling themselves.

Participants identified two benefits of living in this "glass closet." One, they were able to maintain some degree of safety because their identities had not been directly disclosed so they could return to covering and passing if they thought it was necessary. Two, they felt a greater sense of self-integrity because they were not lying or censoring information about themselves. This blend of safety and honesty allowed participants a more satisfying resolution to the conflict between their fear of accusation and their wish for greater self-integrity and integration than either passing or covering did.

Being Explicitly Out. Being explicitly out meant directly disclosing their gay or lesbian identities to selected people at school. This strategy was perceived by participants as the highest risk because, unlike being implicitly out, there could be no retreat to covering or passing once their gay or lesbian identity was directly disclosed.

Participants who chose to be explicitly out did so with a small number of carefully selected colleagues who they anticipated would be trustworthy and accepting. These colleagues included heterosexuals as well as other gay men or lesbians in their schools. At the time of the interviews only two participants were explicitly out to a student, though several were explicitly out to a small number of former students.

Being explicitly out was perceived by participants to be the management strategy that afforded the most self-integrity. Their personal and professional identities could be integrated and the need for secrecy and dishonesty among those with whom they were explicitly out was eliminated.

During the first interview, none of the participants was publicly out at school, although some envisioned and were working towards a day when that might be possible. Not all participants, however, believed that being publicly out was worth the risk of losing either their jobs or their credibility with colleagues and students.

> People wouldn't be able to see beyond my lesbian identity to see me as a good teacher.

* * *

> Dealing with the prejudice and fear would really change teaching for me. It would take too long to rebuild my credibility.

The range of identity management strategies used by participants was quite wide. While a few participants primarily used passing and covering, others believed they were implicitly out to most of their colleagues. Most participants were explicitly out to one or two colleagues at school. In addition, most participants also used more than one management strategy, and sometimes three or four, with different people during the school day. Consequently, these gay and lesbian educators were working within a complicated and everchanging web of different relationships with their colleagues and students that required their constant and careful attention. Since participants perceived the stakes to be high (they could lose their jobs and reputation), choosing the appropriate management strategies was an exhausting and stressful process. All participants talked about the tremendous energy they expended daily in managing their identities.

Inferred Disclosure

There were other ways in which participants believed that they could risk disclosure of their gay or lesbian identities besides directly revealing information about their personal lives. By taking certain actions in school, participants believed that speculation about their sexual orientation among colleagues, students, or parents would increase. These actions are grouped into three categories of potential inferred disclosure: (a) interactional, (b) curricular, and (c) professional.

Interactional. These actions were interpersonal encounters during the school day when participants were faced with the choice of speaking out or not about topics they perceived to be gay-related. They believed that, if they did speak out, others would begin to assume, or at least wonder, if they were lesbian or gay. These interactional inferred disclosures included objecting to gay jokes or homophobic slurs among students or colleagues, discussing with colleagues the need for AIDS education in school, touching same-sex students, speaking out about discrimination against lesbians and gays, and talking to gay or lesbian students who approached the participants for counseling. When confronted with situations when any of these or similar interactional responses were appropriate, participants sometimes chose the safety-making response which was to ignore the situation and say nothing. At other times, they chose the risk-making response which was to speak out.

Curricular. Curricular actions were those the participants took to introduce to either students or colleagues planned educational interventions they thought could be associated with homosexuality. Such curricular actions included teaching classroom lessons on homophobia, sex stereotyping, lesbian/gay writers, or women's studies. Other curricular actions that participants believed risked inferred disclosure included providing resources about homophobia, homosexuality, or AIDS to either students or colleagues. Participants also believed that proposing staff development programs on homophobia or AIDS education, as well as recommending books on gay-related topics for the school library or including gay-related books in the classroom library, would infer that they were lesbian or gay.

Professional. The third type of inferred disclosure discussed by the participants included two categories. The first category was taking some kind of out-of-the-classroom, professionally-related action that increased one's visibility in the school system and consequently provided an increased risk of disclosure, such as filing a sex discrimination suit against the school administrators or running for an office in the state teacher's union. The second category of inferred professional disclosure involved having a professional role that defied traditional gender roles and that might be associated with a gay or lesbian stereotype. Participants believed that being in such a role made them more vulnerable to speculation about their sexual orientation than other gay or lesbian educators might be. Among the women, these roles included a principal, a shop teacher, and a physical education teacher. For the male participants the roles were school librarian and preschool or elementary teacher.

One or two participants consistently took interactional, curricular, and professional risks, while most others chose one or two areas in which to focus their risk-taking. Decisions to avoid risks and opt for safety-making responses were painful. There were occasions for all participants, however, when silence, omission, and the need to blend in were chosen as the most prudent courses of action.

The participants' decisions about directly disclosing or inferring disclosure of their gay and lesbian identities reflect the underlying tension they experienced between the fear of public accusation and their wish for greater self-integrity and integration. This tension resulted in an apparent contradiction in how the participants made sense of the importance of claiming their identity as gay and lesbian educators.

Being Gay Is Incidental
vs. Being Gay Is Special

At some time during the interview, nine of the thirteen participants claimed that being gay or lesbian had nothing to do with their abilities as an educator.

Being a lesbian has nothing to do with being a good teacher. It's no one's business.

* * *

I never really think of myself as different from a straight person, really. I don't think of myself as a lesbian educator.

* * *

I don't think of myself as a gay teacher. I'm just a teacher who happens to be gay.

Their stories, however, revealed ways in which being gay or lesbian did make a difference. Unlike heterosexual colleagues who could choose to share family stories and talk about spouses, the educators in this study carefully controlled all personal information fearing public condemnation or loss of employment.

During a group meeting, participants talked about this apparent contradiction. Prior to the interviews, talking about being a gay or lesbian educator in any depth was unexplored territory for most of the participants. Their lives were compartmentalized into a private life among a circle of trusted friends and a professional life of carefully managed relationships in an overwhelmingly heterosexual environment. Their insistence that being lesbian or gay had nothing to do with being a good educator was a defensive and protective response to the social stigma attached to lesbian and gay people who work with young people. In a society that does not easily accept difference, particularly differences in sexuality, these educators chose to claim that lesbian and gay teachers are no different from heterosexual teachers.

At the same time, these educators believed that the damaging stereotypes about lesbians and gays who work with children had nothing to do with them. They worked diligently to establish themselves as competent and caring professionals who were able to operate effectively in their schools. In this sense, their gay or lesbian identity did not have anything to do with their ability to teach.

Though most of the participants claimed that being lesbian or gay had nothing to do with being an effective educator, all of them talked about how being lesbian or gay provided them with a special perspective. Participants talked about this special perspective toward the end of the interviews when they had, perhaps, moved beyond their public, protective voices. At this level of reflection, participants were able to express their private belief in the value of having gay and lesbian educators in schools without the reflexive defensiveness they had developed to protect themselves.

The special perspective the participants believed they brought to their work grew out of their experience as members of a stigmatized minority group. They believed that their appreciation of what it is like to be marginalized and judged harshly gave them a special sensitivity to differences among students and an awareness of how it feels to be treated like an outsider. This sensitivity was not limited to understanding the experiences of lesbian and gay students, but was generalized to any students who were stigmatized or ostracized in school. Several participants described having a "special mission" or "hidden agenda" in addition to their academic responsibilities. This agenda was not, as anti-gay groups claim, to recruit or molest children. Rather, participants believed that their personal sensitivity to prejudice and intolerance enabled them both to identify with students who were "outcasts" in school and to help other students learn to accept difference rather than fear and ridicule it.

I am sensitive to difference. I know what it's like being on the outside being black and gay. Being unloved creates a capacity to be
loving and caring. I wouldn't even be a pre-school teacher if I was
heterosexual. I'd be socialized out of it.

*   *   *

I'm a better person because I had to work so hard to accept myself. I
have more to offer than subject matter expertise. I can be there for
special ed. kids, acting out kids. I've got room in my heart and
compassion because of my experience as a lesbian.

*   *   *

I have a different perspective. I use my gay energy and creativity in
school. I have a sense of being special. I can identify with people
who feel different. I'm socially concerned. I have a different
agenda, more broad.

The stories the participants shared during these interviews present a
picture of a professional life filled with daily decisions about how much of
one's self to reveal or conceal, driven by an underlying tension between a
fear of accusation and a quest for integrity and integration. In addition to
describing the experiences of the participants, a second purpose of this
study was empowerment through a process of collection reflection and
action. The individual interviews were the beginning of this empowerment process.

THE EMPOWERMENT PROCESS

A three-part definition of empowerment served as the criteria for assessing the success of the project in empowering participants. We wanted
to engender positive feelings about self- and group-identity as gay and
lesbian educators. We also hoped participants would develop a better understanding of themselves as lesbian and gay educators in a heterosexist
society. Finally, we wanted to create an opportunity for gay and lesbian
educators to take action to change their situation, to gain more control
over their work lives. Because empowerment was a goal, participants'
reactions and changes in perception during each phase of the project were
documented.

Doing the Individual Interview

The interview process provided most participants with their first opportunity to reflect on and describe their perceptions and experiences as gay or lesbian educators. Participants described the process as both exhausting and exhilarating. One teacher spoke of the interview as simultaneously "liberating and terrifying." Because they spent so much time separating their personal and professional identities, some group members were initially at a loss about how to talk about these identities as integrated parts of themselves. During the interview one participant responded, "Before joining this group, I never thought of myself as a gay teacher." Another participant said, "Being asked about being a gay educator took a few minutes to compute because I split them so. I had to take off the mask."

In expressing thoughts about themselves and their work, participants experienced an unfamiliar sense of validation: "My experience was important enough to listen to for an hour and a half." One participant talked about how the interview "stirred up" things for him and expressed his frustration with having no one to talk to about these feelings until our next group meeting. The insights participants gained during the interview were elaborated in the next phase of the project: reviewing interviews.

Reading the Interview Transcript and Listening to the Audio-Tape

The participants' reaction to reading and listening to their own words was unexpectedly powerful. In a symbolic way, the transcripts and tapes made their hidden experiences as lesbian and gay educators more visible and more credible, even to themselves:

> Being the center of attention was very affirming. It was stunning to hear my own voice, my passion. I wanted to be interviewed again and again.

*   *   *

> What I have to say is important. I never felt that before.

*   *   *

> It was one of the most meaningful experiences of my life. I felt like a star! I went through the full range of emotions: I laughed, I cried, I applauded. I even said out loud to myself, "You're so gay."

Reviewing the transcripts was a catalyst for changes in how participants thought about themselves as lesbian and gay educators. Some participants described feeling like different people listening to themselves. Others were surprised by contradictions they heard in their interviews:

> In the interview I kept saying that being a lesbian doesn't matter, but when I listened to the tape, it does matter. I've spent so much time building walls to keep from getting hurt, I wasn't aware. It's powerful.

*   *   *

> I was amazed at my defense mechanisms. They're so much a part of me I don't even know they're there.

*   *   *

> I'm furious at what I've given up!

*   *   *

> There were "ah ha's!" Things I never thought about before, that I didn't know I knew.

*   *   *

> I shared the tape and transcript with my partner. It's the first time he really understood what teaching's like for me.

Constructing Profiles

To maintain consistency with our empowerment goals, each participant constructed her or his own profile. This process provided participants with a more in-depth opportunity to individually reflect on their experiences as they read their transcripts and chose what portions to use. Having each participant write her or his own profile also enabled everyone to have control over how their experience was presented to the group. Because participants experienced so much separation between their gay/lesbian and educator identities, they wrote profiles in the first person to encourage integration of personal and professional selves.

Participants reported that this process stimulated changes in how they thought about themselves as lesbian and gay educators. Therefore, some participants found it difficult to stick with their interview transcripts in constructing their profiles. They felt compelled to make additions based on this new personal knowledge so that the profile would accurately reflect their changed self-perceptions.

Sharing Profiles and Identifying Themes of Experience

The profile sharing and the search for themes of experience were collaborative processes in which everyone played an equal role. Participants' reactions revealed that this was the most powerful part of the project so far. Several participants initially were nervous about sharing thoughts they had kept secret, even from themselves in some cases. As one participant said, "It wasn't as bad as having sex the first time, but at least then there weren't 14 people watching!"

This sharing, however, was an essential part of the empowerment process. The profile sharing was described by one participant as a "public witnessing" of our experiences. The isolation gay and lesbian educators feel in school made the opportunity to share with others especially compelling. As a result of this process we developed a strong sense of group identification. Everyone was intently interested in everyone else's profile, and we recognized many similarities in our stories. Participants were no longer isolated and guarded as many of us are in school or even among lesbian or gay friends who do not teach. We were among colleagues who understood and shared each other's experiences. We laughed and cried together as we listened to each other's profiles. Some group members were praised by the group for courageous actions they themselves had never acknowledged.

The process of making themselves visible and claiming their experience was both affirming and frightening. After sharing our profiles, some participants felt vulnerable and exposed. However, the opportunity to overcome isolation was a strong motivation to take the risk of sharing:

> I'm usually afraid to open up (about my experiences at school). Sometimes I'm afraid I'm crazy, but I'm ok. It felt so good to be heard, I just went home and cried.

> *   *   *

> I'm not alone. I'm going to call someone in the group the next time something happens in school and I don't know what to do.

> *   *   *

> I feel scared and excited by what we'll do with all this. I'm afraid it will get back to my school.

> *   *   *

Sharing who I am meant a lot. I've never shared this information before. I loved hearing everyone's stories.

Going Back to School Between Monthly Meetings

Participants described a variety of reactions to returning to school between our monthly meetings. For some participants feelings of isolation were heightened after spending time feeling safe and supported in our group meetings. One teacher reported feeling depressed and angry: "I recognized a smoldering kernel of anger in me." Other participants talked about feeling exhilarated and affirmed by the group meetings and carried this feeling back to their schools. This sense of "the group being right behind me in school," as one teacher described it, encouraged some participants to take new risks. These participants reported such actions as coming out to colleagues, challenging an inservice workshop leader to include lesbian and gay youth in a discussion of teen suicide, talking to colleagues about a partner without changing pronouns, inviting some heterosexual colleagues to dinner without "dedyking" the apartment (hiding books, pictures, and other clues to her sexual orientation), and confronting homophobic comments more directly.

Planning and Carrying Out
Our Collective Action

The group identified two collective actions. The first action was to march as an identified group of gay and lesbian educators in a local lesbian and gay pride march. The second action was to start an organization for gay, lesbian, and bisexual educators in Western Massachusetts. Interest in starting an organization was motivated by two factors: Participants wanted to continue the support and growth experienced during the study and they wanted to share this support with other gay, lesbian, and bisexual educators.

The first priority in planning the march was to find a way for everyone to feel safe participating. Marching together as gay and lesbian educators was a highly visible action in the local community. Each participant had to consider the possibility of being seen by colleagues, students, or parents. Some group members had never marched in a lesbian and gay pride parade, while others had marched, but had not identified themselves as educators. The group decided to support each individual's decision about how identifiable she or he wanted to be. Some participants planned to wear masks or bags on their heads or hats and sunglasses to protect their identities, while others decided not to wear any disguise. Using yellow fabric, the group made a "school bus" to march in. This physical barrier provided an extra measure of security for some participants who were worried about someone trying to take their masks off. We made a large banner that said, "Gay and Lesbian Educators," and we painted posters with such slogans as, "Gay Teachers Are Good Teachers," "Gay Teacher and Proud," and "I'm Your Fourth Grade Teacher." Also, we wrote up a flyer to hand out to spectators describing our group and why we were marching.

In anticipating the march, participants shared their excitement and their fears:

> I don't want to be in disguise. I want to say, "so what?", but it's too risky. I don't have tenure.

> * * *

> I'm not going to march as myself. This is a practical decision. Funding for my program is pivotal next year.

> * * *

> Each year I march as a "supporter" carrying a sign that says, "I support gay and lesbian teachers." I want to march for myself this time.

> * * *

> I wasn't too sure at first about marching, but it's time to be radical. It's time for me to be out there. I've pushed back the fear.

> * * *

> Though I feel really visible in the community, I feel ok about this plan. I feel protected. I can do something I've always wanted to do . . . march in the parade.

All but three group members who had previously scheduled commitments attended the march, and some brought friends, colleagues, or partners to join us. Our banner, posters, and bus attracted a lot of attention among marchers and spectators. Between 25 and 30 people joined us during the march, getting "into" our bus or walking behind the banner. We sang, chanted, and waved our posters. Some people watching the march from the sidewalk cheered for us as we passed. Others just pointed us out to friends and stared. A picture of our banner appeared in the local newspaper the next day, though none of us was recognizable. At our next group meeting we talked about what participating in the march was like. Group members shared several stories:

> It was a wonderful experience. I battled with myself about disguising myself up until the last minute. I decided, "What the hell." I didn't wear one. I saw a boy in the second grade with his mother. She has already requested me as her daughter's teacher next year. She smiled at me.

*   *   *

> I've marched before, but never as a teacher. It felt real scary. I felt supported though. My sweetheart and a friend marched with us. Two people asked if you had to be gay to march with our group.

*   *   *

> I was so high. It was exciting and fun. The march had never felt so celebratory before. I loved singing. I felt so proud of us and so brave about what we were doing together.

*   *   *

> I went through a whole range of emotions. I got more and more nervous as we waited for the march to start. I was terrified when we started out. I was marching right in front of someone supervising an intern at our school who didn't recognize me with my mask. After we got started and people started jumping into our bus, I felt more supported and safe. People said to me, "Are you a teacher? This is so brave of you." It was super. I couldn't have done this without the group.

After the march the group focused on starting a gay, lesbian, and bisexual educators' organization. To introduce other educators to our new organization, we organized a Sunday morning brunch. The 35 people who came were invited primarily through word-of-mouth because we were concerned that publicity about the event would make attendance too risky for most of our lesbian, gay, and bisexual colleagues. We have met monthly since then with attendance ranging from 25 to 40 people. Meetings alternate between a social event one month and an educational program focused on the experience of being lesbian, gay, and bisexual educators the next month. Using primarily word-of-mouth advertising and distribution of flyers at local lesbian and gay events, our mailing list has tripled.

Doing the Group Interview

The group interviews provided participants with the opportunity to reflect back on the 15 months in which we had been involved with the
project and to talk about the changes they experienced over that time.
Participants discussed several changes that can be grouped as follows:
(a) self-perceptions, (b) identification with the group, and (c) actions
taken in school.

Self-Perceptions. Participants talked about feeling more "whole" and
integrated. They were censoring less about their lives and feeling better
about themselves as a result.

> Before we started this group I knew I was an educator, a librarian, a
> gay man, but they never crossed. I never thought of putting them
> together. Now I think of them together more and more. That's been
> the event of the year—becoming a whole person.

*   *   *

> I was always so envious that people had friends at school. The con-
> cept never occurred to me—those parallel lines, your gay life and
> your educator life, they are integrating more and more. I want my
> life together. I'm tired of these split personalities. I'm living my life
> out there now. "Ok, folks, I'm a whole person."

This integration was accompanied with a greater sense of entitlement.
Participants believed that lesbian and gay educators deserved to be treated
with respect, and they talked about beginning to expect that reaction from
their school communities.

The most significant change in self-perception for all participants was
in their fear of being identified as a lesbian or gay educator. Though all
agreed that they still felt fear at school, it was more manageable, less
paralyzing. They felt more in control of their fear and able to act in spite
of it.

> Before last year the fear of being found out was so present. In the
> last year the fear hasn't disappeared, but it doesn't hold me back.
> It's more a part of me. I have more control over it. I'm less con-
> scious of it. Speaking out in the faculty room isn't as much of a risk
> for me anymore. I just do it. My fear used to say, "Stop." It wasn't
> letting me be my whole self. Now it's like a little red flag that goes
> up and stops me sometimes, but it isn't in my way all the time.

*   *   *

I can handle stuff like that (teachers at school knowing he is gay)
better. I'm not feeling so paranoid and so cautious, needing to keep
my cover all the time. I'm feeling more relaxed about it. If people
find out, great. If they don't, who cares? It doesn't seem like that
big a deal.

* * *

I haven't been as self-conscious this year. I conclude from that that
I'm feeling less anxiety and I don't have this internal eye coming out
of my head — looking at me from someone else's point of view to see
how they're reacting to me. I'm just going about my business.

Identification with the Group. Participants developed a strong identification with each other. Together, we celebrated each other's successes
and sympathized with each other's frustrations. Participants felt supported
and used the group as a resource for sharing curriculum information, strategies to address homophobic incidents at school, lists of gay-related library books, and how to safely and effectively counsel lesbian and gay
students.

I really feel like I'm a lot more ok than I was last year. Being a part
of this group I feel like I'm not alone. Before I met all of you, I felt
like the only gay teacher out there.

* * *

I can't believe how many times during the week I'll think of something someone [in the group] said or someone's face. I carry it with
me when I go to school and I know I'm ok.

* * *

The group will always be there. We will change and evolve, but I
know I can call someone up if I need to.

Actions Taken in School. Without exception all participants believed
that they were speaking out more in school about homophobia and being
more open about their lesbian and gay identities. Every action taken was
carefully evaluated to assess the consequences, and most often participants were amazed at the lack of negative responses they received from
colleagues and students. This greater visibility also provided participants
with a means to connect with other gay and lesbian colleagues who had
also been hidden.

My armor is shedding so fast it scares me a little. It's constant coming out. I played mild-mannered Clark Kent — don't do anything to
call attention to myself — for so long. Now, I've worn some pretty
outlandish clothes to school, asked teachers to sign a petition to get
some gay books in the library and no one says anything. I'm ready to
come in with green hair to see if anyone notices.

                          *   *   *

I feel like I've been able to do a lot more talking with people on the
staff to try to get more allies, which has been good. At this point I'm
out to just about everybody on the staff — officially — using the L-
word.

Taking action served as a reality test that helped participants to identify
how their fear of accusation had immobilized them and prevented them
from taking advantage of support that was available in their schools. They
discovered that they could speak out more about homophobia and be explicitly out to more of their colleagues without losing either their jobs or
their credibility among colleagues and students. Participants felt more free
to respond fully and honestly in school rather than censoring anything that
might risk revealing their lesbian or gay identities. Because they had integrated their gay/lesbian and educator identities more fully, they felt less
self-conscious about their sexual orientation as a professional liability.
They felt more entitled to acceptance and more enabled to act from their
emerging integrated sense of identity as gay and lesbian educators.

SUMMARY OF THE EMPOWERMENT PROCESS

We can highlight several ways in which participation in this project was
empowering to group members. The self-knowledge gained through participating in and reacting to interviews and profiles was an important ele-
ment of the empowerment process. Hearing others' profiles also contributed to this increased self-knowledge. These activities helped participants
to elaborate on their self-understanding, to become aware of contradictions in their perceptions, and to better integrate their gay/lesbian and
educator identities.
Participants were able to work toward overcoming invisibility and isolation by deciding to disclose their gay or lesbian identity to more people
at school. One participant has come out publicly to her colleagues and
students. Two others have publicly come out to colleagues. Having allies
at school who "know who I really am and support me," as one participant

said, is an important part of feeling empowered. Moreover, taking the risk of coming out to colleagues was empowering in and of itself. In confronting their fear of self-disclosure and acting in spite of it, participants took more control over their professional lives.

Some participants also took actions to address homophobia in their schools by increasing their challenges to name-calling, anti-gay comments, and AIDS jokes, and by integrating episodes of homophobia education into their classrooms.

Several participants attributed this sense of efficacy to feeling stronger connections with and support from the group. The knowledge that "my experience is not unique and that people like me in other schools share similar experiences" helped participants to strengthen their identification with other gay and lesbian educators. This increased identification empowered them to take more risks in school to confront homophobia.

The consequences of participant empowerment extended beyond their efforts to create a more supportive environment for themselves at school. Several participants expressed the desire to present young people with more accurate images of gay and lesbian people. Furthermore, group discussions reinforced a belief expressed by several participants during the initial interviews: Not only should being gay or lesbian not be grounds for dismissal, it gives one a special and educationally valuable perspective as a teacher. Participants believed that their own experience of being different and overcoming negative social judgments enabled them to be more sensitive to students who do not fit in with their classmates.

To date, no one in the group has had any negative professional repercussions as a result of participation in the project or any of the activities that have grown out of the project. One group member, however, did experience significant personal turmoil. In the interview process and profile sharing he confronted unexplored feelings he had about himself as a gay man and an educator. He was unprepared for the intensity of the angry feelings these activities stimulated, and as a result took a month leave from teaching during the project. In reflecting back on the project now he said, "Knowing now what I do about what this stirred up for me, I don't know if I'd choose to do it again. *And* it was, perhaps, one of the more important experiences of my life. I don't regret participating at all."

DISCUSSION

Though not all of the participants were equally affected by the project, each participant experienced positive changes in her or his self-perceptions and increased connection with a group identity. These internal changes were actualized in the two group projects and in actions taken by participants to address homophobia in their schools.

Based on these internal changes and new behaviors, we believe what this participatory research model was successful in empowering these gay and lesbian educators. Each participant experienced this empowerment differently, however, depending on factors related to their school and community. For example, one teacher worked, lived, and had children attending school in the same small rural district. Additionally, she and her partner, who worked in the same school, had previously been the subject of rumors and anonymous harassment. Not surprisingly, she felt constrained by her situation and was much more cautious about risk-taking than some of the other participants. At the other end of the continuum, another teacher taught in a school district known for its politically liberal perspective in a town that is the only one in the area with a law protecting lesbian and gay employment rights. Though not publicly out, this teacher is used by colleagues as an informal counselor for lesbian and gay students and as a resource on gay or lesbian issues in school. Other contextual factors, such as the general interpersonal climate in the school, whether or not the school attempts to address sexism and racism, or how fair-minded and sensitive the principal is perceived to be, also affected how willing participants were to disclose or risk disclosing their gay or lesbian identities.

Despite differences in school districts, nearly all participants in the project had on-going contact with the fairly large and visible gay and lesbian community in the area. All were involved in lesbian or gay social or political groups or had an informal network of gay and lesbian friends outside of education. The general support provided by these contacts undoubtedly helped to develop the participants' gay or lesbian identities. However, involvement in the local gay community did not necessarily support these participants' identities as educators. For example, one participant said she felt as if she were in a "double closet" because lesbian friends outside of education did not understand why she chose to remain in a work environment requiring such secrecy.

CONCLUSION

The entire educational community has something to gain from the empowerment of gay and lesbian educators. Participants in this study all survived the anti-gay climates of their schools and were effective and dedicated teachers. They found that they could be even more productive if they did not have to expend energy hiding and protecting themselves from the prejudice and ignorance of a homophobic community. In a society committed to social justice, gay and lesbian educators would not be required to sacrifice their sense of self-integrity to remain in their chosen profession. Visible lesbian and gay educators provide colleagues, students, and parents with the opportunity to learn that their fears of and stereotypes about gay and lesbian teachers are not rooted in reality. Perhaps most importantly, young people struggling with their sexual orientation would have more realistic and hopeful expectations about what it means to be gay or lesbian. They would learn that there are gay and lesbian adults, some of whom are respected teachers in their schools, who live happy and productive lives.

REFERENCES

Carr, W., & Kemmis, S. (1986). *Becoming critical: Education, knowledge, and action research*. Philadelphia: Falmer.

Fischer, T. (1983). A study of educators' attitudes toward homosexuality (Doctoral dissertation, University of Virginia, 1982). *Dissertation Abstracts International*, *43* (10), 3294A. (Order No. DA 8228619).

Fogarty, E. (1981). Passing as straight: A phenomenological analysis of the experience of the lesbian who is professionally employed (Doctoral dissertation, University of Pittsburgh, 1980). *Dissertation Abstracts International*, *41* (6), 2384B. (Order No. DDJ 88-28099).

Freire, P. (1970). *Pedagogy of the oppressed*. New York: Seabury.

Griffin, P. (in press). Identity management strategies among lesbian and gay educators. *International Journal of Qualitative Studies in Educaton*, 4(3).

Hall, B. (1975). Participatory Research: An approach for change. *Convergence, 8* (2), 24-31.

Harbeck, K. (1988). Personal freedoms/Public constraints: An analysis of the controversy over the employment of homosexuals as teachers. Vols. I and II (Doctoral dissertation, Stanford University, 1987). *Dissertation Abstracts International 48* (7), 1862A. (Order No. DA 8723009).

Lather, P. (1986). Issues of validity in openly ideological research: Between a rock and a soft place. *Interchange, 17* (4), 63-84.

Mies, M. (1983). Toward a methodology for feminist research. In G. Bowles & R. Duelli-Klein (Eds.), *Theories of women's studies* (pp. 117-139). London: Routledge & Kegan Paul.

Morgan, D. (1988). *Focus groups as qualitative research*. Beverly Hills: Sage.

Moses, A. (1978). Playing it straight: A study of identity management in a sample of lesbian women (Doctoral dissertation, University of California, Berkeley, 1977). *Dissertation Abstracts International*, *39* (2), 1149A. (Order No. 7812461).

Nickeson, S. (1981). A comparison of gay and heterosexual teachers on professional and personal dimensions (Doctoral dissertation, University of Florida,

1980). *Dissertation Abstracts International, 41* (9), 3956A. (Order No. 8105601).

Olson, M. (1986). *From closet to classroom: A perspective on gay and lesbian individuals in U.S. schools*. Available from University of North Dakota Bookstore, Box 8197 University Station, Grand Forks, ND 58202.

Olson, M. (1987). A study of gay and lesbian teachers. *Journal of Homosexuality, 13* (4), 73-81.

Patton, M. (1980). *Qualitative evaluation methods*. Beverly Hills, CA: Sage.

Popkewitz, T. (1984). *Paradigm and ideology in educational research: The social functions of the intellectual*. Philadelphia: Falmer.

Sciullo, A. (1984). Tolls at the closet door: A gay history for teachers (Doctoral dissertation, University of Michigan, 1984). *Dissertation Abstracts International, 45* (2), 497. (Order No. DA 8412076).

Smith, D. (1985). An ethnographic study of homosexual teachers' perspectives (Doctoral dissertation, State University of New York, Albany, 1985). *Dissertation Abstracts International, 46*, 66A. (Order No. DA 8506864).

Woods, S. (1990). The contextual realities of being a lesbian physical education teacher: Living in two worlds. (Doctoral dissertation, University of Massachusetts, Amherst, 1989). *Dissertation Abstracts International, 51* (3). 788. (Order No. ADG 90-22761).

Images of Gays and Lesbians
in Sexuality
and Health Textbooks

Mariamne H. Whatley, PhD

University of Wisconsin-Madison

SUMMARY. Photographs have become a major form of illustration in college level health and sexuality textbooks and may be more memorable than the text itself. Unlike other forms of illustration, photographs are often viewed as objective and unable to "lie." Photographs of individuals from nondominant groups, in addition to being seen as objective representations of reality, are often seen as representing the group to which they belong. To study the representation of nondominant groups in textbooks, it is, therefore, as important to analyze the photographs as the text itself. This paper examines photographs of gay men and lesbians in 14 health and 16 human sexuality college level textbooks. The photographs of individuals present an inaccurate portrait of lesbians and gay men as white, young, and physically-abled. Individual and large group photographs of activism (31% of the total photographs of gay men and lesbians) were positive images that emphasized issues of civil rights. The paper discusses various interpretations of the photographs of gay men and lesbians, subtle homophobia or heterosexism in the texts, and progress that has been made.

Mariamne H. Whatley is Associate Professor with a joint appointment in Women's Studies and the Department of Curriculum and Instruction, University of Wisconsin-Madison. She has written numerous articles on sexuality education, feminist views of science, and women's health. She has co-edited two books: *Women's Health: Readings on Social, Economic, and Political Issues* (with N. Worcester) and *The Ideology of Images in Educational Media* (with E. Ellsworth). Correspondence may be addressed to: Department of Curriculum and Instruction, 225 North Mills Street, Madison, WI 53706.

197

Try to remember a specific famous news story and a news photograph will probably be more quickly recalled than any verbal description. We may see a woman kneeling over a slain Kent State student, men on the balcony pointing towards the assassin of Martin Luther King, Jr., an astronaut landing on the moon's surface. Ask faculty members to examine a new textbook and they will probably flip through the book, looking at the illustrations and reading captions. We are attracted to visual images and are more likely to retain them than the written text, so though it may be difficult for textbook authors to admit, photographs may be more memorable than the text itself.

Photographs have become the major form of illustration in college level health and sexuality texts, replacing other forms of artwork. Photographs may have more impact than drawings because they are seen as objective representations of reality rather than as the artists' constructions (Barthes, 1977). Even though a photograph is as much a construction of the photographer as any other artist's work, there is a "presumption of veracity that gives all photographs authority, interest, seductiveness" (Sontag, 1977, p. 6). The viewer may see the camera as unable to "lie," when, in fact, a photograph may be posed, very carefully selected from hundreds of possible choices at that moment or event, cropped to avoid unwanted elements, or manipulated in many other ways. Rather than recognizing the ways in which a photograph is constructed, readers often believe that the photograph is "true" or "real."

In addition to the objectivity that readers ascribe to photographs, there is an additional weight that photographs seem to carry when they are representing members of a nondominant group. Visual images of individuals belonging to a specific group are often seen as representing that group, especially if there are relatively few such representations (Gilman, 1985). A photograph of a white man, as part of a dominant group in the United States, may be seen as an individual or as a member of a particular subgroup to which he belongs. For example, in a sexuality text, he may be seen as a teenager, a gay man, a transsexual, a father, a person with a spinal cord injury. No generalization is made that transsexuals are all white men or that a white man is likely to have a spinal cord injury, because there is such a diversity of images of white men in the text and in society as a whole. In contrast, however, sexuality texts have so few images of people of color that each carries more weight as being representative of that group. For example, in the sexuality texts I examined in one study, all of the pimps were African-American. The resulting impression is that African-American men are much more likely to be pimps than any other group, whereas a photograph of a white pimp (if one existed in any of these texts) would carry no implications about white men as a group (Whatley, 1988). In the same way, every photograph identified as that of a lesbian or gay man may be taken as representative of gay men or lesbians as a group because there are few such images with little diversity and everyone not *labeled* as gay or lesbian is assumed to be heterosexual.

Photographs can carry connotations, intentional or not, never stated in the text. In spite of the presumed objectivity of photographs, it must be remembered that the selection of photographs is not a neutral process. Just as the selection is a reflection of the author's or editor's agenda, the analysis of these photographs must take into account issues such as audience expectations and dominant meanings in a given cultural/historical context (Whatley, 1988). Because every reader or viewer produces meanings of his or her own, meaning is multiple and is not inherent in the photographic image. There is, therefore, no "correct" or definitive reading or interpretation of textbook photographs. Given a particular historical/political moment, however, it is legitimate to argue for the presence of certain dominant meanings in photographs (Whatley, 1988).

The representation of lesbians and gay men in curricula and texts has not received much attention, though it would seem a logical extension of the many studies on the representation of women and of different ethnic and racial groups. Gary McDonald (1981) investigated introductory psychology textbooks, finding that these failed to address the needs and rights of gays, while perpetuating societal stereotypes. Sex education materials were examined by Whitlock and Dilapi (1983), who found a lack of both inclusion and integration of information about homosexuality, as well as finding homophobia in both blatant and subtle forms. Their paper provides useful guidelines for evaluating texts for homophobia. In extending the examination of homophobia in texts to visual images, Carol Pollis (1986) analyzed the sensitive drawings (line drawings of sexual positions) in human sexuality texts, including the categories of sexual preference, race, class, and age. Her work did not extend to photographs, which, as argued above, provide an important area that needs to be addressed if we are to obtain a complete "picture" of the representation of gay men and lesbians. My purpose in this paper is to provide an analysis that will fill in the gap in this area of study.

I examined photographic images of gay men and lesbians in college level health and sexuality textbooks to determine if there are patterns in the representations that may carry subtle meanings. In previous work I analyzed the ways in which well-intended anti-racist messages in the text may actually be subverted by the images presented (Whatley, 1988). In that paper I argued that an individual photograph that may be taken as neutral or even positive in its representation of African-Americans must be seen in terms of an overall pattern of photographs, including and even emphasizing the gaps and absences. The photograph, in addition, must be seen in terms of its placement in the text, its relationship to chapter titles and captions, as well as to the text itself. By looking for patterns, rather than focusing entirely on the individual image, I identified several themes, including those of "dangerous sexuality" and of Blacks as "exotic." These patterns in turn were placed in the context of the historical moment. For example, the recurring images of African-American men with children could be seen as prescriptive messages when viewed in the context of the blame for economic and social problems placed on the "failure" of the African-American family. In that paper, I attempted to create both a theoretical framework and a methodology for examining the representation of other nondominant groups, which will be used in this paper.

TEXTBOOKS AND PHOTOGRAPHS

Critics have long recognized that textbooks are not objective and factual but are social products with their content open to critical examination. Publishing in the United States is generally controlled by the dominant group—white men, apparently heterosexual—so it is tempting to view the publishing industry as a monolithic machine for reproducing dominant ideologies. However, editors are more interested in high profit margins and financial capital than in imposing an educational agenda (Apple, 1985; Coser, Kadushin, & Powell, 1982). Generally, in the United States, the market for college textbooks, comprised primarily of college professors, would not permit overt sexism or racism. Heterosexism, however, has not received as much attention and is less likely to be seen as a violation of the academic liberal stance. While overt homophobia would probably not be tolerated in textbooks, many forms of subtler homophobia go unnoticed and heterosexism remains unchallenged. In addition, as the authors above have noted, editors from most publishing houses tend to be liberal. They, therefore, would seem unlikely to allow blatantly homophobic texts, but may not be aware of the subtler forms homophobia can assume.

While textbooks are not produced by a conspiracy of dominant groups, the textbook does represent knowledge in part determined by interactions of ideology and economics. The editors often end up maintaining a delicate balance: they will not tolerate overt homophobia but they will be careful not to incur the wrath of conservative groups which oppose the presentation of homosexuality as a viable lifestyle. With increasing attacks by the New Right and the Religious Right on sexuality education, sexuality texts are coming under more intense scrutiny. The topics most likely to lead to negative reactions are abortion and homosexuality. The protective stance of editors, as with many school administrators and classroom teachers, is to minimize controversy by assuming a "balanced" or "neutral" position which presents the basic facts, research, legal and religious issues. There may, in addition, be special features in textbooks designed to stimulate thought and possibly discussion; for example, there may be a "What do you think?" section dealing with gay marriage.

It is interesting to examine textbook photographs to investigate in what ways they may reinforce or undermine this "balanced" position. Generally, textbook authors do not select specific photographs, but may give publishers general descriptions of the types of photographs they wish to have included (e.g., gay or lesbian couple, gay pride march). New photographs are rarely taken specifically for a text because of the great expense and time. Instead photo researchers are hired to find appropriate photographs, drawing on already existing collections. The result is that the choice of photographs depends on what is already available and is therefore partly determined by previous demand. Because the same sources of photographs are often used, identical photographs may appear in competing books. Therefore, although authors may have ideal visions of what the illustrations might look like, the reality may be very limiting. In addition, editors may overrule authors' decisions based on what they think may sell or what may be too "offensive" or controversial (Whatley, 1990).

ANALYSIS OF PHOTOGRAPHS

I selected 14 college level health textbooks and 16 human sexuality textbooks, all published from 1982 through 1989 (References to these texts appear in the Appendix). In several cases, I examined two editions of the same textbook to note any changes. The selection was a convenience sample, but the bestselling textbooks in both categories were included. I examined all the photographs in chapters that focused on sexual preference in the sexuality textbooks and all the photographs from chapters on sexuality in the health textbooks. I then scanned all the photographs in the texts looking for same-sex couples and other possible markers of homosexuality. In addition, I checked the index in each text for all references to homosexuality to find any additional photographs. I recorded a description of each photograph that either was identified as, or appeared to be, a representation of gay men or lesbians. The description included setting, activity, age, and race whenever possible.

Most of the references to and photographs of lesbians and gay men in the health textbooks appeared in chapters on sexuality. In the sexuality texts, almost all these photographs were in chapters that focused primarily on homosexuality and bisexuality, with such titles as "Sexual Orientation," "Sexual Preference," "Homosexuality and Bisexuality." Others appeared in chapters that included other sexual "behaviors" and "preferences," such as fetishes, transvestism, prostitution, and sexual violence such as rape and incest. Several additional photographs appeared in the context of discussions of AIDS in chapters on sexually transmitted diseases. By checking the index of each text, it became apparent that homosexuality was isolated as a topic, rather than integrated into more general discussions of sexuality that included heterosexuality as well. For example, even a chapter labeled as "Sexual Preference" did not discuss heterosexuality, perhaps implying that it is a given but not a preference. The isolation of discussions of homosexuality is a clear reflection of heterosexism, but it is preferable to some of the other textbook approaches. For example, one book included homosexuality in a chapter entitled "Sexual Orientations and Affectional Preferences," along with fetishes, zoophilia, pedophilia and necrophilia (Francoeur, 1982).

The purpose of my examination of the photographs was to identify any patterns of representation. I was interested to see if certain images were more common and whether specific groups of lesbians and gay men were either invisible or dominant. There were a total of 70 photographs in the sexuality texts and 15 in the health texts that appeared to represent lesbians or gay men. Five health textbooks had no photographs of lesbians or gay men.

Gender. Excluding group photographs, which I defined as more than four people, there were a total of 62 gay men and 30 lesbians pictured. The health texts showed 8 individual gay men and no lesbians; the rest were large groups. Given the invisibility of lesbians in many representations of homosexuality, particularly in the popular media, this number may seem appropriate. Given the reality of the numbers of lesbians in this country, however, the imbalance creates a biased portrait of the gay and lesbian population. This is an obvious example of sexism in the texts, which may be seen as reflecting sexism in our society. For example, many may view lesbians not as a group in their own right, but merely as the ladies auxiliary of the gay men's movement. In that case, an occasional lesbian in the text would be more than enough. On the other hand, considering that the heterosexual public seems more open and less hostile to lesbians than to gay men, if there is any attempt made in the texts to gain some degree of tolerance, if not acceptance, for homosexuality, then an increased representation of lesbians seems appropriate. The relative underrepresentation of lesbians was also seen in McDonald's (1981) study of introductory psychology texts. Of the 40 texts that referred to homosexuality, only 14 referred to lesbianism. It appears that while lesbians may be more visible in the texts reviewed in this paper, there is still quite a distance to go before equity is reached, and the explanations and political implications of this imbalance deserve further analysis.

Race. There were several obvious absences in these photographs. Of the total of 100 individual lesbians and gay men, again excluding large groups, there were only three identifiable people of color represented. In large crowd scenes, there were more people of color but only those three seen as individuals. Homosexuality is presented in these texts as the province of whites almost exclusively, which makes invisible the many lesbians and gay men of color. There are numerous African-American, Asian-American, Latino and Native American writers and artists who have raised issues about the intersections of heterosexism, sexism, and racism, and these intersections are clearly demonstrated in these texts.

Age and disability. Besides being almost exclusively white, it would appear from these photographs that gay men and lesbians are almost entirely young and physically-abled. There were no individuals represented with any visible physical disability, except several men with AIDS. There was only one photograph that showed anyone who was clearly old. The health text that showed that photograph was one of the few that deghettoized gay and lesbian images and presented a broadened view about sexuality and aging. On one page, there is an old heterosexual couple and, on the opposite page, an old gay couple with the caption, "A homosexual relationship — like any other — can be stable, long-lasting, and affectionate" (Levy, Dignan, & Shirreffs, 1987, p. 193). Besides these two gay men, there were no old gay men or lesbians. Sexuality texts have generally been weak until recently on issues around aging and disability. However, now that those discussions appear in relationship to heterosexuality, it is necessary to expand them to lesbians and gay men as well.

Children. There were three photographs of lesbians with children and three of gay men with children. Given the increasing numbers of both lesbians and gay men who are having children, often through alternative insemination, as well as those who have children from previous heterosexual relationships, this seems an underrepresentation. One way to reduce the homophobic stereotype of the child molester is to emphasize the number of lesbian and gay families with children. Based on the negative response from some students to the idea of lesbian and gay parenting, it is especially important for texts to present positive images that might counter these beliefs and fears.

Group photographs. Of the 32 group photographs of more than four people, there were four that showed stereotyped activities of gay men: two bar scenes, one scene outside a leather bar, one of a bathhouse (with the latter captioned with the information that most bathhouses had been closed in response to AIDS). Of the remaining group photographs, one showed a mixed group of athletes, apparently at the Gay Games, one showed a gay men's choir, and the remainder all showed political demonstrations, rallies, or marches. Given the voyeuristic pleasure that many people may take in glimpses of gay life (bars and bathhouses, of course, as opposed to doing dishes or walking the dog), it was interesting that only a few photographs were likely to reinforce popular negative stereotypes. This move away from sensationalism can be seen as a positive response to gay and lesbian political activism.

Activism. Twenty-six, out of 85 total photographs (31%), both individual and group, showed activism (such as gay pride marches and demonstrations about AIDS) and specific election-related activities (such as Harvey Milk campaigning). This high proportion raises a number of issues. First, these photographs might be so prevalent because they are readily available from news coverage of these events. Unlike many photographs, they clearly show people who can be assumed to be gay or lesbian. This solves the problem of a source of photographs; it is much easier to obtain these than photographs of couples or individuals who are doing something that can presumably identify them as gay or lesbian. The other option for accessible, identifiable photographs, without the problem of permissions from the subjects, is famous people in the news, so that Harvey Milk and Leonard Matlovich, both pictured in these texts, are obvious possibilities. Interestingly, given the ease of that option, there were only seven famous people photographs, four of them in a series in one textbook.

Whether these activism photographs are used merely because they are available or because they were meant to impart certain information, they do carry significant connotations. The captions accompanying many of them emphasize the importance of activism. For example:

Gay activism: Gays have become politically active in the past decade in their attempt to secure basic civil rights. (Allgeier & Allgeier, 1984, p. 4)

* * *

The emergence of gay militancy is often traced to June 28, 1969, when the patrons of the Stonewall, a gay bar on Christopher Street in New York City's Greenwich Village, vigorously resisted a police raid. (Jones, Shainberg, & Byer, 1985, p. 580)

* * *

The yearly celebration of Gay Pride Week is a strong statement of the gay movement in the United States. (Kilmann, 1984, p. 414)

On one hand, this can be viewed as very positive. Instead of portraying gay and lesbian issues as being focused entirely on sexuality, there is a clear message that there are "basic civil rights" and issues of visibility and pride. These photographs show large numbers of men and women together, including people of color; there are also parents, friends, and children of lesbians and gay men showing support. They project a message of unity, pride, and strength (along with a clear sense of humor). Unfortunately, the high proportion of these photographs is an overrepresentation of the proportion of lesbians and gay men who are actually activists. The image is positive but exaggerated. On the negative side, these are exactly the issues that may be frightening to those who are already strongly homophobic. These photographs may symbolize their concern that it is no longer just isolated couples doing unspeakable things in their bedrooms; there are large numbers of "militant" homosexuals marching down Main Street. These are not just sinners whom religious homophobes might be able to forgive; they are asking for rights, not forgiveness. To the potential conservative critics of the liberal textbook approach to homosexuality, these photographs may be the most frightening.

AIDS. In addition to following up index references to homosexuality, I also checked on all references to AIDS. I expected to find additional photographs of gay men under this topic, given that much AIDS education continues to focus inappropriately on so-called "risk groups." With one exception, all the photographs related to AIDS had to do with activism, that is, pictures of demonstrations and marches. This carried out the positive theme of human rights issues discussed earlier. The exception was a health text (Ensor, Means, & Henkel, 1985, p. 409), which presented a photograph of two white men, one apparently very ill, sitting in a wheelchair, holding a birthday cake. The caption read:

> Kenny Ramsauer with his lover, Jim Bridges, at Ramsauer's 1983 (May) birthday party in New York City. Kenny died shortly thereafter from AIDS.

This particular photograph originally appeared in a British tabloid next to a photograph of Kenny Ramsauer when he was healthy. The caption in the paper read: "Handsome Kenny: His bright eyes show no hint of the agony to come" (Gever, 1989, p. 115). This photograph and others like it play no educational role, but are representative of what Simon Watney (1989) refers to as the spectacle of AIDS:

> It is the principal and serious business of this spectacle to ensure that the subject of AIDS is "correctly" identified and that any possibility of positive sympathetic identification *with* actual people with AIDS is entirely expunged from the field of vision. AIDS is thus embodied as an exemplary and admonitory drama, relayed between the image of the miraculous authority of clinical medicine and the faces and bodies of individuals who clearly disclose the stigmata of their guilt. The principal target of this sadistically punitive gaze is the body of "the homosexual." (Watney, 1989, p. 78)

As this quotation suggests, a photograph of a formerly handsome gay man disfigured by AIDS may do less to create sympathy than to reinforce the view that he was ill because he was gay. The "victim" may be seen by many as a "guilty" victim, who got what he deserved for being gay (and handsome).   Fortunately, all other texts avoided the pitfalls of this kind of representation of people with AIDS; instead, there were numerous images of people with AIDS fighting for basic rights.

Other visual images. In the introduction to this paper, I argued that photographs need particularly close examination because of their aura of objectivity. However, there are other forms of visual representation I will discuss briefly. Sexuality texts often have line drawings that are used primarily to illustrate sexual positions and are referred to as sensitive drawings (Pollis, 1986). Pollis had examined the sensitive drawings in 23 college level human sexuality textbooks. Of these texts, only five included drawings of same-sex couples, with all five showing male-male couples and three also showing female-female couples. There were 224 drawings of male-female couples, compared to six male-male and five female-female. Several of the same-sex drawings were not particularly "sensitive," that is, illustrating sexual positions. Two of the male drawings and one of the female drawings, for example, showed couples (from the waist up only) hugging. In the texts I examined, there were only six such drawings of lesbian or gay couples (there was an overlap of five texts with Pollis' sample). As with the photographs, all the individuals appeared to be white, young, and physically-abled. The fact that there were any sensitive drawings of gay men and lesbians can be seen as positive, especially considering the controversy around discussions of homosexuality. Given that many opponents of sexuality education do not even approve of descriptions of sexual activity that is strictly heterosexual, on the basis that it may give young people "ideas" (on the apparent assumption that if educators do not talk about sex, young people would never think of trying it), representations of female-female cunnilingus would seem to be beyond what they would tolerate. One textbook side-stepped the issue by including six line-drawings of monkeys in same-sex encounters (Katchadourian, 1989, p. 366). This could be interpreted as an attempt to counter the homophobic argument that homosexuality is just not natural; however, my view is that it reduces lesbian and gay sexuality to non-human physical encounters.

Another form of illustration that was very commonly used in earlier sexuality textbooks (over ten years ago) was artwork, often European, but also drawing on Greek, Persian, and various Asian cultures. As photographs of "real" people became more common, the artwork was reduced greatly. The purpose this artwork primarily served was as a visual representation of behaviors that might be too difficult to represent otherwise. For example, Japanese erotic prints appeared, as did Persian drawings of gang rape, classical European paintings representing such topics as bestiality, gang rape, voyeurism, and Greek paintings depicting homosexual encounters. Few of these examples remained in the texts I examined for this paper. However, there were three representations of male-male sexual interactions in Greek art, including on a vase and a cup. There was one drawing of Sappho (not involved in a sexual encounter). One painting appeared three times as an image of lesbian sexuality; "Le Sommeil" by Courbet, which shows two women in bed together, must have seemed to be a "safe" visual image of lesbianism. The one contemporary artwork was the statue entitled "Gay Liberation" by George Segal, which shows a gay male couple standing near a lesbian couple seated on a parkbench. This statue was used in one text completely out of any specific gay or lesbian context. The lesbian couple from the statue appeared as the opener for a chapter entitled "Sexual Organs, Anatomy and Care" (Greenberg, Bruess, and Sands, 1986). It is unclear why this particular photograph was used, unidentified by caption, but it could allow for a wide range of reactions from those who recognized it.

CONCLUSION

The major conclusion that can be reached is that gay men and lesbians are becoming visible in textbooks, but are still isolated and ghettoized. Of course, there may be other gay men and lesbians located elsewhere in the text but there would be no way to identify them except by caption, political buttons, or placement in couples. I did search through all the photographs in all the texts but very few gay men or lesbians appeared outside the chapters or sections clearly labeled as relating to homosexuality. There were twice as many gay men as lesbians represented, so the invisibility, but not the reality, of lesbians in our society is reflected in the choices of photographs.

Based on these photographs, the description of gay men and lesbians that would emerge for a reader would be white, young, and physically-abled. This description, however, excludes a large number of gay men and lesbians and compounds homophobia with racism, ageism, and ableism. These are the same groups that are often excluded from other texts, such as health education texts (Whatley, 1990). The relative paucity of lesbians and gay men with children also was an inaccurate portrayal of the community.

The portrayal of lesbians and gay men as activists, fighting for human rights, is a more positive image than I had expected. The potential negative implications are the additional fears it may arouse in the already homophobic or that it might be a way for editors and publishers to side-step the issue of gay and lesbian sexuality. In a sense, these images convey asexual activists, rather than individuals who are both sexual and politically committed. In addition, the high proportion of such photographs is an inaccurate overrepresentation of the activism of gay men and lesbians. It may also appear that these lesbians and gay men are only activists when it comes to specifically gay and lesbian issues. This latter point could be corrected by inclusion of photographs of contingents in marches with banners such as "Gays for Peace in Central America" or "Lesbians for Choice," which could illustrate the slogan "we are everywhere" in a positive way. That may be a minor quibble compared to the fact that these images show unity, diversity, and strength in a way that photographs of individuals do not.

For authors, editors, and publishers who are considering ways to remove subtle forms of homophobia from textbooks, the first step would be the integration of discussions of homosexuality into all discussions of sexuality. One of the important criteria Whitlock and Dilapi (1983) list for evaluating homophobia in texts is whether information on homosexuality is integrated throughout the text or whether it is isolated in a single section. Chapters on relationships, sexuality and ageing, childhood and adolescence, disability, sexually transmitted diseases, sexual violence, sexual preference, should all include heterosexuality, bisexuality, and homosexuality. The photographs should be used in ways that reflect that same integration. There is no reason why a photograph of an old lesbian or gay couple cannot appear in any section on ageing that shows heterosexual couples. In addition, there clearly has to be both an increased representation of lesbians and a much broader range of individuals, particularly in terms of race, age and disability. These absences are not necessarily homophobic, but reinforce other forms of discrimination in our society.

Textbooks that deal with human sexuality have in the past been improved in response to analysis of these texts in terms of sexism and racism. The beginning steps have been made in terms of heterosexism. Attention to the images as well as the text will advance this work even more.

REFERENCES

Apple, M. W. (1985). The culture and commerce of the textbook. *Journal of Curriculum Studies, 17*(2), 147-162.

Barthes, R. (1977). *Image-Music-Text.* (Heath, S., trans.). New York: Hill and Wang.

Coser, L. A., Kadushin, C., & Powell, W. W. (1982). *Books: The culture and commerce of publishing.* New York: Basic Books.

Gever, M. (1989). Pictures of sickness: Stuart Marshall's *Bright Eyes.* In D. Crimp (Ed.), *AIDS: Cultural analysis, cultural activism* (pp.109-126). Cambridge, MA: MIT Press.

Gilman, S.L. (1985). Black bodies, white bodies: Toward an iconography of female sexuality in late nineteenth-century art, medicine, and literature. *Critical Inquiry, 12*, 204-242.

McDonald, G. (1981). Misrepresentation, liberalism,and heterosexual bias in introductory psychology textbooks. *Journal of Homosexuality, 6*(3), 45-60.

Pollis, C.A. (1986). Sensitive drawings of sexual activity in human sexuality textbooks: An analysis on communication and bias. *Journal of Homosexuality, 13*(1), 59-73.

Sontag, S. (1977). *On photography.* New York: Farrar, Straus and Giroux.

Watney, S. (1989). The spectacle of AIDS. In D. Crimp (Ed.), *AIDS: Cultural analysis, cultural activism* (pp.71-86). Cambridge, MA: MIT Press.

Whatley, M.H. (1988). Photographic images of Blacks in sexuality texts. *Curriculum Inquiry, 18*(2), 137-155.

Whatley, M.H. (1990). The picture of health: How textbook photographs construct health. In E. Ellsworth & M.H. Whatley (Eds.), *The ideology of images in educational media: Hidden curriculums in the classroom* (pp.121-140). New York: Teachers College Press.

Whitlock, K., & DiLapi, E.M. (1983). "Friendly fire": Homophobia in sex education literature. *Interracial Books for Children BULLETIN, 14*(3,4), 20-23.

APPENDIX:
TEXTBOOKS EXAMINED

Sexuality textbooks:

Allgeier, E. R., & Allgeier, A. R. (1984). *Sexual Interactions.* Lexington, MA: D. C. Heath.

Byer, C. O., Shainberg, L. W., & Jones, K. L. (1988). *Dimensions of human sexuality* (2nd ed.). Dubuque, IA: Wm. C. Brown.

Crooks, R. & Baur, K. (1987). *Our sexuality* (3rd ed.). Menlo Park, CA: Benjamin/Cummings.

Denney, N. W., & Quadagno, D. (1988). *Human Sexuality.* St. Louis: Times Mirror/Mosby.

Francoeur, R. T. (1982). *Becoming a sexual person.* New York: John Wiley & Sons.

Greenberg, J. S., Bruess, C. E., & Sands, D. W. (1986). *Sexuality: Insights and issues.* Dubuque, IA: Wm. C. Brown.

Hyde, J. S. (1990). *Understanding human sexuality* (4th ed.). New York: McGraw-Hill.

Jones, K. L., Shainberg, L. W., & Byer, C. O. (1985). *Dimensions of human sexuality.* Dubuque, IA: Wm. C. Brown.

Katchadourian, H. (1989). *Fundamentals of human sexuality* (5th ed.). Fort Worth: Holt, Rinehart and Winston.

Kilmann, P. R. (1984). *Human sexuality in contemporary life.* Boston: Allyn & Bacon.

Maier, R. A. (1984). *Human sexuality in perspective.* Chicago: Nelson-Hall.

Masters, W. H., Johnson, V. E., & Kolodny, R. C. (1985). *Human sexuality* (2nd ed.). Boston: Little, Brown, & Co.

McCary, S. P., & McCary, J. L. (1984). *Human sexuality* (3rd brief ed.). Belmont, CA: Wadsworth.

Nass, G. D., & Fisher, M. P. (1988). *Sexuality today*. Boston: Jones & Bartlett.

Nass, G. D., Libby, R. W., & Fisher, M. P. (1984). *Sexual choices: An introduction to human sexuality* (2nd ed.). Monterey, CA: Wadsworth.

Strong, B., & DeVault, C. (1988). *Understanding our sexuality* (2nd ed.). St. Paul: West Publishing.

Health textbooks:

Bruess, C., & Richardson, G. E. (1989). *Decisions for health* (2nd ed.). Dubuque, IA: Wm. C. Brown.

Carroll, C., & Miller, D. (1985). *Health: The science of human adaptation* (4th ed.). Dubuque, IA: Wm. C. Brown.

Dintiman, G. B., & Greenberg, J. (1983). *Health through discovery* (2nd ed.). New York: Random House.

Dintiman, G. B., & Greenberg, J. S. (1989). *Health through discovery* (4th ed.). New York: Random House.

Edlin, G., & Golanty, E. (1985). *Health & wellness* (2nd ed.). Boston: Jones and Bartlett.

Edlin, G., & Golanty, E. (1988). *Health & wellness* (3rd ed.). Boston: Jones and Bartlett.

Ensor, P. G., Means, R. K., & Henkel, B. M. (1985). *Personal health* (2nd ed.). New York: John Wiley & Sons.

Hales, D. R. (1989). *An invitation to health: Your personal responsibility* (4th ed.). Menlo Park, CA: Benjamin/Cummings.

Hales, D. R., & Williams, B. K. (1986). *An invitation to health: Your personal responsibility* (3rd ed.). Menlo Park, CA: Benjamin/Cummings.

Insel, P. M., & Roth, W. T. (1988). *Core concepts in health* (5th ed.). Mountain View, CA: Mayfield.

Levy, M. R., Dignan, M., & Shirreffs, J. H. (1987). *Life & health* (5th ed.). New York: Random House.

Mullen, K. D., Gold, R. S., Belcastro, P. A., & McDermott, R. J. (1986). *Connections for health*. Dubuque, IA: Wm. C. Brown.

Payne, W. A., & Hahn, D. B. (1986). *Understanding your health*. St. Louis: Times Mirror/Mosby.

Payne, W. A., & Hahn, D. B. (1989). *Understanding your health* (2nd ed.). St. Louis: Times Mirror/Mosby.

Sizer, F. S., & Whitney, E. N. (1988). *Life choices: Health concepts and strategies*. St. Paul: West Publishing.

Teaching Lesbian/Gay Development: From Oppression to Exceptionality

Anthony R. D'Augelli, PhD

The Pennsylvania State University

SUMMARY. Few opportunities exist for young lesbians and gay men to learn about their lives. A university course on lesbian and gay development is described and its impact on students' lives is presented. The course focuses on the exceptional talent of lesbians and gay men in creating lives in a stigmatizing culture. The course's emphasis on how individuals develop or are oppressed by their social environment produces personal change and social action in students.

OVERVIEW

By most accounts, lesbians and gay men label their sexual orientation during adolescence, although many do not act on their feelings for several years and the achievement of a secure personal identity occurs even later. For most, fear of family reaction and peer rejection are important barriers that complement the personal uncertainties of adolescence. Pervasive anti-gay attitudes among teenagers' peers reflect the many biases and stereotypes of the larger society. Accurate information is not readily available for lesbians and gay teenagers. Indeed, few topics in secondary schools' human sexuality curricula evoke such controversy and antipathy as homosexuality. The lack of accurate information perpetuates feelings of inade-

Dr. D'Augelli is a clinical/community psychologist and Associate Professor of Human Development at The Pennsylvania State University. His interests are in lesbian and gay development and the use of community psychology for enhancing lesbian and gay lives. Reprint requests can be sent to the author, Department of Human Development and Family Studies, The Pennsylvania State University, University Park, PA 16802.

quacy and fear, leading most lesbian and gay teens to hide their identity from others. The impact on their personal development during later adolescence is profound: those who conceal their orientation enact variants of a heterosocial identity, and those who reveal their identity are subject to harassment and abuse. Until these teens live independent lives, they are doubly victimized—by the homophobia of their social worlds and by the myths they have internalized. In this process of oppression, they have been implicitly told that their development is abnormal and their prospects for personal and family fulfillment slight. In this sense, they have been deprived of their own development. They have also been deprived of a sense of community, of linkages to other lesbians and gay men. Without the socialization lesbian and gay networks provide, teens are left on their own to construct a social identity. The life tasks of adolescence—the transition from the dependencies of childhood to the autonomies and intimacies of adulthood—can be severely compromised for lesbian and gay youth. Much psychological energy is directed to coping with fears of deviance; social energies are devoted to vigilance to avoid disclosure or exposure. Hidden from friends, families, and helping resources, these teens may consciously postpone exploring their personal identity until early adulthood.

For many lesbian and gay young people, this delayed development is taken up during their years as undergraduate students at colleges and universities. At this point in their lives, lesbians and gay men are intensely interested in understanding their own lives, and reasonably enough, seek to learn about homosexuality. Unfortunately, much of the theory on the development of "sexual orientation" has been dominated by perspectives conditioned by heterosexist attitudes about the development of affectional differences. When young people pursue an understanding of themselves, they do not encounter a literature affirming their lives. Most importantly, when they look to their undergraduate curricula for insights, they find themselves deleted from most relevant courses. They are the "invisible" minority, yet the "hidden curriculum" that devalues the existence and contributions of lesbians and gay men is quite clear. At a time when accurate information and supportive experiences are critical to their development, young lesbians and gay men find few, if any, affirming experiences in higher educational settings. The need for acknowledgement and affirmation is crucial in these women's and men's development, both to overcome the problems of their earlier years and to ensure their successful transition to adulthood.

LESBIAN/GAY DEVELOPMENT

To elaborate on the power of affirmation in the lives of young lesbian and gay men, I will describe my experiences teaching an undergraduate course on lesbian/gay development. Starting with the assumption of the *exceptionality* of lesbian and gay lives, the course has had powerful psychological, social, and political impact on students. The course explores factors that influence the developmental processes of lesbians and gay men, and progresses through a consideration of three levels of analysis: personal change over the life course, the development of close relationships (family, friendships, partnerships), and the impact of society, culture, and history. Individuals are seen as producers of their own development as well as the "result" of a complex set of antecedents. The course is taught from a multidisciplinary perspective, drawing on anthropology, psychology, history, and sociology, although the underlying view is conditioned by my background as a community psychologist interested in how social structures influence mental health.

The course is built upon six conceptual themes. The themes highlight historical patterns of professional, institutional, and personal discrimination, homophobia, and heterosexism. The impact of different levels of bias on individuals' lives and the lives of their emotional intimates is continually emphasized. Instead of a question like "What are homosexuals like?", the themes raise very different dilemmas: "Who says that there are people called 'homosexuals,' and how does this labelling process interfere with how women, men, and their families determine their own socioemotional status?" There is no focus on questions of "etiology"; rather, the emphasis is on documenting creative coping with conflicts caused by those who ask simplistic causal questions. Rather than focusing on the presumed problems that lesbians and gay men have in intimacy development, the focus is on the appreciation of the strengths needed to maintain intimacy in a hostile and unsupportive context. Rather than detailing the sexual contexts that have historically provided the socialization settings for many gay people (especially men), the emphasis is on the diversity of community helping structures that lesbian and gay men have elaborated to promote their own further development.

I. I begin by assuming that the reification of difference into "deviance" and then into personhood ("homosexuals") is intrinsically oppressive by perpetuating a stereotypical mythology of lesbians and gay men.

The historical process which has eventuated in the creation of "homosexuality" allows for the expression of justifiable social concern about how to solve this "social problem." To expose the oppressive structure of this process, I begin the class with a discussion of the "deviance" of "heterosexuality" and the heterosexual "lifestyle," emphasizing its pervasive social pathology (demonstrated by divorce statistics, child abuse and neglect statistics, aggressive behavior patterns, etc.) and raise the question as to methods society might undertake to deal with this increasingly troublesome "social problem." The message from the very beginning of the course is of the importance of determining the relationship between sociohistorical oppression, mythology about lesbian and gay lives, and how this limits personal development. I intentionally do not start with a review of the social scientific "knowledge base" on lesbians and gay men because this is the accumulated wisdom of "homosexuality," with many hidden biases and limitations. Such a review would inevitably lead to a disproportionate emphasis on men and their sexual behavior, reinforcing myths and rendering secondary issues of lesbian life, relationship development, and community involvement.

II. The second theme is exceptionality. I assume the exceptionality of lesbians and gay men, arguing that lesbians and gay men generally achieve a more differentiated developmental status, more variegated personal relationships, and more complex community integration based on their historical need to transcend indifference, neglect, discrimination, and violence.

Contrary to courses in which gay men and lesbians are used as examples of "deviance," "alternate lifestyles," or "contemporary social problems," this course is explicitly affirmative. On an individual developmental level, I argue that gay men and lesbians have been provoked by their socialization patterns, life experiences, and family histories to achieve higher developmental statuses, and more differentiated personal, interpersonal, social, and community lives. The unfolding of lesbian/gay sexual orientation brings with it a generalized sense of difference, a heightened consciousness of self vis-à-vis others. The challenges and pain of authentic personal choice are paramount in lesbian and gay lives in that affectional status can be hidden or disclosed to varying degrees. Choice of revealing a personal status so socially stigmatized demands considerable ego strength, strength that is further developed after disclosure.

Similar arguments are made as far as lesbians' and gay men's relationships with members of their social networks. On a relationship and couple level, for instance, I argue that the task of creating unique dyadic norms due to lack of social ritual encourages lesbian and gay men to achieve a higher level of relational differentiation and integration. The social adhesive of traditional heterosexual roles is unavailable to lesbians and gay men. In contrast, the challenge of intimacy between two same-sexed people creates an inevitable self-consciousness about relationships. This awareness holds the potential for more differentiated social intimacy (and, of course, intensified conflict also). Similar arguments are used concerning lesbian and gay family life: using examples of married lesbians and gay men and lesbian and gay parents, I demonstrate the sophisticated level of interpersonal structure and relationship management that lesbians and gay men must achieve. Finally, I extend the argument to a community level, noting the incredible richness of care provided by organized and informal lesbian and gay networks, the availability of personal help in most urban and even rural areas for lesbians and gay men (help that is not as easily available to heterosexual people), and the quality of the care and empathy provided.

That an analysis of the richness of lesbian and gay lives seldom occurs in other courses on the topic derives in part from the lack of an exceptionality assumption. The argument becomes a mirror image of the deviance model: the pedagogical goal is to describe the many variations of exceptional development among lesbians and gay men, instead of subtly devaluing these differences as disabilities.

III. The third theme is the theme of personal development over the lifespan. Instead of teaching a course about adult women and men between the ages of 20 and 40 ("adults"), I focus on lesbian and gay feelings and experience over the life course as they are gradually expressed and integrated into a personal identity.

The literature on lesbian/gay lives before adolescence is very sparse. Our cultural images are of adult gay people, usually single urban men in their early twenties, most probably because this phase of the lifespan corresponds to those years conventionally presumed to involve the greatest amount of socio-sexual activity. Lesbian or gay teenagers have until very recently been all but invisible in the professional literature. This omission has made the adjustment of lesbian and gay teens exceedingly difficult, and no one has adequately charted the negative consequences on mental health of the suppression or repression of lesbian/gay feelings during the teen years. Many in the class report a strong sense of sexual orientation emerging during their junior high school years, but do not know that there are others with similar feelings. The postponement of adolescence as a developmental experience is an important discussion in the class, since many are entering the psychological equivalent of early adolescence when they disclose their sexual orientation in college.

Reviewing the experiences of older adults who are lesbian or gay has a different impact. Few young adults think about aging; this avoidance seems more pronounced among young lesbians and gay men. The uncertainties of their own adulthood makes thinking about getting old very threatening. Also, the lack of role models of lesbian/gay older adults makes imagery difficult. By discussing aging, the course provides not only a future, but a future worth anticipating. Another interesting effect occurs when young adults read about the lives of earlier generations of lesbians and gay men. After reading narratives of older adults' lives, students appreciate the strength and courage of their predecessors. They see creative coping under much more adverse conditions than they experience. They also gain a critical distance on their own oppression: they can see the history of current oppression, while also modeling the strength of their elders.

The extrapolation of current lifespan developmental thinking to lesbian/gay lives becomes a radical event for students in this class. Human developmental models have been seldom applied to gay men and lesbians in the scholarly or professional literatures. "Taking back" development provides an invigorating and broadening lens on their own lives, as well as the lives of others. The concept of an individual man and woman evolving over decades through a series of affectional and personal feelings, actions, and relationships promotes self-reflection in students. Related to this focus is a subtle but continual focus on questions of plasticity of affectional/sexual development. I do not stress that "sexual orientation" is rigidly and immutably fixed at any particular age since there is no empirical evidence of this. Nor, however, do I argue that crystallization of experience into "orientation" is a social historical fiction. Rather, my emphasis is on understanding social labelling over the lifespan and how labels influence personal experience, relationship experience, and community life. The labelling/action/expectancy process can serve to enrich or limit personal growth. Most gay men and lesbians in the class believe that sexual orientation is innate and that one "discovers" one's sexual feelings. I seek to make students skeptical about such simple biological determinism, noting the complex interplay of multiple factors, but this questioning is intentionally gentle. Most have been exposed to the absurdly simplistic voluntaristic view of affectional orientation, a view that has caused much personal anguish for them.

IV. The next theme is the crucial need for social support for lesbian/gay development.

I assume that individual men and women are always embedded in social networks: we are who we have related to, are relating to, and will relate to, and who has related, is relating, and will relate, to us. In discussing personal development over time, the emphasis is not on a series of "stages," but rather on how *chronological age* and *place in society* engage social, interpersonal, and relational processes. This view reflects the subcomponents of the interdisciplinary science of human development — life-span individual development, relationship development, and community development. Such a framework emphasizing context is an empowering one for oppressed groups such as lesbians and gay men, since it strikes a fundamental blow to the concept of lesbians and gay men as inevitably isolated, "inverted" souls lacking social integrity. The *social loneliness* stereotype is presented as the consequence of social rejection mechanisms, the outcome of a series of interpersonal, personal, and social exchanges in which lesbians and gay men are shaped into isolates and deviants. Another outcome of social rejection is that gay men are shaped into sexual machines and lesbians become invisible. Neither lesbians or gay men then provide a meaningful threat to concepts of heterosocial intimacy. Gay men are dismissed as erotic narcissists; and, lesbians' invisibility leave unthreatened the boundaries of female sexuality. A focus on embeddedness, social identity, social interaction, and social oppression as fundamental to human development encourages discussion of the unconscious dynamics of gay/lesbian oppression. Lesbians and gay men also gain from the social loneliness metaphor: for instance, it allows for separatism, decreases routine contact with oppression, and encourages group cohesiveness.

V. The next theme concerns close relationship development as the normative pattern for lesbians and gay men.

I assume that gay men and lesbians move towards intimacy and commitment in relationships and that relationships move towards couplehood. Couplehood involves integration as a unit into social networks, family life, and community settings. Thus, the course presumes that "normal" development for a lesbian or a gay man evolves to commitment within a relationship that is acknowledged by others in the couple's social world and community. Such couples have a full and rich circle of individual friends (including heterosexual couples); they are fully involved in family life, both within their own *families of origin* and within their *families of creation* (the family of their partners or lovers); they are involved in a rich set of social networks—for example, at work, and in religious settings. They participate as a couple in community groups, and are involved in political and social action toward the larger goal of an egalitarian, multicultural society. Such imagery is crucial since it fuels students' development. The naturalistic fallacy well-known to philosophers ("what is, ought to be") must be short-circuited in educating groups suffering overt as well as subtle oppression. Courses that deal with the data on "homosexuality" are inevitably drawn toward reinforcing stereotypes and oppressive structure, if only because their data are obsolete and reflect an earlier historical time. Sociology courses dealing with "deviance" seldom described the many long-standing couples that would have been found had scholars ventured beyond the "subculture" of gay bars and bathhouses.

VI. The final theme is unstated: the use of the course as a controlled informal support system.

It is not psychologically useful to derail an educational process into a psychotherapeutic one. An effort, conscious or unconscious, to turn a gay or lesbian course into a therapeutic or support group can become a transmission of the oppressive professional culture of psychological deficit or deviance. This can reinforce the concept that lesbian/gay status indicates the need for professional care. Yet, young lesbians and gay men have strong emotional needs; most have spent considerable psychological energy during their earlier years in suppressing their feelings. My solution to the dilemma of addressing need without encouraging dependency is to provide opportunities to explore their own development and factors that might limit their future. There is no discussion of "mental health" problems, counseling, or psychotherapy in the course.

The need for support, however, is not ignored. I encourage personal exploration by requiring short reaction papers on weekly readings. This allows students to "discuss" their lives with me if they choose, and most do. These short papers are windows into oppression, pain, and hurt. It would be entirely too possible to open the window and allow full focus on these issues, and to create clients, which would distract them from a broader analysis of their dilemmas. I refuse to encourage their pathologization, even in a psychological form. By using a life-development perspective, I interfere with the process by which lesbians and gay men have been told by the culture and by well-intended professional people (including many gay and lesbian psychologists, social workers, and psychiatrists) that they are "in need" of psychotherapeutic help.

The goal of an educational process for lesbians and gay men must be empowerment, not psychotherapy. Narrowly "political" education — gay/ lesbian history or political science — pales in comparison to the power gained when lesbians and gay men are educated about the social oppression of their past and are given epistemological frameworks to structure their futures. Teaching gay/lesbian development within an interdisciplinary lifespan human development framework helps avoid the relentless structures of oppression that enshroud educational efforts. Rather, it provokes students to review their past and present, and enables them to plan their futures by a combination of personal power, family integration, and community involvement.

A CLIMATE FOR DEVELOPMENT

I have offered the course since 1984, and it is currently a routine offering at the University. The most recent syllabus is shown in the Appendix. It draws from 25 to 35 students, from a broad range of majors. Most (approximately 80%) of the students are lesbian/gay. They typically divulge this information in the first class, although I never ask. Up until the most recent offering (1990), no heterosexual male had completed the course; two heterosexual men were in the last class. Heterosexual women give two reasons for enrollment: most have a lesbian/gay close relative (usually a brother), and the rest are planning to enter a helping profession. Of the lesbian and gay majority, most have attended lesbian/gay functions on campus before enrolling in the course. Very few — though there are some — use the course as a way to "come out" publicly. Rather, lesbian/ gay students use the course to more fully integrate their orientation into their lives. Most are not open with their parents and families: most have avoided the issue, some have lied. All of the lesbian/gay students seem highly aware of their parents' and families' views, although some of their conclusions have yet to be tested. There is little doubt that entrance to the course represents a turning point in terms of self-consciousness, social disclosure, and commitment to change.

Change occurs in diverse ways in class members, but it is facilitated because the class provides a supportive climate for development. Students report that this is the only course at the University in which lesbian/gay lives are acknowledged in such an extensive way. Most, on the other hand, have experienced homophobic remarks by faculty in courses in which "homosexuality" is mentioned. Many report irrelevant derogatory jokes and remarks about lesbians and gay men. Few describe efforts to assert themselves in these situations, either by requesting more detailed coverage or more accurate presentations, or by confronting a faculty member about a prejudicial remark. Most acknowledge feeling demoralized by these events, and occasionally this feeling emerges as anger. More often, attributions of worthlessness occur, reinforcing years of earlier "socialization." Thus, an explicitly lesbian/gay-affirming classroom environment is emotionally startling, with no precedent in their lives. Most say that they have never been in a social situation in which they could freely discuss their lives; the only exceptions have been conversations held with small numbers of lesbian/gay friends. For many, the simple experience of being asked (indeed, required!) to read lesbian/gay materials — especially fiction — opens up an entire world of information that was unknown to them. (One man told me that he had no idea that there were "gay" novels, except for pornography.)

There are common personal changes students in the course undergo. Most become acutely aware of their own internalized homophobia, appreciating how they too have believed the many myths of the culture. Most begin to understand that lesbian/gay status involves special challenges, and that there are far more supportive resources available than they suspected. Many become active in social settings for lesbian/gay people, using others in the class to ease entrance anxieties. They realize that they must take initiatives to control their own development since little assistance will be provided by heterosexual society. There is a gradual acknowledgement of the pain of their earlier years, and a sense of loss is experienced. On the other hand, when they realize that their earlier experiences were not unique, there is a relaxation of self-judgment and a hopefulness for the future.

This hopefulness often takes the form of efforts to develop relationships and to become more open with families. Many first relationships are initiated, often with considerable emotional intensity. Readings on couplehood help prepare students for the turmoil of first relationships, which appear far more intense for lesbian/gay young people than for their heterosexual counterparts, in my experience. Another common movement is toward greater closeness with parents. If parents are perceived as valued sources of support and affection, students are motivated to share their lives with them, although there is always considerable fear attached to this process. If parents seem likely to reject, students approach others in the family. Their efforts become more direct and assertive over the semester, undertaken after they develop greater personal security and a better-grounded background in lesbian/gay life. Since the course is offered in the spring, many plan to discuss these issues during the mid-semester break. Some report leaving copies of the books for the course in conspicuous places, hoping to provoke a discussion. Over the years, those who have disclosed to parents have been surprised at parents' support, after some initial surprise and denial. Few have reported parental rejection; most who expect this refrain from disclosure, at least at this point in their lives.

In addition to greater openness with families, there is clearly momentum to extend their newly-found strengths to their proximal social world on campus. Students become hyperconscious of the heterosexist assumptions of other students and faculty, and highly attuned not only to exclusionary efforts but also to overt homophobia. As the course describes the richness of lesbian/gay lives, vigilance about others "knowing" is slowly replaced by affirmation. The many opportunities provided by routine social exchange for acknowledgement of lesbian/gay status provoke students to "test the waters"; they are now "armed" with current information, and the knowledge that they can turn to others in the class (and to other resources now more accessible) to process the results of disclosure. Most seem eager to disclose to all of their friends. Many want other students in their classes to know, but this is riskier. Often such a declaration comes in the form of raising questions in classes about lesbian/gay issues. (I encourage this, noting how important — and *legitimate* — this challenging process is, suggesting that many faculty are unaware of their heterosexist views and need to be sensitized to change.) Responses to these comments help categorize, albeit imperfectly, the supportiveness of others. More commonly, disclosure occurs with several in the class who have already been "proven" to have supportive views. The end result is a heightened awareness of the role of one's social network in affirming one's life as a lesbian/gay person. Students no longer perceive "others" as an undifferentiated group of hostile people, but understand the need to determine sources of support and affirmation within their networks. This process helps students avoid developing exclusively lesbian/gay social networks, and encourages the sharing of lesbian/gay status with heterosexual friends, while also strengthening lesbian/gay pride.

As the course focuses on how social networks and social structures facilitate and/or impede development, it inevitably elicits attention to legal and political issues central to lesbian/gay lives. Very few students have any understanding of the complex legal barriers that they face in asserting their rights. When asked about the status of various lesbian/gay rights, few even understand that these issues are relevant to their lives. Most assumed they would live hidden lives or, in a naive way, expected a more fulfilling life in an urban area after graduation. Interestingly enough, the most personal legal issues were of most concern, and readings on wills and power of attorney were met with shock and surprise (especially the ability of hostile natural parents to supplant long-term partners in legal matters). Similarly, readings on parenting, especially custody problems after divorce, and in creating families via donors, found students fascinated at the possibilities for their lives, and simultaneously furious at legal barriers. For most, this process evolved into heightened awareness of law; for others, it led to attempts at political action.

In moving toward legal and political action, most inevitably turned to the University, scrutinizing its formal and informal policies regarding lesbians and gay men. As one of the course's themes encourages consideration of the social systems that most directly influence one's development, the most concerted student activism has become directed toward those units concerned with the residence halls on campus. Training of residence assistants on concerns of lesbian/gay issues was an important concern, as well as policies about harassment. But this focus readily shifted to concern about broader policy—specifically about the lack of formal protection for lesbian/gay students, faculty, and staff in the official equal opportunity policy of the institution.

As the entire domain of lesbian/gay legal matters crystallized, the stance of the municipality surrounding the University also became a focus. Few were aware of the minimal formal protections in basic life recourses—housing, accommodations, employment—that existed in the borough in which the University is located. Indeed, in spring 1989, students in the class attended hearings on a municipal law that would extend protection from discrimination in housing to lesbians and gay men. The refusal of the local authorities to extend these protections—despite the strong support for such extensions by the mayor of the town—was met with incredulity by students, who had not appreciated the legal manifestations of homophobia in their own lives. They had never been so directly exposed to the process by which prejudice and bias rebuffed efforts of lesbians and gay men to obtain basic human rights. In earlier course offerings, these issues were discussed, but the examples were not local. Observing the legal process first hand, particularly after discussions of the impact of such decisions on efforts of lesbians and gay men to become fully integrated into their communities, was experiential learning of the highest order.

A PEDAGOGY OF THE OPPRESSED

My experiences over the last five years has convinced me that teaching this course in the manner I've described is an act of empowerment. In fact, delineating the multiple impacts of personal factors, social process, and culture on lesbian and gay lives for young people at a critical point in their own development is a political act, an act that can provoke turbulent personal reactions to conditions of institutional and community oppression. My analysis of the process has been conditioned by Paulo Freire's *Pedagogy of the Oppressed* (1970). Although Freire's examples are from the history of oppression in South and Central America, his articulation of the radical consequences of informing oppressed people of the structure and parameters of their oppression is directly relevant to the experiences of young lesbians and gay men who are shown the sociopolitical status quo that will dictate their futures. This awareness releases strong anger; such education can unintentionally produce confrontation with the sources of oppression. There are tremendous personal risks in this process, since often these young people move forward in their personal development as a consequence of confrontations with homosexist "authority"—their parents, their friends, their teachers, and their university. Based on my role in this complex process, I feel it critical to inform young lesbians and gay men about barriers to their development, to help them appreciate their exceptionality, and to encourage them to plan their own development in an active, assertive manner. The educational process that I have observed has elicited considerable strength in this group of young adults. Also, the process has unveiled possibilities for the creation of rich, creative lives and partnerships as well as activism for social justice. Unless lesbians and gay men in colleges and universities are offered such pedagogical opportunities, they will remain victimized by the "hidden curriculum" of homophobia, remaining unaware of the power of homophobic mythology, social custom, and legal barriers to rob them of their futures.

REFERENCE

Freire, P. (1970). *Pedagogy of the oppressed*. New York: Seabury Press.

APPENDIX A

Course Outline

Lesbian/Gay Development over the Lifespan

Anthony R. D'Augelli, PhD

TEXTS:

1. Marcy Adelman. *Long Time Passing: Lives of Older Lesbians*. Boston: Alyson, 1986.
2. Gloria Guss Back. *Are You Still My Mother?* New York: Warner Books, 1985.
3. Warren J. Blumenfeld & Diane Raymond. *Looking at Gay and Lesbian Life*. Boston: Beacon Press.
4. Boston Lesbian Psychologies Collective. *Lesbian Psychology: Explorations and Challenges*. Urbana: University of Illinois Press, 1987.
5. Ann Heron (Ed.) *One Teenager in 10: Writings by Gay and Lesbian Youth*. Boston: Alyson. 1983.
6. Frederick Bozett (Ed.). *Gay and Lesbian Parents*. New York: Praeger, 1987.
7. Eric Marcus. *The Male Couple's Guide to Living Together*. New York: Harper & Row, 1988.
8. Keith Vacha. *Quiet Fire: Memoirs of Older Gay Men*. Trumansburg, NY: Crossing Press, 1985.

SCHEDULE:

Section I: Concepts and Frameworks

1. Introduction
2. Development over the Lifespan
3. Relationship Processes
4. History and Culture

Section II: Personal Growth and Development

5. Lesbian Beginnings
6. Gay Male Beginnings
7. Identity Within the Family

Section III: Relationship Development

  8. Women's Relationships
  9. Men's Relationships
 10. Lesbian Parents
 11. Gay Male Parents

Section IV. Development and Culture

 12. Legal and Political Change
 13. Historical Change

Educating Mental Health Professionals About Gay and Lesbian Issues

Bianca Cody Murphy, EdD

Wheaton College

SUMMARY. Despite the large number of clients with gay and lesbian concerns, many mental health professionals remain biased and unqualified to serve them. Mental health professionals are poorly prepared to deal with sexuality in general and with gay and lesbian issues specifically. Education and training about gay and lesbian topics is needed both in graduate schools and in the field. This training should focus on three components: (1) information about sexual orientation, gay and lesbian lifestyles, and community resources; (2) the interface between the gay or lesbian client, his or her sexuality, and the effects of living in a heterosexist and homophobic society; and (3) the interaction between the attitudes, feelings, and sexual orientation of the clinician and of the client.

All mental health professionals should expect that they will see a number of gay men and lesbian women in their practice, and even more clients who have had same-gender sexual relationships or who are concerned about issues of sexual orientation. In order to be effective in their jobs, therefore, mental health workers need to be educated about gay and lesbian issues. From major life events like coming out to parents or being a victim of gay bashing, to everyday activities such as having a romantic dinner out or having the neighbors drop in for coffee, the issues facing gay men and lesbian women' are different from those of heterosexual men and

Bianca Cody Murphy is Assistant Professor of Psychology at Wheaton College and Visiting Research Scholar at Wellesley College Center for Research on Women. Requests for reprints should be sent to: Department of Psychology, Wheaton College, Norton, MA 02766.

The author would like to acknowledge that discussions with Brian McNaught and Gary Drake, LICSW, were helpful in the formulation of many of the ideas presented here. She would also like to thank Joel Hencken, PhD, for his comments on a draft of this article.

women. They are different not because of sexual orientation alone, but because of the heterosexist and homophobic attitudes of the society in which we live. Herek (1986) defines heterosexism as "a world-view, a value-system that prizes heterosexuality, assumes it is the only appropriate manifestation of love and sexuality, and devalues homosexuality and all that is not heterosexual" (p. 925). Homophobia is the prejudice, discrimination, and hostility directed at gay men and lesbian women because of their sexual orientation.

Approximately 10% of the population at any given time, currently over 22 million people in the United States, can be defined as predominantly gay or lesbian (Crooks & Baur, 1990). The Kinsey studies, still among the most comprehensive research studies of human sexual behavior, found that over one third of all men between adolescence and old age had had sex to the point of orgasm with another man (Kinsey, Pomeroy, & Martin, 1948), and that from eight to twenty percent of the women had had some homosexual experience in their lifetime (Kinsey, Pomeroy, Martin, & Gebhard, 1953). While not all of these people would actually *identify* themselves as gay or lesbian, their concerns are often similiar to their lesbian and gay identified counterparts. Matters of sexual orientation are also important to the family and friends of gay and lesbian people, as well as to others who have not had same gender sexual relationships.

Furthermore, the additional burdens of discrimination, oppression, and violence often lead gay men and lesbian women to seek assistance from human service providers. Although there is great diversity within the gay and lesbian community in terms of race, class, age, ethnicity, and physical abilities, all gay men and lesbian women are affected by societal homophobia. The majority of people in the United States see gay men and lesbian women as sick, immoral, criminal, or all three. This prejudice results in discrimination against them in many areas, including jobs, housing, and child custody. In its most overt form, homophobia results in violence ranging from verbal harrassment to murder. Herek (1989) notes: "In recent surveys, as many as 92% of lesbians and gay men report that they have been the targets of antigay verbal abuse or threats, and as many as 24% report physical attacks because of their sexual orientation" (p. 948).

OFFICIAL POLICY

Almost all of the major professional organizations for mental health providers — social workers, psychologists, and counselors — recognize the need to educate their constituents about gay and lesbian issues. In the field of social work, for example, The Council on Social Work Education Curriculum Policy Statement states:

> Special Populations: The social work profession, by virtue of its system of ethics, its traditional value commitments, and its long history of work in the whole range of human services, is committed to preparing students to understand and appreciate cultural and social diversity. The profession has also been concerned about the consequences of oppression. . . . The curriculum . . . should include content on other special population groups . . . in particular, groups that have been consistently affected by social, economic and legal bias or oppression. Such groups include those distinguished by age, religions, disablement, *sexual orientation* and culture. (Council on Social Work Education, 1982, cited in Gochros, 1984, p. 154; italics added)

Similarly, the Human Rights Committee of the American Association for Counseling and Development (AACD) states:

> In order to guarantee that each individual is free to pursue his/her potential, each member of AACD is charged to (a) engage in ongoing examination of his/her own attitudes, feelings, stereotypic views, perceptions and behaviors that might have prejudicial or limiting impact on women, ethnic minorities, elderly persons, *gay/lesbian persons,* and persons with handicapping conditions; (b) contribute to an increased sensitivity on the part of other individuals, groups or institutions to the barriers to opportunity imposed by discrimination; (c) advocate equal rights for all individuals through concerted personal, professional and political activity. (Position paper of the Human Rights Committee of the Association for Counseling and Development, 1987, p. 1; cited in Dworkin & Gutierrez, 1989, p. 6; italics added)

The American Psychological Association (APA) states that it is the ethical responsibility of all psychologists and those in training to:

> maintain knowledge of current and professional information related to the services they render . . . (and to) recognize the differences among people, such as those that may be associated with age, sex, socioeconomic, and ethnic background. When necessary, they obtain training, experience, or counsel to assure competent service or

research relating to such persons. (APA, 1981, p. 643, cited in Buhrke, 1989a, p. 629)

Thus, to be ethical professionals, psychologists have the responsibility to be knowledgeable about and sensitive to the issues and concerns of lesbian and gay people.

Despite the official statements about the importance of sensitivity to sexual orientation, gay and lesbian topics are rarely discussed either in mental health graduate programs or in the field. Part of the problem is that there is little education about human sexuality in general.

CURRENT STATUS OF EDUCATION

General Training in Human Sexuality

Mental health providers frequently have clients who either present with, or eventually discuss in therapy, sexual matters, such as sexual satisfaction, sexual dysfunction, or concerns about sexual orientation. However, most social workers, counselors, and psychologists receive minimal or no education in human sexuality.

Among mental health education programs, social work schools are credited with leadership in providing sex education for their students. They have long recognized the need to incorporate human sexuality education in their graduate training programs (Abramowitz, 1971; Brashear, 1976; Gochros, 1970; Matek, 1977; Schlesinger, 1983). However, in a study of graduate social work programs conducted in the mid-70s, Mazur found that less than two thirds (61%) of social work schools actually offered a course in human sexuality to their graduate students (Mazur, 1978; Zapka & Mazur, 1977). Despite the fact that social work schools are the recognized leaders in sexuality education, they fall far short of their goal of incorporating sexuality education into all graduate school curricula.

Graduate programs in counselor education and clinical psychology offer even less training in human sexuality. Gray, Cummins, Johnson, and Mason (1989) recently surveyed all counselor education programs in the United States. They found that only 44% of the responding departments offered courses in human sexuality, and over 40% of those courses were provided by other departments within the college or university. Only 20% of the offered courses were required for graduation. That means that less than 10% of those departments that responded require a course in human sexuality for graduation. Gray et al. reported that 37% of those who responded said that they had sexuality included only in other general courses. Remarkably, 19% responded that they neither offered a course in sexuality or had sexuality integrated into other courses.

The figures were comparable for clinical psychology. In a thorough survey of APA-approved doctoral programs, Nathan (1986) found that only 37% of respondents said that their department offered a graduate course in either human sexuality, sexual disorders, or sex therapy. Only 41% reported that they discussed sexual issues as part of their general courses.

These findings indicate that the majority of graduate training programs for mental health professionals do not even offer general courses in human sexuality. Those programs that do have general courses in human sexuality often borrow them from other departments. There are serious questions as to whether these courses, offered as they are in other departments, properly address the clinical issues in human sexuality. Is a biology course which focuses on the anatomy and physiology of human sexual organs sufficient preparation for working with the psychological and emotional issues of clients experiencing concerns about masturbation or infertility?

The situation is not much better in field practice settings (Welbourne, 1983). LoPiccolo (1978) reported that less than 10% of clinical training sites teach material on sex counseling and therapy. Recent articles have called for sexual awareness training for counselors (Landis, Miller, & Wettstone, 1975) and for sexuality training for staff in long-term psychiatric hospitals (Cohen & Tannenbaum, 1985). However, until some major changes occur in both graduate schools and field settings, mental health professionals will continue to be poorly prepared to address sexual issues in their clinical work.

Specific Training in Gay and Lesbian Issues

Graduate education and field training in human sexuality for mental health professionals is poor, but training about gay and lesbian issues is even worse. Despite official statements about the importance of sensitivity to sexual orientation, gay and lesbian topics are rarely discussed either in graduate education programs or in the field.

Graduate schools. Dulaney and Kelly (1982) reported that while schools of social work generally offer courses devoted entirely to the elderly and to racial and ethnic minorities, the Newsletter of the Association of Social Work Educators Concerned with Gay and Lesbian Issues reported that only six schools of social work offered a course on homosexuality.

The Committee on Lesbian and Gay Concerns of the American Psychological Association found that only nine percent of the 303 department chairpersons who responded to a survey reported that their programs offered clinical training in the area of sexual orientation; 13.6% of the programs' faculty were doing some gay or lesbian related research; 44% of the departments were willing to sponsor some gay or lesbian related doctoral research; 28.1% had gay- or lesbian-identified students and only 9.9% had openly gay or lesbian faculty members (Carlson, 1985).

In a similiar vein, Buhrke (1989b) reported that almost one third of 213 female counseling psychology students in APA-approved doctoral programs stated that lesbian or gay issues were not discussed in any of their graduate school courses. Seventy percent said they knew of no faculty, 80% knew no supervisors, and 48% knew no students, who were conducting research on lesbian or gay subject matter. The respondents also reported that there were few gay and lesbian role models among faculty and supervisors.

Iasenza (1989) notes that "education is a socialization process which imparts the values of the dominant culture. In this respect, the absence of sexual orientation issues in graduate training reveals the influence of heterosexism and homophobia in our society" (pp. 73-74). It is not surprising then that mental health graduate students have been shown to display heterosexism, homophobia, and ignorance about gay and lesbian issues.

In a survey of 64 graduate counseling students, Thompson and Fishburn (1977) found that only five percent of the participants felt that clinicians were well trained to work with lesbian and gay clients. Glenn and Russell (1986), in a modification of an earlier study of clinicans by Garfinkle and Morin (1978), studied 36 female master's-level counseling students. Each student was shown an audiotape of a role-played intake interview of a female client. The client discussed how her mood was affecting her relationship. In one tape the partner was referred to by a man's name, in another tape the partner had a woman's name, and in the third tape the partner's name and, hence, sex was ambiguous. Glenn and Russell reported that the counseling students in the third situation showed subtle and overt forms of heterosexual bias, e.g., they assumed that the woman's partner was a male. Moreover, in the debriefing process the students said they had not received sufficient training about gay and lesbian issues nor had their heterosexism and homophobia been challenged during their education.

Clinicians in the field. The research literature of the 1970s indicates that clinicians are more likely to have negative attitudes and ascribe pathology to clients whom they believe to be gay or lesbian (Fort, Steiner, & Conrad, 1971; Garfinkle & Morin, 1978; Gartrell, Kramer, & Brodie, 1974). Morin (1977) explains these negative attitudes by pointing out "heterosexual bias in research"—early psychological research frequently compared gay men and lesbian women in therapy or even in prison to heterosexuals in the general population. In 1977, Hencken and O'Dowd noted that clinicians were called upon to help gay and lesbian clients, but there was little research to provide a data base for clinicians to draw on in their work.

Despite recent attempts to correct the heterosexual bias in research and to provide more research for use by clinicians, recent studies of attitudes toward gay and lesbian clients show that mental health workers continue to hold heterosexist and/or homophobic attitudes. Wisniewski and Toomey (1987) surveyed 77 professional social workers in the Columbus, Ohio, area using an Index of Attitudes toward Homosexuals. They found that nearly one third of those social workers who participated in the study earned scores falling within the homophobic range. It has also been demonstrated that stereotyping influences information processing about gay men and lesbian women. Casas, Brady, and Ponterotto (1983) found in a sample of 34 mental health professionals that their subjects were less likely to accurately recall information about gay men and lesbian women than about heterosexual men and women. They also found that their subjects made more errors recalling information that was incongruent with prevalent stereotypes about gay men and lesbian women.

Graham, Rawlings, Halpern, and Hermes (1984) surveyed 400 mental health practitioners in a mid-western city about their attitudes, knowledge, concerns, and strategies in counseling lesbian and gay clients. The results of their study "raise serious concerns about the quality, or rather lack of quality, of services that apparently (sic) many lesbian and gay male clients are receiving. The findings also indicate that therapists who provide services to these two populations, in general, do not have the training to do so" (p. 492). Finally, the Committee on Lesbian and Gay Concerns of APA conducted a survey of over 2,500 psychologists, and concluded: "Adherence to a standard of unbiased practice with gay men and lesbians is variable. Respondents reported substantial numbers of negative incidents involving biased or inappropriate care for lesbians and gay men" (1990, p. iv).

A PROPOSED CURRICULUM

The Educational Context

Although separate courses, workshops, or continuing education may be necessary to remediate a previous lack of education about gay and lesbian issues, it is important not to let these topics be compartmentalized and thereby marginalized. Education about gay and lesbian issues is best accomplished by integrating it into all aspects of the training and professional practice of mental health professionals.

In graduate schools, information about gay and lesbian concerns should be integrated into the curriculum (Iasenza, 1989; Norton, 1982). Gochros (1984) offers some specific suggestions for learning experiences for social work students. Buhrke (1989a) provides a useful discussion of methods that can be used in various counseling courses. For example, she suggests including the coming out process along with traditional developmental issues in a human development course, or including gay and lesbian couples and families in discussions in marriage, family, and/or couples counseling courses. Her compilation of resources can be used by all mental health professionals to improve their inclusion of gay and lesbian material in the graduate curriculum.

In addition, gay and lesbian issues can be addressed in separate courses or in parts of courses devoted to the needs of special populations. Boston University School of Social Work, for example, has a 16-hour course on Oppression in which clinical work with oppressed minorities is discussed; homophobia is included with racism, ageism, sexism, and religious persecution. In Colorado, the state gay and lesbian psychology group has prepared a curriculum on lesbian and gay issues for the graduate psychology programs in the state (L.W. Allen, personal communication, January 19, 1990).

In the field, gay and lesbian topics can be addressed in clinical supervision, case conferences, in-service education, workshops, and continuing education programs (Buhrke, 1989c; Moses & Hawkins, 1985; Nichols & Shernoff, 1985; Peterson, 1985; Schneider & Tremble, 1986).

Components

Over the past fifteen years, I have provided training for human service workers and mental health professionals using a wide range of formats. These have included: as guest lecturer for one-time classroom sessions in graduate social work and counseling psychology programs; as facilitator for day-long in-service workshops for human service agencies and continuing education programs sponsored by APA and by the American Orthopsychiatric Association (ORTHO); as trainer for a weekly education program for professional social workers; and as faculty in graduate counselor education programs. In all of these contexts, I have tried to include three essential components for training human service workers and mental health professionals to work with gay and lesbian clients: "the three I's": Information, Interplay, and Interaction.

Information. Mental health students and professionals need to know and understand a wide range of information about homosexuality. Their education should include definitions of terms, as well as information about what is known and not known about the "causes of homosexuality," lifestyle issues, and community resources (see Blumenfeld & Raymond, 1988, for a comprehensive overview).

It is essential that mental health professionals be familiar with the distinctions between such often-confused terms as *gender identity, sex-role identity,* and *sexual orientation identity.* For example, gay men are often sterotyped as "swishy," "feminine," or that most peculiar and pejorative term "effeminate." Many people therefore assume that gay men want to be women, confusing gay men with male-to-female transexuals.

Training must familiarize mental health professionals with the prevalence of gay, lesbian, and bisexual behavior and with the various theories which attempt to explain the causes of homosexuality. Many of these efforts view homosexual behavior as pathological. Although pathology theories are in disrepute among most professionals, clients and the lay public may ask questions about them. It is not enough to say homosexuality is no longer considered pathological and cite as proof its removal as a mental illness in 1973 from the Diagnostic and Statistical Manual of the American Psychiatric Association. Clinicians need to be familiar with the critique of the psychosocial theories about the etiology of homosexuality of Freud (1905) and Bieber (Bieber, Dain, Dince, Drelich, Grand, Gundlach, Kremer, Rifkin, Wilbur, & Bieber, 1962), with biological theories including the conflicting evidence on the role of hormones in homosexual behavior (Tourney, 1980), with the studies of Ford and Beach (1951) and Churchill (1967) on the widespread prevalence of homosexuality in other cultures and other species, and with theoretical models that account for normal development of gay men and lesbian women (Bell, Weinberg, & Hammersmith, 1981; Kinsey et al., 1948; Storms, 1980). This is necessary in order to be able to discuss, and when necessary refute, negative and pathological views on the "etiology" of homosexual behavior.

Mental heath workers should know of the pioneering work of Evelyn Hooker (1957) and the various studies that have shown that gay men and lesbian women are as "healthy" as their heterosexual counterparts (Bell & Weinberg, 1978). Clinicians also need information about gay and lesbian identity development, coming out, and the relationship between a positive gay or lesbian identity and psychological adjustment (for more references on these topics see Cass, 1985; Coleman, 1987; De Cecco & Shivley, 1985: de Monteflores & Schultz, 1978; Hencken & O'Dowd, 1977; Miranda & Storms, 1989; Sophie, 1982).

Training should include a wide range of information about gay and lesbian lifestyles, including information on gay or lesbian jargon, common sexual practices, health issues, coming out, and the various forms of gay and lesbian families. Bell and Weinberg (1978), Blumstein and Schwartz (1983), and Jay and Young (1979), have all conducted in-depth surveys that address various aspects of gay and lesbian lives. It is important that information be presented that counters prevalent myths and misconceptions such as the stereotype that lesbian couples all play "butch and femme" roles or that lesbian women want to be men.

Mental health professionals should be provided with a list of both local and national resources for a wide range of gay and lesbian concerns. It should include health, legal, religious, social service agencies, and AIDS programs that work with gay men and lesbian women and are lesbian/gay affirmative. It is also valuable to provide a listing of support groups, such as coming out groups at the local women's center; gay fathers' groups; local gay/lesbian Alcholics Anonymous meetings; support groups for heterosexual spouses of gay, lesbian, or bisexual partners; or activity groups for gay and lesbian youth. Many gay men and lesbian women, particularly youth, report a sense of isolation; they need safe, affirmative places to connect with others. Therefore, it is important to list social organizations, gay, lesbian, and feminist newspapers, bookstores, bars, and social clubs, as well as any hotlines or community centers that may exist. It is also desirable to include information on relevant local, state, and national laws: for example, local laws that may protect gay men and lesbian women from discrimination in housing, or state sodomy laws used to prosecute gay men.

Finally, it is essential to have a bibliography on gay and lesbian issues. This bibliography should include general references written for clinicans as well as specific sections on topics like coming out and identity formation; gay and lesbian youth, couples, parents, and families; bisexuality; gay and lesbian sex; and religious issues. The bibliography should include references on material that would be helpful for gay men or lesbian women to read as well as material that is directed toward family and friends.

If one is attempting to integrate this material into a graduate curriculum or other educational programs, the resources and information would be included when discussing specific issues. For example, a course or in-service program on marriage and family counseling would integrate information, resources and readings on gay and lesbian couples and families with the other material presented.

Interplay. Interplay refers to the inextricable link between the individual, his/her sexuality, and society. It is important that training for clinicians emphasize the ways in which the clients' presenting problems are affected by sexual orientation and the effects of living in a heterosexist and homophobic society.

Clients may contact mental health workers because of issues overtly related to sexual orientation, such as coming out to parents, confusion about sexual identity, or having been physically attacked for being homosexual. Where issues concerning sexual orientation are explicit, the therapist must focus on the presenting problem within the context of the larger society and the social stigma attached to homosexuality, as well as within the psychological, familial, and social contexts of the client's life. For example, when a woman decides to come out to her parents, the therapist must address coming out in terms of how family members will respond to the specific information that the daughter is lesbian. The therapist must also help the client explore the effects of her decision to disclose her lesbianism in the context of how her family traditionally handles differentiation of family members, as well as how family alliances and patterns of interaction will either be disrupted or supported by this new information. The ways in which family members deal with a member's lesbian identity are shaped both by the content of the information and by the family's traditional patterns of interaction (Roth & Murphy, 1986).

At other times, the interplay between the presenting problem, i.e., why the client is seeking therapy, and the client's sexual orientation is not as clear. Mental health workers need to be sensitized to the ways in which the lives of gay men and lesbian women are affected by the stresses of living in a homophobic society with people who believe them to be sick, immoral, or criminal. Society's disapproving and sometimes hostile reaction can lead to internalized homophobia (i.e., the individual's acceptance and internalization of society's negative attitudes). This can result in guilt, fear, or self-hatred; it can affect many other, seemingly unrelated, aspects of their lives (Murphy, 1989). A client may seek counseling about career decisions. Although not initially stated, discussion may reveal that she has narrowed her career options because she fears that if she has a public job someone may discover her lesbianism.

Furthermore, the lesbian or gay person must make decisions about secrecy and self-disclosure every day and must cope with the resulting positive and negative consequences. To disclose one's sexual orientation means risking disapproval, discrimination, even outright hostility; to hide means to live a double life, to be wary, self-conscious, and socially isolated; and never to feel truly known or accepted.

For gay men and lesbian women there are few problems that are *not* affected by issues of sexual orientation, heterosexism, and homophobia

(Murphy, in press). "Homophobia inevitably becomes a focus of attention during the treatment process . . . . An understanding of the personal, economic, social and political ramifications of homophobia is essential in working with clients" (Gartrell, 1984, p. 14). Mental health workers need to be taught that issues of sexual orientation and identity management should always be discussed as a part of therapy. It is important to clarify that the client's sexual orientation is *not* the problem. The problem is the homophobia and heterosexism of the larger society, which can and does create difficulties for clients.

Interaction. It is not just therapy clients who are affected by homophobia and heterosexual bias. Mental health professionals are themselves powerfully but subtly influenced by these social forces (Gartrell, 1984; Graham et al. 1984; Martin, 1982; Riddle & Sang, 1978; Stein, 1988). Clinicians must be encouraged to explore their degree of comfort with their own sexual orientation, and the ways in which their attitudes and beliefs about gay men and lesbian women interact with those of their clients. Training programs should raise a number of questions: How does the clinician feel about his/her own sexual orientation and lifestyle choices? How does she/he feel about the sexual orientation and lifestyle choices of his/her clients? How has homophobia and heterosexism affected him/her? What is the relationship between the client and the therapist? How does the sexual orientation of the client and the therapist (gay or straight) affect the therapy?

Education should help clinicians to become conscious of their own homophobia and to overcome their negative attitudes towards and sterotypes about gay men and lesbian women. Mental health workers must be taught to guard against heterosexism and homophobia by scrupulously reviewing the course of therapy and by receiving supervision. A "homophobic or heterosexist therapist, regardless of sexual orientation, cannot be helpful to lesbian and gay clients" (Rochlin, 1982, p. 24). All mental health workers must be taught that *unless they can actively affirm gay and lesbian lifestyles, they cannot ethically work with these clients.*

Education should also focus on the relationship between the clinician's sexual orientation and that of the client (Rochlin, 1982). Although gay and lesbian mental health workers are as susceptible to heterosexism and homophobia as their heterosexual counterparts, being gay or lesbian may be helpful in terms of knowledge about and empathy for the life experiences of gay and lesbian clients. It is again important to remember, however, that there is diversity in gay and lesbian communities in terms of class, ethnicity, and politics. Gay and lesbian clinicians also must guard against overly identifying with their clients.

Training should also include discussion of how the therapist handles information about his/her sexual orientation. Gartrell (1984) and Riddle and Sang (1978) suggest that having an openly identified gay or lesbian therapist who can model a positive gay identity is helpful for the client. What are the implications of disclosing one's sexual orientation to clients? Can straight therapists be helpful to lesbian and gay clients? What are the effects on the client of having a gay or lesbian therapist who hides his/her sexual orientation? To answer such questions requires much clinical and research attention.

Methods

There has not been much systematic research on the effectiveness of various techniques for educating clinicians about lesbian and gay issues. A variety of methods can be used: readings, lectures, films, role plays, experiential exercises, and field research.

A large amount of information can be obtained through reading books and articles on gay and lesbian themes. There are a number of texts for mental health professionals which focus specifically on clinical issues with gay and lesbian clients (Coleman, 1987; Gonsiorek, 1982; Hetrick & Stein, 1984; Moses & Hawkins, 1982; Stein & Cohen, 1986). Gay or lesbian speakers can be invited to give lectures, or participate in small discussion groups. Mental health workers can be encouraged to talk with gay and lesbian colleagues and friends. Analyzing the portrayal of gay men and lesbian women in the media might help us to understand current societal attitudes toward them. In addition, there are popular books and films about gay and lesbian life that might be used to alter stereotypic views. Clinical role-plays and videotapes of interviews with gay and lesbian clients can help therapists both to practice their skills and to explore their feelings about working with various issues that may arise in a helping relationship. Experiential exercises such as guided fantasies can help one to develop empathy for those whose life experiences are different from one's own.

PROFESSIONAL RESPONSIBILITY

As mental health professionals we need to work within our professional organizations (APA, NASW, and AACD) to ensure that they live up to their professional statements about the need to educate their constituents about lesbian and gay concerns. We can work to elect openly gay or lesbian candidates to positions in our professional organizations to guarantee that gay or lesbian voices are heard in important decision-making processes (Brown, 1990). We can work with our accrediting organizations to make sure that when graduate schools apply for accreditation from APA, the Council on Social Work Accreditation, or AACD, they are required to demonstrate that their curriculum includes up-to-date information about gay and lesbian topics. We can work with our certifying organizations to require that agencies seeking to be approved as internship sites demonstrate that they have in-service training and supervision in which they discuss gay and lesbian issues. We can push for our licensing exams to have questions about sexual orientation and to use gay and lesbian clients as case examples. Within our own practice and agency settings, we can request that information and resources for gay and lesbian clients be made available; we can initiate case conferences and in-service education programs where the clinical implications of sexual orientation are discussed; and we can develop homophobia prevention workshops for staff.

CONCLUSION

Mental health professionals are poorly prepared to deal with issues of sexuality in general. Not surprisingly then, they receive little if any education either in their graduate training programs or in their practice in the field which focuses specifically on gay and lesbian issues. Despite the large number of gay men and lesbian women, many mental health professionals remain biased and unqualified to serve them. Education for mental health professionals on gay and lesbian topics is desperately needed. Training should focus on *information* about gay and lesbian issues; on the *interface* between the gay and lesbian client, his/her sexuality, and the effects of living in a heterosexist and homophobic society; and on the *interaction* between the attitudes, beliefs, and sexual orientation of the clinician and the client. We must all work to ensure that training about gay and lesbian issues occurs. Only then can mental health workers practice in a truly effective and therefore professionally ethical manner.

NOTES

1. I use what may seem a redundant phrase — "lesbian women" — for three reasons. First, I reject the generic use of gay to refer to both men and women because it obscures the differences between the experiences of gay men and lesbian women. Secondly, I use the terms gay and lesbian as adjectives rather than as nouns to highlight that sexual orientation is only one aspect of people's lives. Finally, I believe that the use of the phrase "lesbian women" not only parallels

the structure of "gay men" but suggests that lesbian women may have more in common with heterosexual women than with gay men.

REFERENCES

Abramowitz, N.R. (1971). Human sexuality in the social work curriculum. *The Family Coordinator, 20,* 349-354.

Bell, A., Weinberg, M., & Hammersmith, S. (1981). *Sexual preference: Its develonment in men and women.* Bloomington, IN: Indiana University Press.

Bell, A., & Weinberg, M. (1978). *Homosexualities: A study of diversity among men and women.* New York: Simon & Schuster.

Bieber, I., Dain, H., Dince, P., Drelich, M., Grand, H., Gundlach, R., Kremer, M., Rifkin, A., Wilbur, C., & Bieber, T. (1962). *Homosexuality.* New York: Vintage.

Blumenfeld, W.J., & Raymond, D. (1988). *Looking at gay and lesbian life.* Boston: Beacon.

Blumstein, P., & Schwartz, P. (1983). *American couples.* New York: William Morrow.

Brashear, D. (1976). *The social worker as sex educator.* New York: Human Sciences Press.

Brown, L.S. (1990, August). Making psychology safe for gays and lesbians. Paper presented at the 98th Annual Convention of the American Psychological Association, Boston, MA.

Buhrke, R. A. (1989a). Incorporating lesbian and gay issues into counselor training: A resource guide. *Journal of Counseling and Development, 68*(1), 77-80.

Burhke, R.A. (1989b). Female student perspectives on training in lesbian and gay issues. *The Counseling Psychologist, 17*(4), 629-636.

Buhrke, R. A. (1989c). Lesbian-related issues in counseling supervision. *Women and Counseling, 8*(1/2), 195-206.

Carlson, H. (1985, August). Employment issues for researchers on lesbian and gay issues. Paper presented at the 93rd Annual Convention of the American Psycholgical Association. Los Angeles, CA.

Casas, J. M., Brady, S., & Ponterotto, J. G. (1983). Sexual preference biases in counseling: An information processing approach. *Journal of Counseling Psychology, 30*(2), 139-145.

Cass, V.C. (1985). Homosexual identity: A concept in need of definition. In J.P. De Cecco & M.G. Shively (Eds.), *Origins of sexuality and homosexuality* (pp. 105-126). New York: Harrington Park Press.

Churchill, W. (1967). *Homosexuality in males: A cross-cultural and cross-species investigation.* Englewood Cliffs, NJ: Prentice Hall.

Cohen, D.D., & Tanenbaum, R. L. (1985). Sexuality education for staff in long-term psychiatric hospitals. *Hospital and Community Psychiatry, 36*(2), 187-189.

Coleman, E. (1987). *Integrated identity for gay men and lesbians: Psychotherapeutic approaches for emotional well-being.* New York: Harrington Park Press.

Committee on Lesbian and Gay Concerns. (1990). *Final report of the task force on bias in psychotherapy with lesbians and gay men.* Washington, DC: American Psychological Association.

Crooks, R., & Baur, K. (1990). *Our sexuality.* Redwood City, CA: Benjamin/ Cummings.

De Cecco, J.P., & Shively, M.G. (1985). *Origins of sexuality and homosexuality.* New York: Harrington Park Press.

de Monteflores, C., & Schultz, S. (1978). Coming out: Similiarities and differences for lesbians and gay men. *Journal of Social Issues, 34*(3), 59-72.

Dulaney, D. D., & Kelly, J. (1982). Improving services to gay and lesbian clients. *Social Work, 27*(2), 178-183.

Dworkin, S. H., & Gutierrez, F. (1989). Counselors be aware: Clients come in every size, shape, color, and sexual orientation. *Journal of Counseling and Development, 68*(10), 6-8.

Ford, C., & Beach, F. (1951). *Patterns of sexual behavior.* New York: Harper & Row.

Fort, J., Steiner, C., & Conrad, F. (1971). Attitudes of mental health professionals toward homosexuality and its treatment. *Psychological Reports, 29,* 347-350.

Freud, S. (1905). Three essays on the theory of sexuality. In *Standard Editions,* Vol. VII. London: Hogarth Press.

Garfinkle, E. M., & Morin, S. F. (1978). Psychologists' attitudes toward homosexual psychotherapy clients. *Journal of Social Issues, 34*(3), 101-112.

Gartrell, N. (1984). Combating homophobia in the psychotherapy of lesbians. *Women and Therapy, 3*(1), 13-39.

Gartrell, N., Kraemer, H., & Brodie, H.K. (1974). Psychiatrists' attitudes toward female homosexuality. *Journal of Nervous Disorders and Mental Diseases,* 150(2), 141-144.

Glenn, A. A., & Russell, R. K. (1986). Heterosexual bias among counselor trainees. *Counselor Education and Supervision, 25* (3), 222-229.

Gochros, H. (1970). Introducing human sexuality into the graduate social work curriculum. *Social Work Education Reporter,* 18, 47-50.

Gochros, H. L. (1984). Teaching social workers to meet the needs of the homosexually oriented. *Journal of Social Work and Human Sexuality, 2*(2/3), 137-156.

Gonsiorek, J. (1982). *A guide to psychotherapy with gay and lesbian clients.* New York: Harrington Park Press.

Graham, D. L. R., Rawlings, E. I., Halpern, H. S., & Hermes, J. (1984). Therapists' needs for training in counseling lesbians and gay men. *Professional Psychology: Research and Practice, 15*(4), 482-496.

Gray, L. A., Cummins, E. J., Johnson, B. P., & Mason, M. J. (1989). Human sexuality instruction in counselor education curricula. *Counselor Education and Supervision,* 28, 305-317.

Hencken, J. D., & O'Dowd, W.T. (1977). Coming out as an aspect of identity formation. *Gai Saber,* 1, 18-22.

Herek, G. (1986). The social psychology of homophobia: Toward a practical theory. *Review of Law & Social Change,* 14(4), 923-934.

Herek, G. (1989). Hate crimes against lesbians and gay men. *American Psychologist,* 44, 948-955.

Hetrick, E., & Stein, T. (Eds.). (1984). *Innovations in psychotherapy with homosexuals.* Washington, DC: American Psychiatric Press.

Hooker, E. (1957). The adjustment of the male overt homosexual. *Journal of Projective Techniques,* 21, 18-31.

Iasenza, S. (1989). The challenges of integrating sexual orientation into counselor training and research. *Journal of Counseling and Development,* 68(1), 73-76.

Jay, K., & Young, A. (1979). *The gay report.* New York: Summit Books.

Kinsey, A., Pomeroy, W., & Martin, C. (1948). *Sexual behavior in the human male.* Philadelphia: Saunders.

Kinsey, A., Pomeroy, W., Martin, C., & Gebhard, P. (1953). *Sexual behavior in the human female.* Philadelphia: Saunders.

Landis, C.E., Miller, H.R., & Wettstone, R.P. (1975). Sexual awareness training for counselors. *Teaching of Psychology,* 2(1), 33-36.

LoPiccolo, J. (1978). The professionalism of sex therapy: Issues and problems. In J. LoPiccolo & L. LoPiccolo (Eds.), *The handbook of sex therapy* (pp. 511-526). New York: Plenum Press.

Martin, A. (1982). Some issues in the treatment of gay and lesbian patients. *Psychotherapy: Theory, Research and Practice,* 19(3), 341-348.

Matek, O. (1977). A methodology for teaching human sexuality to social work students. *Journal of Education for Social Work,* 13(3), 50-55.

Mazur, C. (1978). *A descriptive study of social work education in human sexuality: Curriculum design and instructor characteristics.* Unpublished master's thesis, Honolulu: University of Hawaii.

Miranda, J., & Storms, M. (1989). Psychological Adjustment of Lesbians and gay men. *Journal of Counseling and Development,* 68(1), 41-45.

Morin, S. F. (1977). Heterosexual bias in psychological research on lesbianism and male homosexuality. *American Psychologist,* 32, 629-637.

Moses, A.E., & Hawkins, R.O., Jr. (1982). *Counseling lesbian women and gay men.* St. Louis: The C.V. Mosby Company.

Moses, A. E., & Hawkins, R. O., Jr. (1985). Two-hour service training session on homophobia. In H. Hildago, T. L. Peterson, & N. J. Woodman (Eds.), *Lesbian and gay issues: A resource manual for social workers* (pp. 153-157). Silver Spring, MD: National Association of Social Workers.

Murphy, B.C. (1989). Lesbian couples and their parents. *Journal of Counseling and Development,* 68(1), 46-51.

Murphy, B.C. (in press). Counseling lesbian couples: Sexism, heterosexism and homophobia. In S.H. Dworkin & F. Gutierrez (Eds.), *Journey to the end of the rainbow: Critical incidents in counseling gay, lesbian, and bisexual clients.* Alexandria, VA: AACD Press.

Nathan, S. (1986). Are clinical psychology graduate students being taught enough about sexuality? A survey of doctoral programs. *Journal of Sex Research,* 22, 520-524.

Nichols, M., & Shernoff, M. (1985). Some guidance and advice for a continuing education session on gay and lesbian issues. In H. Hildago, T. L. Peterson, & N. J. Woodman (Eds.), *Lesbian and gay issues: A resource manual for social workers* (pp. 148-151). Silver Spring, MD: National Association of Social Workers.

Norton, J. L. (1982). Integrating gay issues into counselor education. *Counselor Education and Supervision, 21* (3), 208-212.

Peterson, T. L. (1985). A prototype for a comprehensive continuing education program on gay and lesbian issues. In H. Hildago, T. L. Peterson, & N. J. Woodman (Eds.), *Lesbian and gay issues: A resource manual for social workers* (pp. 145-147). Silver Spring, MD. National Association of Social Workers.

Riddle, D., & Sang, B. (1978). Psychotherapy with lesbians. *Journal of Social Issues,* 34(3), 84-100.

Rochlin, M. (1982). Sexual orientation of the therapist and therapeutic effectiveness with gay clients. *Journal of Homosexuality,* 7(2/3), 21-29.

Roth, S., & Murphy, B.C. (1986). Therapeutic work with lesbian clients: A systemic therapy view. In M. Ault-Riche (Ed.), *Women and family therapy* (pp.78-89). Rockville, MD: Aspen Press.

Schlesinger, B. (1983). Teaching human sexuality to graduate social work students: A decade review 1971-1982. *Journal of Social Work and Human Sexuality,* 1(3), 7-17.

Schneider, M. S., & Tremble, B. (1986). Training service providers to work with gay or lesbian adolescents: A workshop. *Journal of Counseling and Development,* 65(2), 98-99.

Sophie, J. (1982). Counseling lesbians. *The Personnel and Guidance Journal,* 60(6), 341-345.

Stein, T. S. (1988). Theoretical considerations in psychotherapy with gay men and lesbians. *Journal of Homosexuality,* 15(1/2), 75-95.

Stein, T.S., & Cohen, C. (Eds.). (1986). *Contemporary perspectives on psychotherapy with lesbian and gay men.* New York: Plenum.

Storms, M. (1980). Theories of sexual orientation. *Journal of Personality and Social Psychology,* 38, 783-792.

Thompson G. H., & Fishburn, W. R. (1977). Attitudes toward homosexuality among graduate counseling students. *Counselor Education and Supervision,* 17, 121-130.

Tourney, G. (1980). Hormones and homosexuality. In J. Marmor (Ed.), *Homosexual behavior* (pp.1-58). New York: Basic Books.

Welbourne, A. K. (1983). A review of the current status of human sexuality training programs for professionals. *Marriage and Family Review,* 6(3/4), 61-77.

Wisniewski, J. J., & Toomey, B. G. (1987). Are social workers homophobic? *Social Work,* 32, 454-455.

Zapka, J., & Mazur, R. (1977). Peer sex education training and evaluation. *American Journal of Public Health,* 67, 450-454.

HIV Education
for Gay, Lesbian,
and Bisexual Youth:
Personal Risk, Personal Power,
and the Community of Conscience

Kevin Cranston, MDiv

Massachusetts Department of Education

SUMMARY. Adolescent gay and bisexual males face a higher risk of infection with HIV than most other young people because of their behaviors and because HIV prevention programs have failed to address their unique concerns. Ironically, current efforts to heighten public awareness about the AIDS pandemic may be nullifying the potential for gay, lesbian, and bisexual young persons at high risk to form the support networks needed to modify their behavior. The personal and group empowerment of gay, lesbian, and bisexual young people is a necessary prerequisite to their ability to make healthy behavioral choices around HIV and other health issues. This paper proposes a comprehensive health education model for HIV prevention for gay, lesbian, and bisexual adolescents. Current health education efforts would be augmented by broader self and group empowerment training that would develop self-esteem, social skills, support networks, and access to risk reduction materials. An integrated system of care involving school-based programs, multi-service youth agencies, and self-help groups would be in a position to deliver appropriate educational, mental health, medical, and social

Kevin Cranston is AIDS/Health Education Consultant to the Massachusetts Department of Education, a visiting lecturer at Harvard Divinity School, and a member of the Adult Advisory Board of the Boston Alliance of Gay and Lesbian Youth, Inc. (BAGLY). Correspondence may be addressed: Massachusetts Department of Education, Bureau of Student Development and Health, 1385 Hancock Street, Quincy, MA 02169-5183.

support services. Such a system of care presents gay, lesbian, and
bisexual youth with their best chance to reduce their risk of infection
with HIV and develop into emotionally healthy individuals.

In the past few years, public and scientific awareness of the threat posed
to young people by the AIDS/HIV pandemic has grown, in part because of
an increase in the number of adolescents who have been affected by the
disease. Along with other groups of individuals at significant risk of HIV
infection, adolescents have been the subject of specialized behavioral research and vigorous HIV prevention efforts. Within the adolescent population, however, the special needs of gay and bisexual males have received little attention, despite the fact that they are at very high risk of
infection. The complex personal and community issues that heighten the
risk of HIV infection in gay and bisexual males require specialized educational interventions and targeted services. This paper will address the neglect of gay, lesbian, and bisexual youth in current health education programs and make recommendations for developing more effective
approaches to HIV prevention within this population. The work of Brazilian educator Paulo Freire (1970) lends itself to this model that has as its
goals the personal and group empowerment of lesbian, gay, and bisexual
youth. Authentic personal empowerment, in the context of a community
of shared values and experiences, is a prerequisite to effective HIV risk
reduction for these young people. One important question to be addressed
is whether gay-specific HIV programs hold the promise of serving the
needs of young lesbians as well.

TERMINOLOGY

In this paper, the terms *gay* and *lesbian* refer throughout to male and
female individuals, respectively, who identify or are in the process of
identifying according to a primarily or exclusively homosexual orientation. The term *bisexual* refers to male or female persons who identify
according to a sexual orientation that is directed to a significant degree
toward members of both sexes. The term *sexual orientation* is inclusive of
affectional attachments as well as sexual feelings, fantasies, and behaviors. The terms *adolescent* and *adolescence* refer to individuals age 11 to
24, but may also include individuals sharing the developmental concerns
of this age group who are somewhat older or younger.

HIV infection includes both symptomatic and asymptomatic states,
while *AIDS* refers strictly to the medical diagnosis of acquired immune
deficiency syndrome. *Risk behaviors* are those that allow for the transmis-

sion of HIV from one person to another, including blood-to-blood contact (e.g., the sharing of injection needles) and sexual intercourse (anal, vaginal, or oral). *HIV prevention* refers to strategies for avoiding initial infection with HIV. One of these strategies is employing *safer sex*, which here means a range of sexual behaviors that pose lower risks of sexual transmission of HIV including, but not limited to, various non-intercourse sexual behaviors and/or the use of condoms, dental dams, and other barrier methods.

KEY CONCEPTS IN ADOLESCENT HIV PREVENTION

The current state of research into adolescent HIV prevention does not provide conclusive statements about what works. Just as risk of infection is multi-factorial in its origins, the capacity of persons to reduce their risk has multiple sources. Nevertheless, theorists and practitioners in the field of adolescent risk reduction have identified likely components of a successful approach.

First and foremost, HIV related information needs to be presented within the larger context of comprehensive health education. In order for young people to address their risk of HIV infection they need to have a broader understanding of personal health and wellness, especially of related risk behaviors (e.g., alcohol and substance use), of anatomy and physiological function, of human sexuality and sexually transmitted diseases. In schools, comprehensive health education also refers to a continuous, planned, sequential approach to the broad range of health issues across all grade levels.

The self-esteem of young people underlies the comprehensive health education approach. Self-esteem is considered the linchpin to the ability to utilize the content of health education. Put another way, young people cannot be expected to choose healthy behaviors, whether it is observing good nutrition, wearing seat belts, or opting for safer sexual practices, if they do not possess a strong sense of personal worth. Furthermore, health education is only effective if it provides quality counseling and other support services to those young people whose self-esteem has suffered most.

Beyond a fundamental love of self, young people need to learn a set of personal skills around all health issues that enable them to make choices that preserve their well-being. Among these are skills in decision-making, communication, relationship-building, and the negotiation/refusal of behaviors. While these capabilities have relevance to a number of health concerns, they are crucial to the prevention of HIV and other sexually transmitted diseases (STDs). The capacity to choose safer sex, for example, requires that a young person be effective in expressing personal needs, deciding on an acceptable level of risk, maintaining an intimate relationship, and discussing the options of sexual expression with a partner. Other necessary skills include knowing how to correctly use condoms and other barrier forms of disease prevention, how to identify health problems, and how to get help when problems are identified.

High self-esteem and competency in certain personal skills combine to create a sense of self-efficacy, the belief that one possesses the ability to use the learned skills in defense of personal well-being. Self-efficacy emerges in much of the research into adolescent HIV prevention as a crucial component in the successful adoption of risk reducing practices. Other beliefs and belief systems apparently related to the ability to make healthy behavioral choices are the acceptance of personal susceptibility to HIV infection, the recognition of the severity of HIV infection, and the expectation that the chosen behavior(s) will actually reduce risk.

THE FAILURE OF HIV EDUCATION
FOR SEXUAL MINORITY YOUTH

The above described model for HIV prevention in adolescents that includes a comprehensive health education approach, a focus on self-esteem and social skills development, the availability of support services, and access to safe sex materials, has been poorly applied to gay, lesbian, and bisexual young people in mainstream settings. To date, sexual minority youth have few appropriate resources available to them. In fact, the majority of recent HIV prevention services directed at adolescents have actively excluded the concerns of gay, lesbian, and bisexual young people. The reasons for this exclusion have their roots in institutional heterosexism and in our country's historic experience of the pandemic.

Because Americans equated AIDS and HIV infection with the gay male community at the outset of the pandemic, health education experts observed that heterosexual individuals often dismissed their risk of infection. To counteract this misperception, many health educators have felt the need to stress that "AIDS is not a gay disease." Furthermore, there seems to be a growing trend for schools to request that guest speakers who discuss AIDS refrain from discussing homosexuality. While this approach may help instill a sense of personal susceptibility to HIV infection and deflect some of the homophobic responses that many adolescents accord HIV prevention efforts, it has the unfortunate effect of eliminating one of the few educational situations in which gay, lesbian, and bisexual issues can be discussed. If homosexuality is acknowledged in these programs, it is often done with the assumption that the concerns apply to just a few individuals, rather than to a sizeable percentage of persons. These factors have combined to cause the "degayification" of HIV disease, which, in turn, obscures the concerns of a significant number of gay, lesbian, and bisexual young people present in these settings.

GAY AND BISEXUAL YOUTH
AND THEIR RISK OF INFECTION

Until recently, epidemiological studies of the AIDS/HIV pandemic have concealed the true risk facing gay and bisexual young males, in part because studies have often failed to distinguish between youth and adult populations in various risk categories, and because greater attention has been paid to AIDS diagnoses cases over HIV infection rates. In light of the relatively small number of adolescents (both gay and non-gay) who have received a diagnosis of AIDS during their adolescence, when contrasted with the very large number of adult gay and bisexual men who have been diagnosed to date, it is easy to overlook the risk facing gay and bisexual adolescents.

As was discussed above, those advocating for AIDS/HIV education of young people take great pains to dramatize the risk to heterosexual youth. One common approach is to point out that the rate of "heterosexual" transmission among adolescents is twice that of adults (approximately 8% versus 4%). It is rarely pointed out, however, that the great majority of sexually infected adolescents were infected as a result of homosexual contact.

Recently, more accurate rates of infection and risk behavior among gay and bisexual males has become available. At the Fifth International Conference on AIDS in San Francisco, the U.S. Centers for Disease Control released data from an on-going seroprevalence survey (seroprevalence is the estimated rate of infection with HIV in a given population at a given point in time) of clinics and facilities serving adolescents. Across all the sexually transmitted disease clinics surveyed, the rates of HIV infection in gay and bisexual males age 20-24 ranged from 4% to 47%, with a median rate of 25%, a rate of infection ten times higher than the next highest risk group, young urban black males (Wendell, Onorato, Allen, McCray, & Sweeney, 1990).

Additionally, the San Francisco Board of Health reported on a seroprevalence survey of young gay and bisexual men visiting gay dance clubs in the city (Lemp, Nieri, & San Francisco Dept. of Public Health, 1991).

Of the 258 men age 17 to 25 who consented to HIV antibody testing (along with Hepatitis B and syphilis screens), 12% tested antibody positive. Particularly high rates were observed in the 17 to 19 and the 20 to 22 year old groups (14.3% and 14.0%, respectively, testing positive), and among African-American and Latino men across the entire age group (22.9% and 14.3%, respectively).

What accounts for the increased risk among young gay and bisexual males? Primarily, it is a result of engaging in unprotected anal and oral intercourse and shared injection drug needles and paraphernalia. For example, the San Francisco study found that 43% of the respondents had recently engaged in unprotected anal intercourse (both insertive and receptive). Secondarily, these risk behaviors are more likely to result in HIV transmission in a population where there are high rates of infection already present. While sexual and drug use contact with older gay men may at one time have been solely implicated in the heightened risk of younger gay and bisexual males, contact outside of the adolescent community is no longer a necessary factor in the risk equation. There are now significant levels of infection in the gay and bisexual youth population so that unprotected intercourse and needle sharing with peers are extremely high risk behaviors.

Risk of HIV infection is not limited to gay and bisexual males, or to male-to-male sexual contact. Any members of the gay, lesbian, or bisexual community who engage in injection drug needle sharing, other blood-to-blood contact (e.g., blood rituals, or practices such as ear piercing or tattooing where a needle is shared), or unprotected intercourse of any kind with a male or female partner may become infected. Certainly young lesbian women have contracted and will contract the disease, although as a group lesbians have a significantly lower level of infection rates.

A strictly behavioral/epidemiological model of HIV risk among lesbian, gay, and bisexual youth misses a number of developmental, historical, and psychological factors that further increase the likelihood of HIV infection in this population, and complicate attempts to address and influence their risk. Gay and bisexual adolescents are at higher risk for sexually transmitted diseases, and, along with lesbian youth, are at higher risk for a host of other threats to their health (e.g., suicide and alcohol/substance abuse). Being gay, lesbian, or bisexual in a heterosexual world is difficult for any individual, and being an adolescent as well greatly complicates the situation.

The so-called "tasks" of adolescence, including the search for personal identity, the development of meaningful peer relationships, the integration of physical and emotional changes, the differentiation from parents, and various forms of personal experimentation may be complicated by a sexual orientation not in keeping with social norms. Schools and other youth settings generally operate under a presumption that adolescents are heterosexual. Gay, lesbian, and bisexual adolescents in these settings may lack opportunities to practice social skills crucial to their development and to establish authentic systems of peer support for their emerging identities.

Historically, lesbian, gay, and bisexual youth have a different experience of the AIDS/HIV pandemic than their adult counterparts. Adult gay men were targeted from the early 1980s with materials and programs designed to address their particular risk behaviors, within a frame of reference specific to their culture. Today's lesbian, gay, and bisexual youth, however, have come of age at a time when the AIDS education message has gone mainstream. While most adult gay men and lesbians connected with the community have watched as friends and lovers have become infected, sickened, or died of HIV disease, relatively few younger gay people have been so personally affected. Personal loss is known to be a significant factor in the unprecedented behavioral changes within the gay male community. Most young gay, lesbian, and bisexual community members have not had equivalent experiences that would compel them to modify their risk behaviors. Unlike most adult members of the organized lesbian, gay, and bisexual communities, younger members can still maintain the belief that they are not susceptible.

Similarly, lesbian, gay, and bisexual youth are at increased risk because of their lower self-esteem. A body of evidence exists to document higher rates of suicidal ideation and suicide attempts in this population compared to heterosexual adolescents, a problem believed by most researchers to be secondary to low self-esteem. Gary Remafedi, of the University of Minnesota, the Hetrick-Martin Institute for the Protection of Lesbian and Gay Youth in New York City, and the U.S. Department of Health and Human Services Report of the Secretary's Task Force on Youth Suicide each confirm this heightened suicide risk. Associated risks include higher rates of alcohol and substance abuse, violent victimization, school problems, and family conflict related to sexual orientation issues. The comprehensive health education model predicts that a person with a poor sense of personal worth has less ability to pursue healthy behavioral options. If the use of alcohol or other drugs is linked with sexual activity, unsafe sexual practices are more likely to occur (AIDS Action, 1991).

THE GOALS OF AIDS/HIV EDUCATION
WITH SEXUAL MINORITY YOUTH

Following the general model of HIV prevention education outlined above, it is possible to sketch out goals and strategies for addressing the risk of HIV infection facing gay, lesbian, and bisexual youth. Attention must be paid to their low self-esteem and other personal problems. There needs to be a mental health system staffed by professionals who are aware of the unique issues of gay, lesbian, and bisexual youth and skilled in effective therapeutic approaches. Clearly, suicide prevention services need to make special efforts to reach out to gay, lesbian, and bisexual youth.

These adolescents also require access to affordable, confidential, and sensitive health care. Given the growing number of HIV-infected gay and bisexual youth, those who provide health care to the lesbian and gay community need to advocate for an equivalent level of care for its adolescent members. Early intervention and clinical trials of promising treatments need to be available to infected young people.

In addition to helping these young people cope with their coming out experiences, educators and service providers need to create safe and supportive environments within which gay, lesbian, and bisexual youth may engage in the process of learning about HIV prevention. We must set as a goal the creation of authentic communities of young gay, lesbian, and bisexual persons, youth-focused social milieux that promote self-love and reinforce the risk reduction message. This is a theme that will be addressed further below.

Just as their heterosexual counterparts require a set of personal skills in order to operationalize safer sex instructions, gay, lesbian, and bisexual youth need to develop competency in a similar, but not identical collection of skills. Young lesbians and bisexual women need information that is relevant to sexual expression between women. Gay and bisexual males need additional content specific to the risk associated with anal and oral intercourse. Both groups need to learn how to build friendships and romantic relationships in a world that often compels secrecy about sexual orientation. These socialization skills are more about the process of coming out than they are about risk reduction, and they are a necessary prerequisite.

HIV educators addressing the risk of gay, lesbian, and bisexual youth should attempt to evaluate the young person's sense of self-efficacy concerning these skills. If someone feels ill-equipped to negotiate safe sexual practices, she/he must have a secure context within which to work on this personal development. The ability to refuse behaviors, to choose abstinence from drug use or sexual expression, for example, is critical to health and well-being.

Finally, HIV education for sexual minority youth needs to make appropriate safer sex and other risk reduction materials readily available. Adolescents consistently report that lack of access to condoms is a significant barrier to having safer sex. This turns out to be no less true for gay or bisexual young men (AIDS Action, 1991). Providers of health education and support services play a critical role in making available the materials necessary for sexual risk reduction. This means providing free access to dental dams and condoms (both lubricated and unlubricated condoms are needed), bleach, sterile syringes, and clearly written risk reduction literature.

A FREIREIAN MODEL OF AIDS/HIV EDUCATION FOR SEXUAL MINORITY YOUTH

Paulo Freire's educational work with the Brazilian poor serves as a model for the development of self-empowering communities of gay, lesbian, and bisexual youth committed to survival and growth. His pioneering work was based on the contention that poor, unschooled peasants were capable of coming to terms with their lives in critical and authentic ways through a learned process of questioning and evaluating their status in the world and the societal structures that have led to that status. A Freireian approach rejects knowledge as a fixed entity and sees this instead as a tool of the majority to protect the status quo and their power. Through the use of a "banking" analogy, he demonstrates the power of the traditional educational/knowledge system. In that system those in power "deposit" information into the passive minds of the oppressed by defining and controlling the content of education. Through this mechanism, the world view of the powerful becomes the world view of the oppressed, thus diminishing the likelihood that the oppressed will question the unfairness of their life circumstances.

Many educational approaches to AIDS/HIV education with adolescents use the "banking" model. The facts about AIDS/HIV are static entities inserted into the minds of learners. The decisions educators want students to make are made for them in advance, and students are drilled on the correct responses (e.g., "sexual abstinence is the surest way to reduce the risk of HIV infection"). Learners are not critically engaged in the educational event, which serves to support the power of the interest group that the AIDS educator represents. In the area of sexuality education, for example, students consistently express a desire for more information about homosexuality, and yet most sexuality education curricula offer minimal content in this area. The very absence of specific information about gay, lesbian, and bisexual individuals is itself the content that informs learners that sexual minority youth either do not exist or they are not important. Controversies around school-based sexuality curricula point to the conflicting forces attempting to gain control over the educational content. If students had control over sexuality curricula, every school in the United States would actively engage in discussions about homosexuality in health classes and elsewhere.

In an educational model that has as its goal personal and collective empowerment, we need to help communities of lesbian, gay, and bisexual young people enter into a critical dialogue about their lives in the presence of both HIV and heterosexism. Freire introduces the concept of the community of conscience, the committed human society devoted to the development of a critical consciousness about their oppressed status and the forces that conspire to preserve that status. The community of conscience is a tool to be used by sexual minority youth to wrest control of their relational and sexual lives, to examine where their education needs supplementing, and to promote the development of a system of care that serves their needs.

Such a community is a challenge not only to conservative heterosexist forces, but also to well-meaning adult helpers who seek to "do for" gay, lesbian, and bisexual youth. Adult providers must be prepared to examine their power over young learners, and to work with an empowered community of adolescents who can effectively command the terms of their own education. Critical questions for the community of conscience might be, "What does it mean to be a gay, lesbian, or bisexual young person? What draws us together? Why are we at risk? Why haven't our needs been addressed?" These questions need to be answered prior to introducing the traditional content of AIDS/HIV education.

The process of building critical consciousness among gay, lesbian, and bisexual youth is inextricably linked with that of the lesbian, gay, and bisexual liberation movement(s). The historical process by which issues of sexual orientation have moved out of the moral, legal, and medical realms into the socio-political arena is "required reading" for the community of conscience. For example, a great deal can be learned by examining the early days of the AIDS/HIV pandemic in terms of the experiences of the lesbian and gay community (see, for example, Randy Shilts' *And The Band Played On*). Young gay, lesbian, and bisexual community members asking themselves, "Why haven't our needs been addressed?" is as powerful as Freire's villagers asking themselves, "Who owns the well?"

The community of conscience does not exclude the adult gay, lesbian, and bisexual community. Rather, it engages the adult community in authentic mutuality. Lesbian, gay, and bisexual adolescents benefit from the experience and perspective of the adult community, while also sharing their own lived reality with these adults. As gay, lesbian, and bisexual youth define themselves and their world, they can offer fresh and unique approaches to coping with a dominant culture that has passively watched the AIDS/HIV pandemic rob us of life and health.

MULTIPLE SETTINGS: A SYSTEM OF CARE

The three institutional settings that appear to have the potential for utilizing a Freireian model for effective AIDS/HIV prevention for gay, lesbian, and bisexual youth are: schools, multi-service agencies, and self-help support groups. School-based programs have the advantage of ready access to and by the greatest number of sexual minority youth. Programs, such as PROJECT 10 at Fairfax High School in Los Angeles, adhere to the political and ethical position that public education and related services are the right of all students. This perspective requires a commitment to address the unique needs of all students, including gay, lesbian, and bisexual youth. Programs modeled after PROJECT 10 are being developed across the United States. They represent an attempt to more equitably use public resources on behalf of minority youth, and to provide support and educational services that promote justice and equity in the school community. These programs recognize the presence of gay, lesbian, and bisexual young people, and in doing so also have the opportunity to build critical consciousness among all students within the school community around issues of diversity, tolerance, and human rights. A potential drawback is the tendency of traditional school governance models to be invested in a power-over relationship, such as, administration to faculty and faculty to students. Insofar as programs such as PROJECT 10 seek power-sharing governance structures within traditional educational settings, they serve as a model for this new vision of educational ownership.

To date, multi-service agencies have carried the burden of reaching out to and addressing the needs of gay, lesbian, and bisexual youth. Over the past decade, complex systems of social service provision for sexual minority youth have been provided from within the gay and lesbian communities and through the use of public funds. Agencies, such as the Hetrick-Martin Institute in New York City and the Gay and Lesbian Community Services Center in Hollywood, have led the way in the development of educational (including AIDS/HIV prevention education), mental health, social support, housing, and medical services for gay, lesbian, and bisexual youth. These adult providers are trusted and respected by the young people they serve. Modeled after the best mainstream youth service and child welfare agencies, they offer comprehensive and integrated systems of care. Furthermore, they have been strong advocates for gay, lesbian, and bisexual adolescents in the child welfare and youth services community. This latter approach has served to legitimize the service needs of gay, lesbian, and bisexual youth. To the degree, however, that it replicates power-over relationships between providers and adolescents, it can sacrifice the development of the community of conscience. The risk is that sexual minority youth may not have the power to influence the provision of services in these settings or to establish an authentic communal presence.

Finally, self-help groups constituted by gay, lesbian, and bisexual youth have emerged as critical places for youth empowerment. Modeled after the women's health movement and other non-professional organizations of persons seeking liberation and empowerment, youth-controlled organizations wield power over their own process of the development of personal awareness and communal support. In the area of HIV prevention, self-help groups can create a social milieu that supports and reinforces a reduction in high risk behaviors. Invited adult educators provide current information to be processed by group members personally and in collective discussion. Unfortunately, these groups rarely have the structure or resources to provide for the tangible needs of their members, such as in areas of housing, counseling, and health care. Similarly, by the very nature of their purpose and composition, they lack broader political and social influence within their communities. But, as sites for youth empowerment, they cannot be equalled.

A comprehensive approach to effective HIV prevention education for gay, lesbian, and bisexual youth draws on the strengths and resources of all three of these service modes. School-based programs can educate the entire student population about gay, lesbian, and bisexual concerns and about HIV/AIDS related issues. They also are in a unique position in terms of both access and resources to address the needs of sexual minority youth who participate in our educational systems. Multi-service agencies can offer more intensive, targeted programs and services for young people at highest risk. And self-help groups can build the community of conscience that will empower and sustain these young people. With a multifaceted system of care in place, gay, lesbian, and bisexual youth stand a better chance of creating for themselves a sense of self-worth, a community of support, and a future of possibilities.

REFERENCES

AIDS Action Committee of Massachusetts (1991). *A survey of AIDS-related knowledge, attitudes, and behaviors among gay and bisexual men in Greater Boston*.
Freire, P. (1970). *Pedagogy of the oppressed*. New York: Seabury Press.
Lemp, G., Nieri, G., San Francisco Department of Public Health AIDS Office (1991). *The young men's survey*. A presentation to the San Francisco Health Commission.
Shilts, R. (1987). *And the band played on: Politics, people, and the AIDS epidemic*. New York: St. Martin's Press.
Wendell, D., Onorato, I., Allen, D., McCray, E., Sweeney, P., and state and local health departments (1990). *HIV seroprevalence among adolescents and young adults in selected clinic settings, United States, 1988-90*. Paper presented at the Sixth International Conference on AIDS, San Francisco, CA.

Index

ableism, 6,197,203,208,209
abolitionist, 83
abortion, 128,201
accreditation, 242
Acquired Immune Deficiency
   (AIDS), 6,16,20-22,25-26,
   33,61-65,71-72,90,91,98,99,
   107,108,132,153,173,180,
   193,202-206,238,247-259
administrators
   conservative, 2,130,131,133
   powers of, 2,4,26-27,32,39,121,
      123-126,130,132,133,135,
      141,143
adoption, 106
advising, faculty, 110
affirmative action, 133
Afghanistani, 21
Afro-American, see Black
ageism/aging, 6,197,199,203,
   207-209,218,231,233,236
Alcoholics Anonymous, 238
Alcott, Amos Bronson, 124
Alcott, Louisa May, 124
Alliance for Health, Physical
   Education, Recreation and
   Dance, 163
alumni, 116
American Association for
   Counseling and
   Development, 231
American Educational Research
   Association, 7
American Federation of Teachers, 7
American Law Institute, 125

American Orthopsychiatric
   Association, 236
American Psychological
   Association, 132,233,
   235-236
anatomy, 233,249
anti-discrimination statement, 83,
   117,127,135,162,224
Anti-Saloon League, 83
anti-Semitism, 13
anti-war, 83,173
Armenian, 21
artwork, see illustrations
Asian, 21,97,134,203,207
association with gays/lesbians
   by college employees/students,
      86,90,93,98,100,108,109,
      221
   by educators/counselors, 38,46,
      47,53,63,67,71,73,156,161
athletics, 5,99,110,117,141-166,204
attitudes of gay/lesbian youth
   towards teachers, 3,9,21,29-37,48
   towards counselors, 3,9,21,29-32,
      37,71,72,
Attitudes towards lesbians and gay
   men
   administrators, 32,39
   beginning teachers, 29-55,59-70,
      73,74
   change of, 60-74,128,130,142,
      161,163
   mechanisms for, 60-74,161,163
   college/university

The Publishers gratefully acknowledge the efforts of Karen M. Harbeck in the preparation of the Index and Table of Cases for this volume.

administrators, 86,93-95,100,
    105,115,133
faculty, 86,89,93,99,100,110,
    112,113,115,133,200,
    222-224,236
employees, 4,81-95,114-119
service, 86,112,224
students, 4,40,81-86,95-119
counselors, 29,30,32,37-39,42,
    43,49,53-63,70-73,235
development of, 18
general student population, 3,
    9-11,21,24-26,134
judiciary, 122
mental health workers, 234-235,
    240,250-251
negative, 7,12,13,16,18,32,
    38-42,49,53,55,60,66,73,
    168,191,193,201,204,208,
    234,240
attitudinal scales
Attitudes Towards Homosexuality
    Scale, 30-31,40-42,55,58,59,
    66-69
Homosexuality Knowledge Index,
    49-52,66-69,72
Index of Homophobia, 30,31,
    40-42,55,58,59,66-69
Likert, 30
methodology, 30,85,147
Professional Attitudes Index
    Scale, 65-69
sampling, 84,85,113
attorneys, 122,123,130

bathrooms, 99,104,109,126
bestiality, 207
blackmail, 125,129
Blacks, 1,10,18,21,32,37,40,53,54,
    65,73,83,97,198,200,203,
    251,252
Boston, MA, 142
Boston University School of Social
    Work, 236
Brazilian, 248

Bridges, Jim, 206
Briggs, John, 129,131
British, 123,124,206
Brown, Willie, 128-129
Bryant, Anita, 122,128-129

California, 122,124-126,128-129
California State Board of Education,
    126
California State Education Code,
    125
California State Penal Code, 125
California State Supreme Court, 126
Campaign to End Homophobia, 60
captions, textbook, 198,200,204,208
career, 134,239
Catholic, 147
Caucasian, 15,21,23
censorship, self, 81,91-93,108,109,
    113-115,176,178,190,192
Central America, 208,225
certification area, 43-45,53
certifying organization, 242
change, *see also* attitudes, change
    legal, 122,126-127,130
    social, 1,122,126,128,130,169
    technological, 1
child pornography, 128
Chinese, 15,21
Christian, 34,61,93,124,128-129,
    146,201
Christopher Street, 205
church, 14,15,84,117,128
civil rights, 1,55,59,60,73,83,
    127-128,133,197,205-206
class, social, 29,60,61,82,145-147,
    199,230-231,240,255
clergy, 11,111,128,129,131
Cleveland, OH, 84
co-education, 83
Courbet, 207
colonial times, 1,122,123
"Coming Out," *see* "Out"
comments, degrading, 88,89,98,

105,116,117,144,160,162, 174,180,187,193,222,230
Communism, 125,146
community, 2,84,122,131,132,135, 174,187,194,208,214, 216-221,224-225,237,240, 248,250,252-254,256-257, 259
computer, 121-122,124
concealment strategies
  college/university, 101,114,115
  distancing from others, 141,150, 152-153,160,173,174,182, 184,191
  distancing from homosexuality, 141,150,153-155,160,171, 173-174,180,184
  gay and lesbian youth, 11,14,15, 19,23,214
  teachers, 5,141-166,168,171, 173-182,191,194
condoms, 249-250,255
confidentiality, 37,72,105,254
conservative, 1,2,122,128-131,133, 201,205
contraceptives, 128
Council on Social Work Education, 231
counseling, 20,25,62,63,155,180, 191,220,231,234-236,249, 258
counselors, 3,6,11,26,29,30,32, 37-39,42,43,49,53-63,70-73, 169,194,230-232,234-236
couplehood, 215,219-222,225,236, 238
courses, gay/lesbian, 98,213-227, 235
credential revocation, *see* employment concerns
criminal, 124-126,127,132-133,141, 145
cultural factors, 1,11,26,81,82,118, 121,124,145,199,220,231, 234,237,253

institutional, 83
culture, gay/lesbian, 87,88,98,123, 225
curricula, 4,6,61-62,67,71,135,143, 199,214,225,231-232,242, 255
  college, 6,135,214
  graduate training, 229-246
  intervention, 67-68,180,191, 235-236,238,242
  teacher education, 60,65,67,135, 163
custody, 142,224,230

Dade County, FL, 128-129
date rape, 23,26
dating, 15,23,143,150,156,175
dean's office, 110
death penalty, 123,124,129
degayification, 251
demographic variables, 38,53,84,86
dental dams, 249,255
detachment, 33,153-154
developmental process, 13,127, 213-227,237-238,252-253
deviancy theory, 145,215-216,220
differentiation, 217,253
discrimination, 82,85,105,107,112, 113,118,135,154,167,180, 216,230-231,239
  educational benefits, 14,99,103
  governmental, 14,224
  housing, 14,224,230,238
  medical assistance, 14,25,231
  occupational, 14,88,89,94, 131-134,224,230
  sex, 180,238
disease, contagious, 133
dismissal, *see* employment concerns
divorce, 216,224
dorms, 82,100,103,106,109,112
drawings, *see* illustrations
drop-out prevention, 18,20,25

educators, *see* school personnel
egalitarian, 220
ego identity, 12
elementary years, 19,31,39,40,43,
    51-54,65,122,124,147,163,
    169,171,181
Emerson, Ralph Waldo, 124
employment concerns of educators
    accusations, 88,89,167,171-174,
        178,181-182,192
    credential revocation, 2,4,121,
        125,132
    dismissal, 2,4,5,93,118,121,
        125-127,130-133,141,143,
        148-150,168,171-172,175,
        179,181,192-193
    exposure, 88,89,104
    general harm, 104,115,131,144,
        171-172,175,179,192
    hiring, 89,90,121,126,127,
        130-133
    imprisonment, 124
    ostracism, 88,89,171-172,175,
        179,181,182,192
    promotions, 89
    raises, 89
    recommendations, 109
    reputation, 2,88,126,144,
        171-175,179,181,192,194
    resignation, 124,131,132,134
    retention, 121,122,126
    rights, 121-140,143,194
    suspension, 125,141
    tenure, 2,86,88,89,93,131,132
empowerment, 135,154,248,258
    conservatives, 129
    education, 6,247-248,256
    process, 5,167-196,247-248
encounters with gays/lesbians, 30,
    31,38,39,46,47,53,71,73,82,
    98,108,109
enculturation, 13
English, *see* British
epidemiological studies, 251-252
equal rights, 81,83,116-118,231

Equal Protection, 127,130
ethnicity, 13,18,82,87,96,97,112,
    114,115,118,133,145,199,
    230-231,233,240
European, 207
exceptionality, 6,213-227
exclusion, 81,104,115,116
Executive Branch, 128
evangelists, 61

faculty development, 60,68-71,180
Fairfax High School, 9,10,19,21,24,
    26,257
Falwell, Jerry, 131
family, *see* parents
father, 198
Federal courts, 127,128
felonies, 132
fetishes, 202
Filipino, 21
financial ruin, 124
First Amendment, 127,130
Florida, 122,126,128
foster care, 142
freedom, personal, 1,5,121,122,126,
    127,134,142-143,163
friends, 94,95,100,111,112,115,
    153,176,182,205,214,215,
    219,225,230,238,241,254
Fuller, Margaret, 124

gay bashing, 10,229-230,238
Gay and Lesbian Counseling
    Services Center, 10,257
Gay/Lesbian Liberation Movement,
    122-123,126,202,205
gay/lesbian rights, 49,60,109,117,
    118,122,123,127-128,130,
    170,194,224,256
gender, 1,4,13,29,43,45,53,56-58,
    60,61,81,82,95,112,114,
    134,144,162,163,176,178,
    180,202
genitalia, male, 106

German American, 97
Georgia, 61
graffiti, 88,98,99,116
Greek, 207
gubernatorial, 122,129
guest lecturer, 60,236,241,250
gym/physical education
    facility/teams, 110,117,143,
    153,155,157

Hawaii, 42
health, 16,25-26,145,237-238,
    247-250,253-256,258
    textbooks, 197-221
Helms, Jesse, 61
Helms, Mary, 129
heterosexual
    orthodoxy/heterosexism, 81,
    93,109,116-118,160,
    162-163,197,200,203,209,
    214,230,234,239-240,242,
    250,256
heterosexual privilege, 132,141,
    160-161,223
Hetrick-Martin Institute, 257
hiding, 2,5,13-15,106,115,146,149,
    160,194,213-214,239
Hispanic, 18,21
Hollywood, CA, 129,257
homes, residential, 10,22
homophobia in schools, 10,11,17,
    18,24,25,100,143,149,153,
    160-163,169,173,180,
    191-195,197,199,234
    definition, 38,40,144,230
    detrimental consequences for
        youth, 3,10-12,16,19,27
    abuse, 3,10,11,14,17,22-24,27,
        82,214
    academic failure, 3,10,17
    alienation, 11,217-218
    criminal, 10,17
    drop-out risk, 3,10,11,14,17,
        19,22,23,27,253
    HIV/AIDS, 3,21,247-259

homelessness, 3,10,11,17
    isolation, 3,11,13,14,17,19,24
    parental rejection, 3,10,11,13,
        17,21,22,222-223
    physical violence, 3,10,14,82,
        214,253
    self-esteem, 3,11,14,19,25,27,
        162,217-218,222,247,249,
        253-254
    sexual abuse, 3,17
    sexual promiscuity, 3,11,14,17
    sexually transmitted diseases,
        3,16-17,21-22,202,249-252
    stress, 17
    substance abuse, 3,11,17-19,
        21-23,26,252-253
    suicidal ideology, 3,17,22,23,
        253
    suicide, 3,11,17-19,22,23,
        26-27,161,162,187,252-253
    institutionalized in schools, 11,12,
        160
    internalized, 2-5,7,38,124,144,
        160,214,222,239
homosexuality
    advocacy, 122,129,201
    and education books, 2,201-202
    origins of, 12, 237
    views of
        changing, 122,126
        crime, 1,124,142,230,239
        genetic defect, 1
        learning disability, 1
        mental disorder, 1,124,142,237
        sickness, 1,33,142,230,239
        sin, 1,32,55,59,65,66,93,117,
            124,142,205,230,239
housing, 108,109,112-114,224,258
hotline, 20,238
HIV, *see* AIDS

illiteracy, 145
illustrations, 197-211
immoral conduct, 122,125,127,130,
    132

incest, 202
infertility, 233
inservice training, 6,67-69,235-236,
    238,242
Institution for the Protection of
    Lesbian and Gay Youth,
    Inc., 17
insurance, health, 94
integration, 68,83,171,173,175-179,
    181-182,185,190,192,199,
    202,209,217,221,235-236,
    253
interdisciplinary, 123,215,221
internship sites, 242
interviews, 30,121,147,167-168,
    170-171,179,182,184-185,
    190,192-193,234
intolerance, 2,116,158,182,202
invisibility, 2-3,13,121,123,161,
    167,186,192,202-203,205,
    208
isolation, 81,91,95,104,113,152,
    160-161,186-187,191-192,
    202,208,219,238-239
Italian, 97

Japanese, 207
Jewish, 97
job retention, 4-5
jokes, 61,88,105,154,174,180,192,
    222
judiciary, 123,125,127,129-130,133
junior high school, 11,17,22,25,30,
    70,121,141,147,169,171,218

King, Martin Luther Jr., 198
knowledge, of gays/lesbians
    counselors, 4,6,29-32,39,49,72
    general public, 127
    professionals, 4,6,29,49-52,54,
        66,87,88,229-246
    self, 192,218
    teachers, 4,6,29,31,32,39,49,
        50-52,54,66-68

Lane, Charles, 124
Latino, 97,203,252
legal issues, 67,121,122,142,201,
    223-225,238,256
legal protections, 4,27,123,171
Legislative Branch, 128-129
legislators, 122,123,128-129,132,
    135
lesbians, lesbianism
    attitudes towards youth, 38,40,43
    experiences of youth, 18,21,23-24
lewd conduct/vagrancy, 124,126
liberal, 4,81,84,116,127,142,174,
    194,200,205
library, 99,110
library materials, 20,180,191,192
licensing examinations, 242
litigants, 127
litigation, 121-140,142,168
lobbyists, 125,127,135
Los Angeles Times, 20
Los Angeles Unified School District,
    9,10,18,20

magazines, 94
magnet schools, 20
males
    attitudes towards youth, 38,40,43,
        51-52,54,59,67
    experiences of gay, 21-23
    suicide rates of gay, 17
Mapplethorpe, Robert, 61
marital status, 43,45
march, pride, 187-188,201,204-205
Massachusetts, 132-133,187
Massachusetts Gay Rights Law, 170
masturbation, 233
Matlovich, Leonard, 204
McCarthy, Joseph, 125,126
medical issues, 67,206,247,256
medical practitioners, 11,15,25,26,
    95,110
Melville, Herman, 124
mental health professionals/services,
    6,11,16,22,110,111,127,

215,217,220-221,229-247,
254,258
Miami, FL, 129
Midwest, 38,100,235
Milk, Harvey, 204
minority groups, 1,6,13,135,142,
146,154,182,197,198,236
minority rights, 1,126-127,130,
133-134
Minnesota, 123
Model Penal Code, 125
Modern Language Association, 7
molestation, 132,133,142,143,146,
148,167,171,172,182,204
moral development, 1,143
multicultural, 220
municipal boards, 127,224

narcissist, 219
National Association for Girls and
Women in Sport, 163
National Association for Sport and
Physical Education, 163
National Education Association, 127
National Endowment for the Arts,
61
National Gay and Lesbian Task
Force, 17
Native American, 97,203
necrophilia, 202
needles, 249,252,255
needs of gay/lesbian youth
AIDS prevention, 20,25,71,
247-259
counseling services, 20,62,63,71,
258
emotional support, 11,247,249
faculty development, 68-71,74
health care/education, 16,247,
249-250,254-255,257-258
hotline, 20,68
information, 11,18,20,24,62,
68-71,247,250,254-255,258
in school discussions, 24,62-65,
68-71
integrate curriculum, 62,67-72

non-judgmental support, 19
outreach, 24,68-69
parental education, 69,71
peer support, 11,16,18,247,253,
257-258
programs, 61-62,68-71,249
referral services, 11,247-248,250,
254,257-258
role models, 16
safe environment, 18-19,62,66,
254,257
safe sex devices/needles, 249-250,
255
safe sex education, 25-26,62,
247-259
scholarships, 20
self-esteem development,
249-250,254
self expression, 15
sex education, 24,247-259
shelter, 17,22,257-258
social skills development,
249-250,253-254
substance abuse
intervention/education, 25,
249
suicide prevention, 25,254
negotiation, 4,130-131,134,249
neighbors, 95,117,229
newspapers, 94,99,121,131,238
"New Wave", 10
New York City Gay/Lesbian
Community Clinic, 16
New York Governor's Task Force
on Bias Related Violence, 85
New York Governor's Task Force
on Lesbian and Gay Issues,
17
New York State Task Force on Gay
Issues, 17
North Carolina, 42,60
nutrition, 249

Oberlin College, 81-119
Oberlin Gay Liberation, 83
Oberlin Inn, 88

obligations
  ethical, 6,11,27,231-232,257
  professional, 11,27
Ohio, 42
Oklahoma, 122,128-130
oppression, *see also* homophobia
  internalized, 2,4,5,7,124,214,
    222,239
  societal, 6-7,163,213-215,
    218-221,225,230-231,256
  theory, 6,145-146,236
Orange County Department of
  Education, 133
"Out", 2,5,83,88,89,94-95,131,
    134,168,169,172,173,
    175-179,192,194,229,234,
    237-238,254

Pacific Islander, 97
parents, 10,11,14-16,21-24,84,94,
    111,112,115,117,123,
    141-142,148-149,168,181,
    187,195,200,203-205,
    213-215,219,229-230,236,
    238-239,253
participatory research, 168-169,194
"passing," *see also* concealment,
    11,13,15,19,33,101,103,
    141,143,148,150-152,
    175-179
Peabody, Elizabeth, 124
peasants, 255
pederasty, 123,202
peer pressure, 37,213
peer support networks, 6,16,19,161,
    167-196,219-220,223,238,
    247,253
Pennsylvania State University, 84,
    114
Persian, 207
personality traits of homophobics,
    38
Phenomenological, 4,144,147
photographs, *see* illustrations
physical educators, 4-5,141-166,181
physically challenged, 13,230-231

physicians, *see* medical practitioners
pimps, 198-199
police, 89,110,125,205
politics, 91,92,107-109,117,121,
    122,126-129,132-133,142,
    146,162,169,194,199,
    204-205,208,215,220-221,
    223-224,240,257-258
pornography, 222
postal authorities, 125
poverty, 145
Powell, Justice, 130
power of attorney, 224
prejudice, 2,4,13,14,26,29,60,66,
    72,122,127,132,142-144,
    154,161-162,167,182,194,
    222,224,230-231
pre-school, 169,171,181,182
prison, 235
privacy, 83,117,126,127
private schools, 123,128
procedural rights, 125-126
professional activities, 30,31,62-74
program status, 43-45,53
progressivism, 83,118
PROJECT 10, 3,9-28,257
promotion, *see* employment
    concerns
Proposition Six Initiative, 122,129
prostitution, 3,11,202
Protestant, 147
psychiatrists, *see* mental health
    professionals
psychology, 6,199,203,232-233
publishing/publishers, 200,208-209
punk, 10

Questionnaires, *see* attitudinal scales
questioning sexual preference, 86,
    87,96-98,101,103-106,110

race, 4,13,18,29,35,40,43-45,51-54,
    56-61,65,73,81,82,85-88,91,
    92,96-116,118,132-134,
    145-147,169,182,197-200,

202-203,205-209,230,233, 251
racism, 6,13,35,60,93,173,194,200, 203,208-209,236
Rafferty, Max, 133
Ramsauer, Ken, 206
rape, *see also* date rape, 202,207
Reagan, Nancy, 129
Reagan, Ronald, 129
recommendations, 109
Reconstruction, 122
recruitment, 142,143,167,171,172, 182
religion, 1,83,93,116-118,201,220, 231,236,238
residential college, 84
residential services, 110,224
risk of HIV infection, 247-255,258
risk taking, 149,155-162,174-181, 187-188,192-194,223,225
ritual, 217,252
role models, 1,5,12,16,25-26,106, 110,126,127,132,155,161, 193,195,218,234,241
rural, 30-32,38,67,70,147,169,194, 217
Rutgers, 84,114

"safe sex", 3,22,25-26,247, 249-250,253-254
safety, 2,175,178,180-181,187,238
St. Paul, MN, 128
San Francisco, CA, 7,252
Sappho, 207
Save Our Children, *see* Bryant, Anita
school-based intervention, 3,9-28
    funding of, 20
school board, 27,125,127,131,135
"school bus", 188
school, boarding, 123
school climate, 30
school district, 4,174
school personnel
    administrators, 2,4,26,27,32,39, 121,123-126,130-132,135,

141,143,169,173,181,194, 257
    beginning teachers, 3,29-55, 59-70,73,74
    counselors, 3,29,30,32,37-39,42, 43,49,53-63,70-73
    gay/lesbian teachers, 39,62-63, 66-67,106,121-196
    general, 122
    janitor, 37
    negative attitudes, *see* attitudes
school prayer, 128
Sears, James, 7
seat belts, 249
secondary, 31,39,40,43-44,51-54, 65,70,122,124,169,171,213
Segal, George, 207
self-esteem, 5,153,156,162,182, 193,239,249-250,254
self monitoring, 15
seminar, 60
senior high school, 11,17,18,22, 30-33,35,39,54,71
seroprevalence surveys, 251-252
sex, with students, 132-133,142, 171-172
sexism, 6,13,60,173,194,200, 202-203,209,236
sex role inventory scale, 168
sex-segregated, 123
sexual harassment, 81,103-106, 112-116,118,158,160,194, 214
sexual intercourse, *see also* safe sex, 249,252
sexual orientation development, 12-14,127
sexual rebels, 32
sexual revolution, 126
sexuality education/discussions, 12, 24-25,30,34,60-74,83, 197-211,213,232-234, 247-259
sexually transmitted diseases, *see also* AIDS and HIV, 3,16, 17,21,22,202,209,249-252

Shack, Richard and Ruth, 128
social development, 11-14,19
social entitlements, 1
social historian, 123
socialization process, 13
social mores, 122,125
social ostracism, 88,104,115,116
social policy, 67,123
social work, 6,221,230-232,235-236
Socrates, 121
South American, 225
South Carolina, 30,32,42,61
South Carolina Guidance Counseling
    Association, 30
Southern, beliefs, 29-79
Sparta, 123
special interest litigation groups, 4,
    122
splitting/separation, 5,11,19,168,
    174-178,182,184,190
spouse, 94,128,132,181
stereotypes
  of gays/lesbians, 12,13,88,98,99,
    105,116,134,141,142,
    148-150,162-163,172,176,
    180,182,195,199,204,215,
    219-220,222,230-231,235,
    237-238,240-241
  sex role, 11-12,17,19,84,99,116,
    118,142-145,148-150,
    162-163,168,180,237-238
stigma, 13,16,148,167,182,206,239
stigmatization, 12-16,19,26,146,213
Stonewall, 205
student
  general population, attitudes, 3,
    9-11,21,24-26
  organizations, 111
  services, 85,110
suburban, 147
surveillance, 125

teachers
  abuse by, 10,22
  beginning, 29-55,59-70,73,74

college/university, 86-89,93,99,
    100,112,113,115,234
constraints on, 1
gay/lesbian, 39,62-63,66-67,106,
    121-196,234
as minority group, 1
tenure, 2,86,88,89,93,131,132,174
textbooks, 4,5,12,61,135,197-211,
    241
Thoreau, Henry David, 124
transcendentalists, 124
transsexuals, 198,237
transvestism, 202

unconstitutional, 126,127,130
unions, 4,122,127,130,132,134,180
United States Supreme Court, 130,
    131,135
University of California, Berkeley,
    134
University of California, Santa Cruz,
    85,113,114
University of Illinois,
    Champagne/Urbana, 84,85
University of Massachusetts,
    Amherst, 84
unprofessional conduct, 4
urban, 147,169,217,224,251

victimization, 7,26,81-83,85,88,89,
    99,100,103,105,113-115,
    117,158,214
violence, 216
  against gays/lesbians, 17,60,82,
    84,85,88,104,105,116,
    142-143,230,239
  by gays/lesbians, 99,128
  types of at college/university
    assault/battery, 89,103-105,
    113-114,202,209
    followed/chased, 89,104-105,
    114-115
    spat on, 104-105,113-114
    property damage, 89,104,114
    verbal abuse, 88,89,95,99,100,